BEST *SEASHORE* NATURE SITES

Drawing by Louis Agassiz Fuertes. (Courtesy of Whitney Oppersdorff)

Barred owl (Aegolius acadicus).

BEST *SEASHORE* NATURE SITES
OF MIDCOAST MAINE

PUBLIC PRESERVES FOR
MARINE AND UPLAND EXPLORATION

Des FitzGerald   Tony Oppersdorff   Kyrill Schabert

Photography by
Tony Oppersdorff
and as noted

With a Foreword by
Philip Conkling

and Epilogue by
Bob Steneck

Waterline Books
Jefferson, Maine

This is a **Waterline** Natural History Book

Waterline Books
15 Mariner Lane
Jefferson, Maine 04348
(207) 549-7805
waterlinebks@gwi.net
http://bestnaturesites.webs.com

ISBN: 978-0-9764275-1-3

Design and Composition: Victoria Waters of Hughes Publishing Services
Editorial Coordinator: Ava Goodale
Proofreader: Cathy Kulka

Front Cover: La Verna Preserve, Bristol (photo: Tony Oppersdorff)

Spring beauty (Claytonia virginica).

Contents

Reid State Park, Georgetown.

Living on the Edge of the Sea

ECOLOGISTS ARE FOND OF POINTING OUT THAT EVERY SPECIES HAS A DISTINCT NICHE—a unique combination of habits, habitat, foraging strategies and protective cover that allows enough individuals to sustain themselves long enough to reproduce— even thrive.

Ecologically speaking, we are a littoral species; that is, of all the habitats into which humans have radiated, we occupy the edges of the water more tenaciously than any other. And of all of the shoreline habitats we frequent, the largest numbers of us are drawn ineluctably to the edge of the sea. Today in America, almost 60 percent of us live in coastal counties—and that percentage continues to increase decade by decade.

In ecological terms, the littoral zone is by definition, an "edge" habitat—comprising a boundary area between two separate ecological zones—land and water. Edge habitats support higher species diversity by virtue of supporting creatures from the two habitats that intersect here. Along Maine's coastal littoral zone, we find creatures like crabs and urchins that emerge from the marine environment to forage on land between the tides, while creatures from land, like raccoon and mink, feed on such creatures along these shifting borders.

At the shore we, of course, expect to find shorebirds, wading birds and waterfowl, but there we also find land birds like hawks and eagles, even owls waiting to feed on the unwary. And two of the nation's greatest migratory flyways—along the Atlantic and Pacific coasts—bring waves of neo-tropical migrants past those who take pleasure in wandering along a littoral zone. Edges are alluring.

To add to the allure, the Maine coast is what geologists call a "drowned coast-line," not because, as my boys once imagined, so many mariners have lost their lives in the tempestuous weather the coast can experience. Rather, rising sea level following the melting of a vast continental ice sheet filled the basin of what is now the Gulf of Maine, leaving isolated hilltops as an "archipelago" of islands just offshore and a series of brackish estuaries that trend far inland from the mouths of rivers and streams that pour off Maine's dissected coastal plain. These rivers—part fresh, part salt—add another dimension of ecological complexity to the diversity of coastal habitats.

Because the Gulf of Maine basin tapers at its easternmost end at the head of the Bay of Fundy, tides are amplified by the pull of the moon as one heads west to east. Think of a bathtub where the water level piles up at one end when you slosh yourself back and forth to create a little wave. Along the Maine coast, eight-foot tides at the New Hampshire border increase to ten- to twelve-foot tides along Midcoast Maine and then double that range—24-foot tides—when the wave reaches Eastport.

Another important driver affecting the Maine coastal ecosystems is the influence of the dominant oceanographic current, an offshoot of the Nova Scotia Current, which is itself an offshoot of the Labrador Current. A refreshing dip into Maine's ocean waters is a character-building experience for most of us. But the effect on marine systems is quite different. In contrast to warm tropical water, colder water holds more dissolved oxygen and carbon dioxide, the building blocks of all marine food webs. We are used to the idea that terrestrial productivity—or "biomass"—tends to increase as we head toward the equator. But for marine ecosystems, this relationship is reversed: by and large the further toward the poles you go, the more productive the marine ecosystems.

Thus the interplay of topography, oceanography and temperature is constantly changing along the Maine coast, depending on the state of the tide, the phase of the moon, the season of the year, even the time of day. No two expeditions to any place along the Maine coast will ever be the same. The scenery and the diversions never repeat and the imagination is never dulled.

Not so long ago, Maine ranked near the bottom of the list of states with lands open to the public. But more than 25 years ago, Maine voters established the Land for Maine's Future Program and have passed five bond issues to fund the purchase of public land, including many parcels along the coast to increase access to Maine's stunning diversity of coastal environments. In addition, almost 100 different local land trusts have protected many thousands of more acres and miles and miles of undeveloped coastline, much of which is available to those interested in the treasures of Maine's natural beauty.

Today many Americans seek out coastlines with gently sloping beaches protected by shark nets and lifeguards, where clean white sand is brought in by the truckload and then carefully manicured to create the impression of timelessness. But then to keep the beach in place, the shores need to be barricaded, armored and de-natured, so the experience tends to feel manufactured, like a ride at a theme park. But the Maine coast is completely different. Beginning with the Romantics, painters and poets have always preferred the rocky shores as places to experience the sublime—and Maine offers the most expansive and sublime rocky shores along the entire Atlantic coast.

The Maine coast is made for walking and exploring, and for finding pieces of nature's wondrous works to stuff in a pocket—a feather, a stone, a shell, Aristotle's lantern. Set out on your own expedition, helped along by this guide, and take in all these diverse wild and natural experiences that the Maine coast offers you for free.

—Philip Conkling, 2014

Reid State Park, Georgetown.

Introduction

THE SEASHORE IS THE FOCUS OF THIS SECOND VOLUME OF *BEST NATURE SITES*. Though much of Maine's 3,400 miles of shoreline is either difficult to approach or legally inaccessible, our book points the way to public preserves on the Midcoast with descriptions, photographs, maps and articles related to the natural history of each location. Maine's coastline is highly variable, with bays and inlets offering numerous possibilities for interpreting natural ecology and human history. We wrote this book for the pure pleasure of such discovery and to bring what we enjoyed to the attention of other "curious travelers."

The 20 chapters that follow cover 32 sites from Freeport to Searsport, along the major rivers and the peninsulas that divide them, highlighting the "best" ones and what's to be found there (see maps, pp. xviii–xxiii). In these pages, we have shifted the emphasis from the Route 1 corridor of our previous book to the saltwater coast, but we have included a few non-seashore spots. In Chapter 14 we present Hidden Valley Nature Center, which offers a thousand acres of upland, lowland, a bog with boardwalk and pond habitat. Chapter 20 offers three paddling destinations where a canoe or kayak is recommended: Sandy Point Wildlife Management Area (WMA), St. Clair Preserve, and Ruffingham Meadows WMA. Each site is a destination worthy of several visits, and collectively they offer a thousand opportunities for exploration, observation or quiet rambling in the countryside.

Sidebar articles, printed on tinted pages following each site description, are meant to showcase topics specific to the site or of a general nature. The topics often came to mind with a question that one of us posed during our fieldwork and so result from our own curiosity. It would be fair to say that we "write to learn." Many of the articles are by experts in the field (*see* Contributors, p. xiv), and they give this publication a gravitas that, as generalists, we could never offer.

Being able to "sit by the sea" is largely dependent upon the generosity of many individuals, families and organizations that have chosen to acquire, protect, preserve and maintain a particular piece of land. These efforts are ongoing, and they benefit all of us. None of this work should be taken for granted, nor should anyone assume that financial obligation incurred by land trusts and non-profits is all paid for. Conservation organizations need the active support of everyone who takes pleasure in walking down a path, through a forest of old trees, to view the sun rising or setting over a far horizon.

— D. F. T. O. K. S.

Nature's sculpture garden.

Acknowledgments

Besides the many contributors (*see* below) who generously made time to tailor their expertise to our needs, we thank the following who helped "behind the scenes." Our spouses—Whitney Oppersdorff, Susan Spinney and Lucinda Ziesing—offered essential evaluation as the work progressed, helping to hasten an all-too-slow process.

Very much "on the scene," was Victoria Hughes Waters, who as designer and compositor, transformed our words and photographs into book pages, on both this volume and the last. Ava Goodale wrote sidebars, acquired photographs, liaised with the land trusts, and proofread (in addition to teaching full time and having her second child). Cathy Kulka proofread the final version and copyedited the sidebars, providing feedback along the way. Rodney Hook was indispensable in enhancing digital photographs that needed help. For plant and fungus identifications, we thank, respectively, Beedy Parker and Greg Marley. And Ken Demmons helped in finding insects and other species to photograph.

In addition, the following experts guided our efforts: Brian Beal and Daniel Belknap of the University of Maine; Markus Frederich and Barry Costa-Pierce of the University of New England; Pamela Hunt of New Hampshire Audubon; Nancy Sferra of The Nature Conservancy; Jim Sterba, author of *Nature Wars*; and Gail Wipplehauser of the Maine Department of Marine Resources.

Many photographers, including David White, (*see* below) donated shots of plants and animals that would have been otherwise unavailable to us. And fundamental to the book, the staff members of Land Trusts and governmental agencies, notably the Maine Department of Inland Fisheries and Wildlife, responded to our needs with alacrity.

Contributors

These willing and generous individuals, so much more knowledgeable than we in their respective fields, have enriched this guide with their natural history articles.

Archie Bonyun lives and works on Westport Island in Maine and gave us a guided tour of Bonyun Preserve, chapter 11. He is a member of the Westport Island Planning Board and on the Board of Directors of the Kennebec Estuary Land Trust.

Philip W. Conkling (p. viii) is the founding publisher of *Island Journal* and the monthly coastal newspaper, *The Working Waterfront*, where he continues to contribute as a columnist. He is the author of *Islands in Time, A Natural and Cultural History of the Islands of the Gulf of Maine; Lobsters Great and Small;* and the editor of *From Cape Cod to the Bay of Fundy: An Environmental Atlas of the Gulf of Maine.* After stepping down as founder and president of the Island Institute in 2013, Conkling advises a variety of clients as part of Philip Conkling and Associates.

Chris DeSorbo (pp. 6, 86) is the Director of the Raptor Program at the Biodiversity Research Institute (BRI) in Gorham, Maine. Chris's research has emphasized contaminant evaluations in birds (particularly bald eagles and common loons) and movement studies using color bands and satellite tracking technology. Chris received a B.S. at the University of New Hampshire, and an M.S. at Antioch University.

Alison C. Dibble, Ph.D. (p. 108) researches native bee pollinators of low bush blueberry through the School of Biology and Ecology, University of Maine, Orono. Through her consulting firm, Stewards LLC, she conducts ecological inventories for land trusts, agencies and private landowners.

Dennis Dunbar (p. 107) currently serves as Board President of the Kennebec Estuary Land Trust and Treasurer for the Westport Island Conservation Commission. Prior to his retirement in June 2002, after 35 years of service to Lockheed Martin, he served as Vice President and Chief Technical Officer for International Launch Services (ILS), which provided commercial and government space launch services worldwide.

Melissa Duron (p. 32) graduated with a B.S. in Biological Sciences from the University of Southern Maine in 2004. She now works at Biodiversity Research Institute (BRI) in Gorham, Maine, and is director of the Forest Songbird Program.

Ava Goodale (p. 96, 134) graduated from Cornell University with a degree in Natural Resources. With a professional background in conservation biology and field ecology, she taught science at Riley School in Rockport and now teaches environmental science at Millbrook School in New York.

Erik Hargreaves (maps, pp. xviii–xxiii) is Senior Cartographer at Delorme Mapping in Yarmouth, where he has been for the last 25 years. He moved to Maine from Virginia in 1987 and has lived in New Gloucester for the last 20 years.

Alicia Heyburn, (p. 60) a self-designated "friend of the fish," supports organizations through event management, project planning, public outreach and grant writing. She was Project Director at Kennebec Estuary Land Trust for many years and serves on the board of Harpswell Heritage Land Trust.

Ron Joseph (p. 182) worked as a Maine wildlife biologist for 33 years before retiring in 2010. He keeps busy volunteering for land trusts and leading birding trips, as well as writing on environmental topics for various newspapers.

Jake Maier (p. 108) is a consulting forester in Orland, Maine. Originally from Germany, his work focuses on increasing average tree size and forest health.

Ashley Malinowski (p. 198) is employed by the Maine Department of Inland Fisheries and Wildlife.

Annette Naegel (p. 102), who takes great pleasure in doing anything outdoors, is the Georges River Land Trust's Conservation Program Manager, with 24 years of experience working for environmental non-profits in Maine, including the Island Institute. She has a background in environmental science.

Beedy Parker (p. 99), an environmental activist and gardener, has lived in Midcoast Maine for 35 years. She is the author/illustrator of *A Natural History of Camden and Rockport*, and an inner city natural history, *Life in Boston*. She is watching climate change in the garden and by the roadside.

Abby O. Pearson (p. 131) completed her master's degree at the University of Southern Maine in salt marsh restoration ecology with a focus on how terrestrial arthropods respond to changes in the plant community. She currently works as a lab instructor at Colby College in the Environmental Studies Program.

Ralph Perkins (p. 50) has degrees in zoology and biology and his professional background focused on wetland protection programs, specifically the identification and mitigation of proposals upon vernal pools. Since his retirement and relocation to Maine, he has participated in many vernal pool explorations with local schools and the local watershed association.

Peter Ralston (p. 42), co-founder of the Island Institute, is a widely collected and exhibited photographer whose work is principally available through Ralston Gallery in Rockport, Maine.

Marietta Ramsdell (p. 176) is a founding member and current President of Friends of Sears Island and stewards the 601-acre easement on Sears Island. Marietta's background is in education and she holds an M.A. in Communications.

H. Bruce Rinker, Ph.D. (p. 204) is a forest ecologist, science educator and explorer native to the Shenandoah Valley of Virginia. His publications include *Forest Canopies* (2004) and *Gaia in Turmoil* (2010).

Bob Steneck, Ph.D. (p. 207) is a marine ecology professor at the University of Maine in the School of Marine Sciences. He studies coral reefs in the Caribbean and Indopacific oceans and kelp forests in North America.

David White (p. 18) retired as president of a computer consulting company in 2005 and now is an avid wildlife photographer, splitting his time between Brunswick and Florida.

*This alert young **red fox** (Vulpes vulpes), one of six in this particular litter, has not yet left its den and remains dependent on its mother for food, an omnivorous diet of small mammals, both living and dead, birds, turtles, vegetation and carrion. Red foxes are the largest members of the genus and may weigh as much as 30 pounds.*

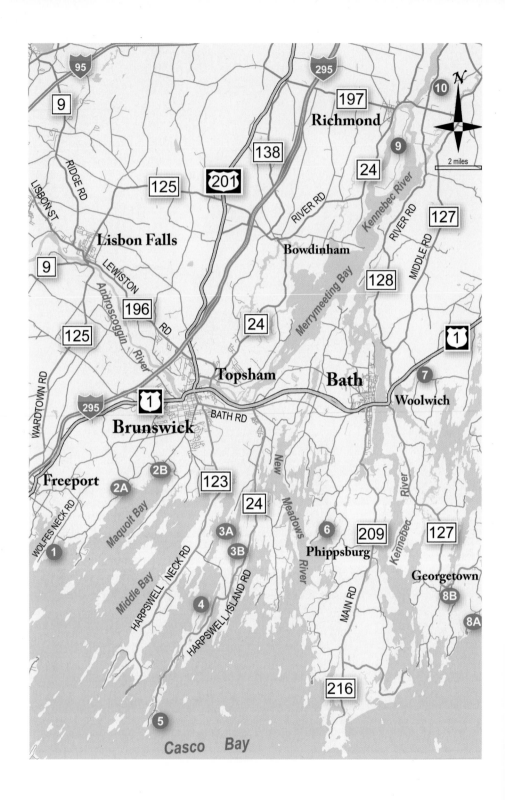

1. **Wolfe's Neck State Park**
State of Maine, Division of Parks
and Public Lands
207-287-3821
www.maine.gov/dacf/parks/index.
shtml

2A. **Maquoit Bay Conservation Land**
Town of Brunswick, Department of
Parks and Recreation
207-725-6656
www.brunswickme.org/depart-
ments/parks-recreation/

2B. **Maquoit Landing (Wharton's
Point)**
Town of Brunswick, Department
of Parks and Recreation
207-725-6656
www.brunswickme.org/depart-
ments/parks-recreation/

3A. **Cliff Trail Preserve**
Town of Harpswell
207-833-5771
www.harpswell.maine.gov

3B. **Long Reach Preserve**
Harpswell Heritage Land Trust
207-721-1121
www.hhltmaine.org/

4. **Bowdoin College Coastal Studies
Center Preserve**
Bowdoin College
207-725-3396
www.bowdoin.edu/coastal-studies-
center/

5. **Giant's Stairs**
Harpswell Heritage Land Trust
207-721-1121
www.hhltmaine.org/

6. **Green Point Preserve**
Kennebec Estuary Land Trust
207-442-8400
www.kennebecestuary.org/

7. **Nequassett Fish Ladder**
Bath Water District
207-443-2391
www.bathwd.org/

8A. **Reid State Park**
State of Maine, Division of Parks
and Public Lands
207-287-3821
www.maine.gov/dacf/parks/index.
shtml

8B. **Josephine Newman Audubon
Sanctuary**
Maine Audubon
207-781-0974
www.maineaudubon.org/

9. **Swan Island Wildlife
Management Area**
Maine Department of Inland
Fisheries and Wildlife
207-287-8000
www.state.me.us/ifw/

10. **Pownalborough Courthouse
Preserve**
Lincoln County Historical
Association
207-882-6817
www.lincolncountyhistory.org/

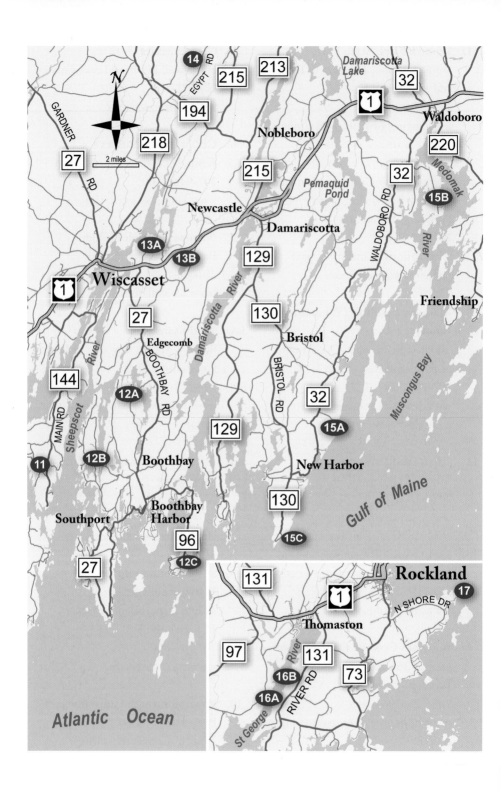

11. **Bonyun Preserve**
Kennebec Estuary Land Trust
207-442-8400
www.kennebecestuary.org/

12A. **Ovens Mouth Preserve**
Boothbay Region Land Trust
207-633-4818
www.bbrlt.org/

12B. **Porter Preserve**
Boothbay Region Land Trust
207-633-4818
www.bbrlt.org/

12C. **Linekin Preserve**
Boothbay Region Land Trust
207-633-4818
www.bbrlt.org/

13A. **Griggs Preserve**
Sheepscot Valley Conservation
Association
207-586-5616
www.sheepscot.org/

13B. **Marsh River Preserve**
Sheepscot Valley Conservation
Association
207-586-5616
www.sheepscot.org/

14. **Hidden Valley Nature Center**
207-586-6752
www.hvnc.org/

15A. **La Verna Preserve**
Pemaquid Watershed Association
207-563-2196
www.www.pemaquidwatershed.org/

15B. **Osborn-Finch Preserve**
Pemaquid Watershed Association
207-563-2196
www.pemaquidwatershed.org/

15C. **Pemaquid Point Lighthouse Park**
Town of Bristol
207-677-2492
www.bristolparks.org/lighthouse.
htm

16A. **Fort Point Preserve**
Town of St. George, Department
of Parks and Recreation
207-372-6363
www.stgeorgemaine.com/town_
parks_rec.html

16B. **Town Forest Preserve**
Town of St. George, Department
of Parks and Recreation
207-372-6363
www.stgeorgemaine.com/town_
parks_rec.html

17. **Owls Head State Park**
State of Maine, Division of Parks
and Public Lands
207-287-3821
www.maine.gov/dacf/parks/index.
shtml

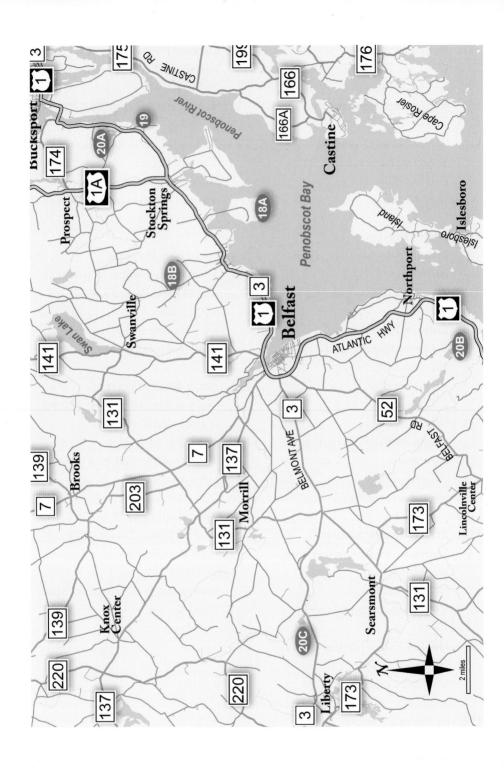

18A. Sears Island
Maine Coast Heritage Trust
207-729-7366
www.mcht.org/

18B. Long Cove Headwaters Preserve
Coastal Mountains Land Trust
207-236-7091
www.coastalmountains.org/

19. Sandy Point Beach Park
Town of Stockton Springs
207-567-3404
www.stocktonsprings.org/

Luna moth (Actias luna, photo: Barbara Favicchia).

20A. Sandy Point Wildlife Management Area
Maine Department of Inland Fisheries and Wildlife
207-287-8000
www.state.me.us/ifw/

20B. St. Clair Preserve
The Nature Conservancy
207-729-5181
www.nature.org/ourinitiatives/regions/northamerica/unitedstates/maine/

20C. Ruffingham Meadows Wildlife Management Area
Maine Department of Inland Fisheries and Wildlife
207-287-8000
www.state.me.us/ifw/

Bird banders have the opportunity to see the intricate detail of their temporary charges, such as this male **Wilson's warbler** (Cardellina pusilla), *banded during spring migration on its way to more northerly breeding grounds. During spring and fall, the second growth forest at the Park hosts many such members of the warbler family, Parulidae.*

◆ I ◆   Wolfe's Neck State Park

During a July thunderstorm of 2013, the osprey nest on Googins Island just offshore toppled with three five-week-old chicks, all of which were found by rangers in the following two days and returned to the nest platform, 50 feet up, to continue their maturation without delay.

OFFERING A WELCOME RESPITE TO NATURE SEEKERS, weary of the consumerism in downtown Freeport, this preserve lies but five miles from L.L. Beans's Big Boot, just right for an impromptu picnic lunch at the seaside and a walk along the rocky coastline and through the many loop trails that interlace the woods. This site will do nicely as the southerly start of the curious traveler's odyssey along Midcoast Maine. It spans the glacially carved peninsula that ends at Moore's Point, with shore frontage on both Casco Bay and the Harraseeket River.

Though this site is in part attuned to family outings with picnic areas and restrooms, there is no shortage of nature here along its coastline and inland wooded trails. Come here in May and trillium will be blooming in places along the roadsides and the ospreys will have returned to breed once again (*see* pp. 4–7 and p. 8). The botanical ecology of this site is summarized by the park as containing "varied ecosystems, including climax white pine and hemlock forests, a salt marsh estuary, and the rocky shorelines."

Education is an important component of the park. Interpretive signs are placed at various points describing important facets of the ecosystems, such as one explaining the life of the ospreys. Nature programs throughout the summer offer guided walks, talks and youth-oriented activities essential in today's society to fostering an awareness of natural history, the best antidote to "nature-deficit disorder."

For another perspective on this area of upper Casco Bay, take a drive along Burnett Road on the right shortly after leaving the park and stop by the bridge crossing the Little River, a good place for water birds. If you're heading on to Maquoit Bay in Brunswick, the next sites in this book, continue on Burnett Road to Flying Point Road that follows the shoreline through a rural landscape.

Not far to the north of the park on Burnett Road is a good vantage point at the mouth of the Little River to scan for shorebirds at low tide, or ducks when the tide is in. The osprey nesting site at the park on Googins Island is visible in the upper right.

Directions: Wolfe's Neck State Park, Freeport, 200 acres, State of Maine, Division of Parks and Public Lands

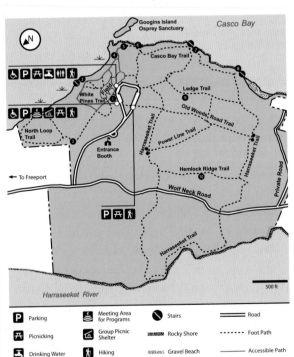

Take Exit 22 off I-295 in Freeport and turn east on Mallet Drive. Turn right at the traffic light onto Main Street. After 0.2 miles, turn left on Bow Street and continue for 2.3 miles. Turn right onto Wolfe's Neck Road and follow to the park entrance on the left after 1.4 miles. Dogs allowed on leash.

WebSource: www.maine.gov/cgi-bin/online/doc/parksearch/search_name.pl?state_park=31

Natural "sculpture" along the shore results from thousands of years of waves eroding the intermixed layers of bedrock, which themselves took hundreds of millions of years to form. These exposures hold the "story" of the earth's history, but even without much knowledge of the geological facts, they are aesthetically pleasing to behold.

Shaded paths bordered by moss-covered outcroppings topped by ferns thread through woods of spruce and oak. The trail network covers much of the interior over to the opposite shore along the Harraseeket River.

One of a Kind

Have you ever tried to capture a trout with your hands? Or hold onto a wriggling five-pound bass? Or dived off a dock at a perch? If so, then you know it's not easy to catch a fish. But that's what an **osprey** *(Pandion haliaetus)* does all the time. According to the Cornell Lab of Ornithology, "Over several studies, ospreys caught fish on at least 1 in every 4 dives, with success rates sometimes as high as 70%. The average time they spent hunting before making a catch was about 12 minutes..." That's a success rate that any fisherman would envy.

A diving osprey displays the "two-by-two" arrangement of the talons prior to striking a fish. (photo: David White)

What's the secret? Or, rather, what specialized features have evolved to allow this raptor, also known as a fish hawk, to become such an effective, "top-dog" predator of an elusive, underwater prey? Other important questions are: what has happened to allow this creature to rebound so dramatically from the edge of the DDT cliff during the 1960s and '70s? And what does the future hold for this fish-eating, long-distance migrant? Fortunately, answers may be forthcoming, as the osprey is one of the most well studied of all the raptors.

Every species is an evolutionary assemblage, but in a sense, the osprey is unique in terms of its taxonomy: literally in a "class" by itself. While it is a member of the accipiters *(Order Accipitriformes,* made up of four families of some 225 species), it is the single species within the single genus *Pandion,* found on every continent except Antarctica, a notable geographical spread for a single species.

Another unique trait of the osprey is that it is the only North American raptor that depends on a diet of live fish. To hang onto that slimy prey while maintaining its iconic head-forward position, this bird has developed several unique characteristics of its toes and talons. Most importantly, the osprey has an ability to switch its four toes around so that there are two in front and two in back. (Other hawks maintain the three-in-front, one-behind arrangement.) With binoculars you can sometimes see the toes change position just as the bird's feet reach down into the water. Another adaptation is that the talons are round rather than grooved,

Captured fish are always transported head-first for minimal wind resistance. (photo: Sharon Fiedler)

presumably to prevent the fish from escaping its grasp. Finally, the pads adjacent to the talons are barbed, making it further unlikely that the mackerel or trout will escape.

Appearances to the contrary, this moment is a vulnerable one for *P. haliaetus*. That is when it's subject to theft by its imperial raptorial cousins. Here in Maine, this is usually the **bald eagle** *(Haliaeetus leucocephalus)* although there is the occasional **golden eagle** *(Aquila chrysaetos)*. A lumbering eagle roars down upon the smaller osprey, turns upside down and then attacks from beneath in a high-speed battle with a fish for a prize. An osprey has a five- to six-foot wingspan and weighs around four pounds, while the eagle has a wingspan that may exceed seven feet and can weigh nearly fourteen pounds. Even viewed from a distance, this battle of the titans is thrilling to watch. But while this interspecies *kleptoparasitism* benefits the eagle, it does not harm the osprey: the only likely damage to either party is the loser's ruffled feathers.

There are, however, other dangers. Great horned owls prey on osprey. Raccoons and other furry mammals steal eggs from their nests, and, of course, there are humans. Fish farms are a magnet for ospreys, and, though the bounty may be beyond the wildest dreams of any osprey, so too is the ire of the farmer. Birds of prey are protected in this country, but elsewhere the osprey may be shot, trapped or poisoned with impunity.

—T. O.

Connecting the Dots: Osprey Migration

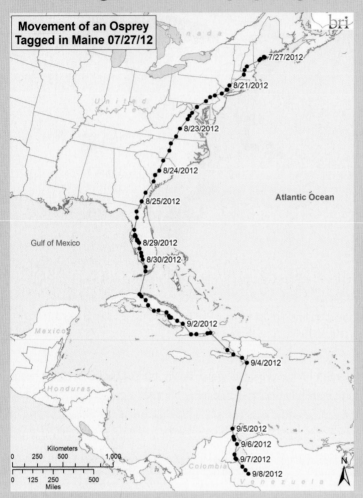

**Movement of an Osprey
Tagged in Maine 07/27/12**

7/27/2012
8/21/2012
8/23/2012
8/24/2012
8/25/2012

Atlantic Ocean

Gulf of Mexico

8/29/2012
8/30/2012

9/2/2012

Mexico

9/4/2012

Honduras

Kilometers
0   250   500   1,000

0   125   250   500
Miles

9/5/2012
9/6/2012
9/7/2012
9/8/2012

Colombia

Venezuela

N

(Courtesy of Biodiversity Research Institute)

This map shows the fall migration path of an osprey tracked to its wintering area. In July 2012, biologists from Biodiversity Research Institute fitted an adult female osprey with a backpack-mounted GPS tracking device. Biologists were able to track this individual to its winter haunts in Venezuela and document the route it used to get there. Almost exactly one year later, the biologists recaptured her to remove her transmitter following yet another successful breeding season in Wiscasset, Maine.

Ospreys are one of the most commonly observed raptors in Maine. Often observed along the coast, these striking, large black-and-white birds are typically found where fish are abundant.

Evolution has "molded" a beak superbly designed for consuming fish. (photo: Chris DeSorbo)

Ospreys are one of several raptor species whose populations declined precipitously due to the devastating effects of the pesticide DDT that caused catastrophic reproductive failures in birds—especially top-level predators. Following the banning of DDT in 1972, and other protections, their populations have made a strong recovery throughout much of their range, and Maine is no exception. One characteristic that unquestionably helped osprey populations recover is their uncanny willingness to build nests on human structures including nest platforms, buoys, towers and power poles. Ospreys often arrive in Maine during early to mid-April and depart for warmer climes in late July into August after their young have fledged.

— Chris DeSorbo

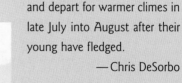

Up and away goes a briefly captured bird wired to transmit its travels. (photo: Chris DeSorbo)

The name "wakerobin" comes from the perceived common timing in spring of the plant's flower and the bird's eggs.

Trillium erectum: a Flower Worth Finding

They say that this trillium blooms when the robins arrive, but in these days of scrambled climates this truism holds less true. I am certain of this because in Midcoast Maine I have photographed robins' eggs and the flowering trillium on the same day, anytime between mid-April and early May. Hence wakerobin may not be the best of the several names traditionally given this spring ephemeral. Nor does "stinking Benjamin" do it justice, even if the flower does smell of rotting meat. But those names, at least, begin the story.

Who was Benjamin? There was no Benjamin, at least not a human one. The name comes from the Indonesian gum benjamin tree, *Styrax benzoin,* or "kemenyan" in the Malay language. The gum was rendered to oil then blended with frankincense and sandalwood, among other sweet-smelling ingredients, to make incense and perfume. Over time benjamin became synonymous with these happy odors, so we have a name that boils down to "stinking perfume."

Why the stink? That answer is more obvious: to attract pollinators. This flower may look as if it was dipped in wine from Burgundy, but to a flesh-eating fly, the flower smells and looks like rotting meat. The attraction does not reward the plant alone, however, as a visiting fly may enjoy a vegetarian meal. But in "flying" off it distributes its host's pollen.

A better name? Poor Benjamin. He cannot easily escape an unfortunate name, at least not to the level of elegance this arresting spring beauty deserves. In fact he has acquired many names, which more or less speak for themselves: nosebleed, birthroot or Beth root (for menstruation), trinity lily, three-leafed nightshade, Jew's harp plant, Indian shamrock, and rattlesnake root, among others. Some feel there is insufficient evidence to rate the medicinal effectiveness of poor stinking Benjamin, though Native Americans and colonists are said to have used its astringent quality to stem bleeding. Perhaps it's sufficient to simply enjoy this harbinger of warmer days. *Trillium erectum* is not listed as threatened in Maine, but he/she does not transplant and is somewhat rare: a true ephemeral.

—T. O.

◆ 2 ◆ Maquoit Bay:
World of the Tidal Flats

Old apple tree at the Wharton Point Landing frames the outlet of a small tidal creek, a favored foraging area for shorebirds.

COME DOWN TO THIS BAY FROM BUSY BRUNSWICK for a look at the saltmarsh and mudflat environment essential to the species that thrive in this setting. Birdwatchers will likely find wading birds such as snowy egrets, great blue herons and various shorebirds (*see* p. 18) feeding and resting along the shoreline, as well as songbirds such as the saltmarsh sharp-tailed sparrow known to breed in the area. Those who wish simply for quiet contemplation of the world around them will find few people at either of these two sites and a long vista extending to the southwest down which to gaze.

Preserving as much as possible of shoreline property is vital to the health of Maine's marine environment and for the well-being of those of us who *must* have access to the natural world. And a protected ecosystem is also essential to the livelihoods of those who harvest the resources of the sea, specifically in this case, the soft-shell clams that live in the muddy substrate of bays such as this one.

Brunswick benefits greatly from the Town's land conservation program, backed by federal and non-profit agencies.

Seagulls use Rocky Point as a drop zone to break apart clams and mussels. High tide view, looking northeast to Wharton Point Landing.

The bay also supports eelgrass beds—a true flowering plant as opposed to sea-weeds that are more primitive algae—that are critical to many marine species, such as described in this Seagrant excerpt:

> Eelgrass supports several commercial fisheries by providing structure, shel-ter, and foraging habitat in mud flats, mixed sediment or sand flat environ-ments. American lobsters, blue mussels, soft-shell clams, razor clams, blood worms, sand worms, rock crabs, sand shrimp, periwinkles, and winter flounder all benefit from eelgrass beds.
>
> (http://seagrant.mit.edu/eelgrass/eelgrassscience/importance.html)

But of late both the eelgrass and soft-shell clams have suffered marked declines in a changing climate, in part due to a commensurate increase in one particular species, the green crab (*see* p. 13). This predator of clams and other marine invertebrates, for-merly rare north of Cape Cod, has attained record numbers on the Midcoast, with Maquoit Bay and contiguous areas being hotspots of the green crab "invasion," por-tending an uncertain future for commercial clammers. Soft-shell clam landings in Maine have shown a downward trend from a high of 40 million pounds in 1977 to about 10 million pounds in recent years.

According to George Augustus Wheeler in the *History of Brunswick, Topsham, and Harpswell, Maine* (1878), Maquoit means "bear place," and though you won't see that spe-cies here anymore, there are still many species to find on a trip to the following two sites.

Maquoit Bay Conservation Land

The ½-mile trail runs down a spine of land with drop-offs on either side before emerg-ing onto a point with a good overview of the bay. The plant inventory and topography of the site by the Brunswick-Topsham Land Trust notes a variety of trees in the upland section, including,

> white pine, red oak, red maple, red spruce, hemlock, paper birch, and large-toothed aspen. There are three steep gullies where hemlocks are generally

Masses of dead eelgrass blow ashore in the prevailing southwest winds of summer.

A shoreline uncluttered by buildings is a sight worth preserving. Looking southwest to Bunganuc Point.

dominant, though a hardwood stand of relatively mature beech, ash, red maple, and birch is found along the northen reaches of the middle gully. In the gullies are freshwater streams bordered by strips of narrow wetland predominated by mixed ferns and sedges [that] transition from bulrush-sedge wetlands upland, to spartina salt marsh towards the coast, which then open out to tidal mud flats. The forests are generally 30 or 40 years old, with older trees more frequent in gullies and closer to Rocky Point.

Directions: Maquoit Bay Conservation Land, 124 acres, Town of Brunswick, Department of Parks and Recreation

From downtown Brunswick, take Maine Street south past Bowdoin College campus; then bear right on Maquoit Road for 1.9 miles; then right onto Woodside followed by quick left onto Bunganuc Road to parking area on left. Dogs must be leashed at all times. Please note that hunting is permitted in this park.

WebSource: www.brunswickme.org/departments/parks-recreation/

Commemorative plaque at the landing is a quick history lesson, describing activity at the site from the days of the Native Americans to the present. (photo: Brunswick Parks and Recreation Department)

That should pique the interest of curious travelers with an eye to the plants, while birders will have equal opportunity for both songbirds in the woods and waterbirds on the bay. And those out for a quiet walk will find cool shade from the tree canopy overhead.

Maquoit (Wharton Point) Landing

The landing is both a place to view nature and a working waterfront for the clammers, wormers and other fishermen. It has long seen use by humans, starting with native Abenaki people who portaged back and forth from the Androscoggin River, and starting in the later 1600s by European migrants, including Thomas Wharton who owned the land at that time.

Today it is a handy vantage point to "glass" the bay for wildlife in all seasons, or just to enjoy the coastal breeze on a hot day in summer. Or launch a boat and go exploring down the bay.

The ramp is used year-round by clammers, some of whom use airboats to navigate the miles of mudflats.

Directions: Maquoit Landing, Town of Brunswick, Department of Parks and Recreation

From downtown Brunswick, take Maine Street south past Bowdoin College campus; then bear right on Maquoit Road for 1.9 miles to landing parking area. Dogs must be leashed at all times

WebSource: www.brunswickme.org/departments/parks-recreation/

This species thrives in a variety of habitats, as in this rocky tide pool amid red and green marine algae.

The Green Crab in Maine: "Mean, Green, Eating Machine"

As a child summering in Maine, I used to delight in the ability to turn over a fan of sun-dried seaweed on a rocky shoreline and find skittering greenish brown crabs to grab before they grabbed you. They were fast and not shy about defending themselves. I had no idea then that what I was seeing—and assumed to be a part of Maine's natural shoreline environment—was, in fact, not native to our coast but rather a 200-year-old transplant that, with increasing sea temperatures, would become a major disruptive force to our near-shore marine ecology.

The **European green crab** (*Carcinus maenas*) is on every top-100 list of the worst invasive organisms worldwide. This not-so-august group includes the likes of the brown tree snake, the cane toad, the Asian catfish, kudzu, the zebra mussel, the Norway rat and the domestic cat. This crustacean is silently munching away on anything its size or smaller, and armed as it is with a think-tank's array of attributes to survive, it has proven that adaptation through generalization can win the day.

It is believed that the primary vector for the spread of these animals into non-native waters was off-loaded ship ballast, first in the form of stones in the early 1800s, and later simply ballast water. There may well be many other more recent transport means for this adaptive species, such as the use of seaweed as packing material for the transport of live seafood.

This European invasive is rather small and, in fact, not always green. Shell (carapace) size rarely exceeds 3.5 inches by 2.5 inches, and its color can run from dark kelp green to brown and even a rusty red, depending on the substrate and whether it's male or female. The creature can most easily be identified by the five tooth-shaped shell protrusions (spines) behind each eye. This is, in fact, the easiest way to distinguish it from its closest cousin, *Carcinus aestuarii,* also a native of the Mediterranean.

This crustacean has been so successful at conquering new habitats around the globe that it is now referred to simply as the "green crab." It broke the bonds of the European continent long ago; green crabs were first sighted on the east coast of the United States in Massachusetts in 1817. From that humble start, *Carcinus* has moved inexorably north and south, eating its way into new habitats. Its range on the east coast is now from South Carolina, where warm waters inhibit its movement further south, to as far north as Newfoundland, where cold water, for now, holds it back. The US west coast has seen a far quicker expansion. The green crab was first noticed in San Francisco Bay in 1989; remarkably, by the late 1990s, it was found as far north as British Columbia and south to the Baja peninsula.

Green crabs are now found globally. They have invaded virtually every major land mass shoreline that has temperature conditions within its wide tolerance. Only New Zealand now remains to be conquered, which is probably only a matter of time. In some marine environments, they are only one of many voices in the choir, but in most places green crabs are writing the score for all to follow.

This animal is the perfect study in adaptation. Its key to success is a diabolical assembly of both disruptor and conqueror characteristics. The green crab can tolerate a wide range of water temperatures (called *eurythermic*), from 32 to 86 degrees F. It can thrive in an equally broad range of salinities (called *euryhaline*). It prefers muddy or sandy bottoms but proliferates on rocky shores as well. It likes to be in shallow water but can be found as deep as 40 feet and may be able to go even deeper. Add to this list the facts that *Carcinus* can go for up to three months without food, can live out of water for up to 10 days, and is prolific, with an average-sized female producing upwards of 185,000 eggs at one time.

On top of all of this, *Carcinus* can eat almost anything it comes across in its new habitats. Studies performed for the Global Invasive Species Database suggest that up to 158 separate genera are on the menu for this invasive. In order to have such a wide range of food available to it, the green crab is gifted with an extraordinary set of skills. Here's how the Washington State Department of Fish and Wildlife characterizes their new invasive crab: "The European green crab is capable of learning and can improve prey-handling skills while foraging. The crab is quicker, more dexterous, and can open shells in more ways than other species of crabs." What exactly are we up against here?

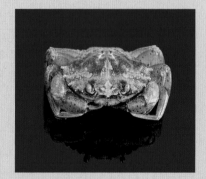

Green crabs are in the Order Decapoda, meaning "10 legs." (photo: Brian Beal)

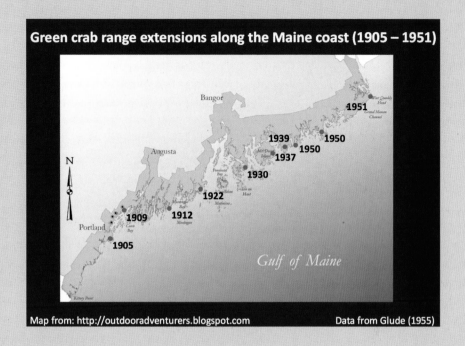

Green crab range extensions along the Maine coast (1905 – 1951)

Map from: http://outdooradventurers.blogspot.com   Data from Glude (1955)

These adaptive characteristics would enable any creature to prosper, but the green crab also has the ugliest of temperaments. There is emerging evidence that the original green crab invaders of the early 1800s came from southern European stock, but a second wave of *Carcinus*, from more northerly origins, has appeared since the 1970s and 1980s. This new genotype was first seen in Nova Scotia and seems to not only be more cold-tolerant but also to sport a far more belligerent attitude. Its aggressive, take-no-prisoners behavior allows it to elbow its way into many varied ecosystems and become a force to be reckoned with. Thank goodness it doesn't grow to the size of Dungeness or king crabs, or tidepool exploration in this part of the world would become a painful pastime.

Crustaceans like the green crab share the physiological need to grow by shedding their hard outer shell, called molting or shedding, and then re-growing it over a period of time. This is generally when they would be most vulnerable to predation by other crustaceans, as well as fish. The green crab has, however, evolved a behavior to minimize the risks of this time period. As the female green crab begins the process of molting, the male of the species, which is usually larger, will embrace the female within his intimidating claws and hold on to her until her shell has hardened; in some instances, they will also mate. This "spooning" behavior both protects the females at their most vulnerable period and also probably insures that the largest males will have sole genetic claim to a female.

What has put this Maine invasive so high on the lists of global invasives is not so much how adaptive it is but, really, how much and what it eats. The green crab is a voracious, generalist hunter of marine mollusks, other crabs and small fish. It seems to have a special taste for soft-shell clams, scallops and mussels, and while it preys on them in their spat (early juvenile) stages, it can also crush and eat adult forms as big as itself. It is thought that one green crab in a single night will feed its epic appetite with as many as 40 half-inch clams. Clam flats in many regions along the Maine coast have been severely impacted by the green crab, and this important fishery is at risk.

There is a growing concern that if green crabs eat their way through Maine's shellfish populations, they may next turn to small or postlarval lobsters to satisfy their prodigious appetites. Much more needs to be understood about their interactions in the wild to know how large an issue this could become. Some early studies have shown that green crabs outcompete and devour lobsters their same size in controlled conditions. What we don't know is if lobsters are especially vulnerable when they shed and become "soft shells," but one could expect that to be the case (*Journal of Experimental Marine Biology and Ecology*, Vol. 329, Issue 2, 21 February 2006, pp. 281–288).

Evidence now shows that the green crab is also impacting Maine's coastal marsh communities. As the populations of these crustaceans have spiked in warming ocean waters, scientists are seeing damage to sea grasses like eelgrass and marsh grasses like spartina, due to both the grazing and burrowing activities of these crabs. It is known that they snip the grasses off at the base in order to better hunt for the varied organisms that might be hiding in the vegetation. They also will burrow extensively into the mud below, creating large galleries of tunnels that can cause diebacks of marsh grasses, as well as severe erosion and bank collapse. Scientists studying the damage to marsh grass communities in the upper Damariscotta River system and at other sites are now seeing evidence that *Carcinus maenas* may also be eating grasses as a part of its diet. Because the crabs feed at night, marine biologists have been relying on stomach contents and trapping to prove this theory. It is not known if the green crab normally eats marine vegetation or if this is caused by their proliferating numbers and reduced primary prey.

The important take away from the green crab problem is that we have lived with these invaders for over 200 years, and they are probably here to stay; we will not get rid of them. Ocean temperatures directly affect their populations, and as the temperatures rise, so do the number of green crabs and their impact on our coastal communities, both natural and human. "Most people don't know it, but water temperature in the 1950s was as warm as it is now," marine biologist Brian Beal said. "That temperature, combined with green crabs, wreaked havoc on the [clam] population. Then in the 1960s, we had a period of three years with heavy snow and it knocked green crabs on their ass, and the clam population started to return. We just haven't had a repeat performance of what we had in the 1960s" (*The Forecaster*, Dec. 11, 2012).

Maine now appears to be caught in the pincers of an established southern green crab population that is expanding north as waters warm and a more northerly population from

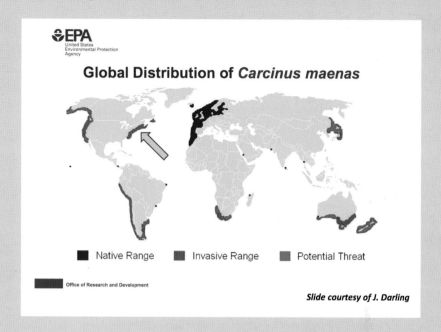

Global Distribution of *Carcinus maenas*

Native Range   Invasive Range   Potential Threat

Slide courtesy of J. Darling

Canada that is expanding south. We have managed through overfishing to eradicate most of the natural fish species that would have dined on this new invertebrate, and so the table is quite literally set.

Efforts are underway to try to control green crab numbers in some way while protecting economically important shellfish stocks. Trapping these animals is easy but at present not economical. In order to allow a bay to recover, every crab has to be trapped and then the bay fenced off—a tall order at best. There has been some limited success using netting laid over clam flats to protect the growing shellfish stock from these invaders, but that too is costly and problematic.

Carcinus has very little meat in proportion to shell, so what would be the most elegant solution—for we humans to eat it—has so far not been realized. There is no established market for green crabs as a fertilizer, a source of animal feed or even bait for lobsters. We can hope for colder winters, but few climatologists would say that is likely.

In its native European and North African habitats, there are several natural population controls for *Carcinus*, including a parasite in the barnacle family that interferes with the male crab's reproductive functions, a greater number of other crab species that help keep populations in check, and a wider diversity of fish and bird predators than here on the Maine coast.

However, as much as it would be nice to end on a note of hope for the US situation, there is currently no apparent solution. This invader in our midst has the upper hand just now, and it's everywhere we look.

— D. F.

Gallery of Maquoit Bay Waders

In the warm months, nature photogapher David White walks a regular beat with his camera in the Brunswick area, and follows the birds to Florida in the winter. He has encountered all these species at Maquoit Bay. His online offering of nature shots is at http://davewhitewildlife. blogspot.com. (all photos: David White)

Lesser yellowlegs *(Tringa flavipes)* snares a sandworm.

Short-billed dowitchers *(Limnodromus griseus)* forage in the spartina grass.

Willets *(Tringa semipalmata).*

Red knot *(Calidris canutus)* in fall plumage.

Great egret *(Ardea alba)* descends for a landing at the water's edge among snowy egrets.

Snowy egrets *(Egretta thula)* hunt in formation, at times spreading their wings to rouse fish from hiding.

19

◆ 3 ◆ "Twin" Preserves on the Long Reach

Cliff Trail Preserve rewards curious travelers with one of the finer views in the Midcoast area.

Maine has bays, sounds, harbors, coves and pools. It also has a few reaches, famously Eggemoggin and this one, Long Reach, upon whose east and west shores lie two preserves that face one another. Along with Doughty Preserve not far to the north, much of the land has been conserved by the Town of Harpswell and the Harpswell Heritage Land Trust, land that would have otherwise been highly sought after by developers, given the secluded nature of the area so close to the densely populated Brunswick/Topsham environs less than ten miles to the north.

As in many of the water bodies in the area, much of Long Reach drains entirely at low tide exposing acres of muddy gray sediments, the silty, almost liqui–d substrate so favored by marine invertebrates, such as soft-shell clams and clam worms, both important species for those who work the sediments for a hard-won source of income.

These two sites on Great Island are among many other preserves in the Harpswell area—including the Bowdoin Coastal Center Preserve (chapter 4) and the Giant's Stairs (chapter 5)—all listed on the Town's and Land Trust's websites shown below the map.

Cliff Trail Preserve

When you reach the top of the Cliff Trail, the only sign of human development will be the large hangar building at the former Brunswick Naval Air Station far off in the distance. Through a variety of easements by several agencies, land on both sides of Long Reach remains the largest undeveloped area in Harpswell, to the obvious benefit of both wildlife and humans who value such preservation.

What forces of nature bent these trees across the path?

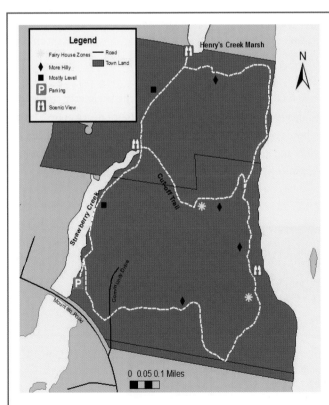

Directions: Cliff Trail Preserve, 200 acres, Harpswell, Town of Harpswell

From the center of Brunswick, take Rte. 123 south 6.2 miles, then left onto Mountain Rd. 1.3 miles to Harpswell Town Office on left. The trailhead is located behind the office on Mountain Road at the far corner of the parking lot near Strawberry Creek. Dogs on leash.

WebSource: www.harpswell.maine.gov/
http://hhltmaine.org/conserved-land

Above: Trees give way to bedrock that gives way to the "ooze" of Strawberry Creek, with only a sinuous rivulet at low tide. Within the sediments thrives a community of marine invertebrate species—crustaceans, mollusks, worms—most of which are known only to ecological researchers. Right: From atop the 150-foot overlook on the Cliff Trail, looking east to the Long Reach Preserve on the opposite shore, the extent of the tidal flats is evident. Clammers work the area for the iconic "steamer" clams.

Two contiguous loop trails, totaling about 2 ½ miles, cover the perimeter and center of the preserve, with three scenic views marked on the map, the best one, of course, at the cliff summit, as well as at the heads of Strawberry and Henry's Creeks, where birders can scan the tidal marshes for waders and ducks in the various seasons. And, as in all preserves, the quiet solitude of walking a forest path is reward unto itself for a trip to this site.

Outcrops of quartz are bright spots among the otherwise mossy green and pine-needle brown of the forest floor along the trail.

Red spruce spread shallow roots not much deeper than a foot in the thin forest soil, termed "duff," where the most nutrients are to be had, and so are susceptible to windthrow. New seedlings will soon emerge in the presence of increased sunlight.

Long Reach Preserve

As stated on the land trust's description, the preserve "is a classic example of Harpswell's folded bedrock geology. Two steep bedrock ridges separated by peat-filled wetlands run north-south along the property. Long Reach itself [considered a high-value estuarine habitat] is another submerged valley that is now tidal mudflats." It is a logical adjunct to the Cliff Trail, with reciprocal views across the Reach from the respective shorelines. Three loop trails provide access to the various habitats within the preserve, each with its own community of plants and animals.

The northeast section of the preserve is the southern terminus of Long Marsh that extends over two miles to the north, gradually transitioning from a freshwater to saltwater ecosystem. Here, it is described as a shrub-scrub freshwater wetland, defined as shallow wetlands and water bodies with short woody vegetation less than 20 feet high. On the western side of the site is a narrow bog wetland that runs almost a quarter mile parallel-ing the loop trail. On our May visit we

Fiddleheads of ferns develop underground sometimes for years, emerging finally in a spurt of growth. The cells on the inner side of the coil grow faster than the outer side, causing the young plant to unwind.

*The blooming of **trailing arbutus** (Epigaea repens), with its fragrant flowers and distinctive evergreen leaves, is one of the many rewards of May in Maine. Native Americans made a tea of the leaves for stomach and kidney ailments, and the plant does contain a substance, arbutin, used as a urinary antiseptic, according to the* Peterson Medicinal Plants guide. *And its presence requires a particular micro-habitat:*

> *The sensitiveness of Ericaceae [its family] has been shown to be connected with the fact that their roots grow in a sort of mutually helpful parasitic relationship with certain fungi, which themselves are prevented from thriving unless the soil is too acid for the growth of most bacteria. (William Trelease,* Winter Botany*)*

Burls are nature's sculptures, caused by trauma to the bark of a tree from mechanical injury, insect, bacteria, or virus. As described on the U.S. Forest Service website, "Once damaged, the cambium [inner bark] cells continue to produce abnormal xylem [transport system from roots to leaves], resulting in burls which enlarge throughout the life of the tree."

were lucky enough to find trailing arbutus blooming, along with many of the other so-called spring ephemerals, the small, forest-floor flowers that "gladden the heart" of the winter weary.

In the very southwest corner, you will have a view across the water to the Cliff Trail preserve and its 150-foot overlook. Low tide will reveal the acres of mudflats and perhaps clammers and wormers with "beached" boats working the sediments; at high tide ospreys or eagles may be seen overhead or perched in trees.

Northern section of the bog.

Early spring in the bog: the sphagnum substrate is greening and ferns are uncurling, while the deciduous shrubbery has yet to leaf out.

Directions: Long Reach Preserve, 93 acres, Harpswell, Harpswell Heritage Land Trust

Long Reach Preserve is located on the Harpswell Islands Road (Route 24) about 3 miles south of the Brunswick-Harpswell town line and adjacent to the Trufant-Summerton Ball Field on Sebascodegan (Great) Island. The trail head is to the right as you drive into the ball field. Dogs allowed on leash.

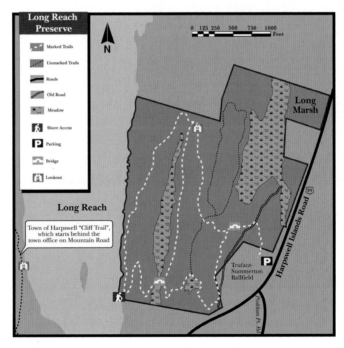

WebSource: http://hhltmaine.org/conserved-land/public-access/long-reach-preserve/

Description of Long Marsh ecosystem:

http://hhltmaine.org/wp-content/uploads/2013/04/HHLT-Fall11-Newsltr.pdf

Trebuchet in the Woods

The eternal boy—*puer aeternus,* myself included—is likely to enjoy a lingering fascination with trebuchets, those ancient Roman catapults. So when a magazine article about a plant referenced

one, I kept reading. My curiosity led me to an article in *Nature* (May 12, 2005), which revealed the surprising ability of the common **bunchberry dogwood** *(Cornus canadensis).* This is the unmistakable, green-and-white, five-inch herb that carpets the damp ground of our Midcoast forests. Beautiful and easy to recognize, bunchberry thrives in acidic soil, sharing the dappled light with various mosses, lichens and patches of false Canada lily. The four white petals of the flower that come out as early as May are in fact specialized leaves, called bracts, that surround the true, pale-green flowers. As spring turns to summer, a cluster of bright red berries replaces the bracts and flowers.

Flower, leaves and fruit of the bunchberry, a common woodland plant, are reminiscent of its much larger relative, the **flowering dogwood** *(Cornus florida)* of more southerly climes.

As pretty as these may be, they are hardly worth collecting as food as they have no taste and are filled with seeds. By autumn the six to eight true leaves turn a rusty blood-red. But this information is available in plant guides. What's not is the subject of study by four Oberlin College researchers: the spellbinding method of pollination by which the tiny flowers and their stamens spread their seeds. These are the botanical trebuchets.

A trebuchet is a specialized catapult first used by the Roman military to hurl boulders at walls or fire at the enemy. The physics is simple, but as applied to plant pollination it provides an exquisite example of botanical evolution.

Imagine a basic playground seesaw with an off-center pivot such that one side is longer than the other. A heavy counterweight is raised and suspended from the end of the shorter, elevated arm, while the longer one, holding a relatively lighter projectile, is held down near the ground. When the weight is suddenly released, the long end flips up tossing the missile rapidly into the air. Tuck a sling between tracks under the longer arm and the catapult becomes a trebuchet, a device that combines the power of a slingshot with the rotational acceleration of a sling. For two thousand years—even after the invention of gunpowder and cannon—this was the most destructive siege weapon in the world, and remains a testament to human ingenuity in the art of fighting.

Even so, a trebuchet doesn't hold a candle to the "simple" bunchberry whose spring-loaded stamens have been catapulting pollen into the air for millennia at speeds too fast for the eye to see. The plant wins, hands down. It is, according to the authors "the fastest movement so far recorded in a plant."

Each of the tiny flowers is about a tenth of an inch tall, with four diminutive petals and stamens. In the closed position, the stamens are contained by the petals folded together and fused at the tip. With the touch of a passing insect, the hinged, cocked and armed stamens release their load of pollen into the sky. They snap outward with incredible velocity: the stamens accelerate at 24,000 meters per second squared (m/s2), according to the authors of the Nature article. This occurs with a relative force that is 800 times greater than what is experienced by astronauts at lift-off.

The action propels the pollen about an inch into the air. This may not seem like much, but it's enough to pepper the insect whose touch initiated the sequence. In a flash the insect has pulled the trigger and transformed itself into a target: a symbiotic dance of pollination.

A bunchberry trebuchet releases its pollen in less than 0.4 milliseconds. That's 125 times faster than the strike of a chameleon's tongue or 333 times faster than the closing of a Venus's flytrap. How do we know? We know because Associate Professor Marta Laskowski, used a camera that records 10,000 pictures per second. Her results are visible at www.oberlin.edu/news-info/05may/expflower.html. Not long in the event. Eons in the making. It's a compelling, watch-it-again movie.

Take a walk next spring with a pine needle or a bit of button thread stiffened with saliva. Looking through a set of jeweler's spectacles or a magnifying glass, touch a bunchberry flower. You might just see the oldest and tiniest trebuchet in the woods.

— T. O.

Here to Stay?

A common but unwanted plant to be seen in Maine is the non-native **Japanese barberry** *(Berberis thunbergii)*, introduced to the US in the late 1800s as an ornamental. (It is distinct from the native **common barberry** *(Berberis vulgaris)*, no longer common, and purposefully eradicated in some areas because of its role in spreading wheat rust.) This native of Asia first arrived at Boston's Arnold Arboretum as seeds from Russia in 1875. It is tolerant of shade and sun and can grow in many soil types up to six feet high in a densely packed bush, armored with piercing spines. It prefers disturbed settings but will grow and invade undisturbed forest stands or clearings. It is resistant to browsing deer, and in the fall it produces a large number of lovely red berries that the birds will eat. (The genus name means "fruit" in Arabic.) Birds are, in turn, its primary form of seed dispersal, but a branch in contact with the ground can also take root to create another bush. Japanese barberry leafs out earlier in

the spring than most other native plants and retains its leaves longer in the fall. It cannot be killed by cutting, but needs to be pulled from the ground root and all to be certain of eradication. Directed fire on the root system is also effective once the primary bush has been cut down.

To top it off there seems to be evidence now that deer mice, the host to larval deer ticks, prefer the protective habitat that this thorny bush offers, and for this reason has now become a vector point for Lyme disease. Where it is controlled, there are fewer incidences of deer mice, deer ticks and Lyme. In one Connecticut study it is thought that tick populations can reach 120 ticks per acre in a stand of barberry bushes as opposed to the norm of closer to 10 ticks per acre. This adds another more lethal layer to the term invasive.

— D. F.

Japanese barberry bushes grow from two to six feet high and wide. Birds eat the fruit and spread the seeds, said to have a 90% germination rate. (photos: Des FitzGerald, *top*; Alison C. Dibble, *bottom*)

◆ 4 ◆ Bowdoin College Coastal Studies Center Preserve

Intertidal area reveals acres of rockweed and exposed bedrock along the Long Cove trail.

THIS SECLUDED NECK OF LAND, BOUNDED ON BOTH SIDES BY WATER, is not only a nature site but a nature research facility, as well, for aspiring scientists at nearby Bowdoin College, with a marine science laboratory housing aquaria and a solar-powered terrestrial science laboratory for interdisciplinary purposes. Imagine what the former residents of the 1800s, farmers and fishermen, would think upon seeing the place today, with its modern buildings and much of the cleared land returned to forest. Consider spending some time here, with a series of trails totaling 3 ½ miles spread over 118 acres of diverse habitats, with an interpretive trail guide (see web link below map) listing biological and historical aspects at 19 marked stations.

If you arrive at low tide, head for Wyer Island, an islet on the west side connected by a gravelly spit, a good vantage point over Harpswell Sound. On the spit itself are dense layers of shells from clams and snails, collected here by the prevailing current. The guide describes the island as a "harsh environment characterized by high winds, full sun, and constant ocean spray," clustered thickly with its main vegetation of poison ivy, bayberry, beach rose, birch and spruce. Here a small embayment harbors a quiet pool where seagulls ply the intertidal shallows for clams, crabs and other invertebrates.

A pine, fallen some years ago, has transformed a branch into its trunk. Thick carpets of pine needles throughout much of the preserve make for comfortable walking.

From Wyer Island, a clockwise walk around the periphery of the peninsula leads to Brewer Cove—site of a spring that provides water to animals and in former days to humans—and on to Dog Head, before turning south to skirt the shore of Long Cove, ending at the edge of the meadows that are cut late in the season to promote ground nesters such as bobolinks, and small grassland mammals such as voles and jumping mice.

Visitors with an affinity for butterflies can scan the meadows for various species working the flowers for nectar, including the swallowtail butterfly (*see* p. 34) and luna moth (p. 32). This fine piece of Maine's geography has been conserved under the aegis of the College for all to explore for perpetuity and awaits curious travelers in their peregrinations along the many miles of the Midcoast.

On the west shoreline Dipper Cove trail, walk the connector out to Wyer Island to see clam and snail shells of many species, such as periwinkles and oysters, amassed by incoming tidal currents on the north side of the spit.

Seaside Plantain (Plantago maritima), *highly salt tolerant, grows along the shoreline even in the meager sediments collected in rock crevices.* **Glasswort** (Salicornia europaea), *the ashes of which were formerly used in glassmaking, is an edible succulent, also adapted to the rocky seashore environment.*

Directions: Bowdoin College Coastal Studies Center, 118 acres, Orr's Island

From Route in Cooks Corner, go south on Route 24 for 10.7 miles. Turn right onto Bayview Road, about 1.7 miles south of the Orr's Island Bridge. After approximately 1 mile, the road ends and parking is available in designated spaces. Do not drive on to farm property. Dogs allowed on leash.

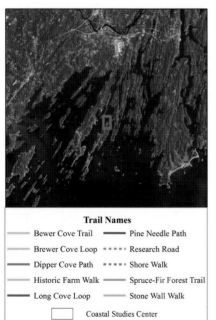
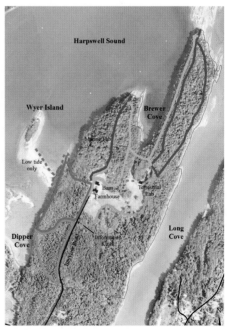

Trail Names

Bewer Cove Trail	Pine Needle Path
Brewer Cove Loop	Research Road
Dipper Cove Path	Shore Walk
Historic Farm Walk	Spruce-Fir Forest Trail
Long Cove Loop	Stone Wall Walk
Coastal Studies Center	

WebSource: www.bowdoin.edu/marine-laboratory/location/history-trail-guide.shtml

Luna Moths: Winged Elegance

The not-often-seen underside of a male luna moth shows the "furry" body and exquisite antennae. (photo: Melissa Duron)

Of all moths, the **luna moth** (*Actias luna*) is one of the more captivating and curiosity-eliciting lepidopteran species, with its sizeable sea-green colored wings, long hind-wing tails, robust furry body and large feathered antennae. In the Northeast, adult luna moths appear from May to July with the sole goal of reproducing before their fat reserves are gone, since they do not feed as adults (Tuskes et al. 1996). Luna moth success is dependent on food availability, predator avoidance, habitat integrity and environmental conditions.

Most field guides will list multiple deciduous tree species as food sources and declare the luna moth to be a generalist. However, a study conducted by Tallamy et al. (2010) wanted to determine the effect of non-native plants on native moths such as the luna moth. The luna moths either did not survive on alien plant species or did not have the same biomass as their counterparts that were reared on native plants. Furthermore, luna moths reared on native plants had mixed survivorship and lower biomass on their purported host plants, which possibly indicates regional host plant specificity. As much as food availability is important, so is nutritional content. Lindroth et al. (1995) found that experimentally raised carbon dioxide levels, such as those expected with climate change, led to changes in the chemical composition of birch leaves. This resulted in increased time spent feeding, presumably to obtain the same amount of nutrients found in leaves grown under normal carbon dioxide levels. A well-nourished, fat caterpillar is necessary to complete the luna moth life cycle and important to the health of the overall food web by providing nourishment to predators.

Predator avoidance in both adults and caterpillars is necessary to ensure luna moth success. Since adults cannot feed, they are short-lived and must conserve fat reserves by staying inactive until a mate is found. Inactivity and short life span reduce their chances for getting eaten before they've had a chance to find a mate and lay eggs (Tuskes et al. 1996). Caterpillars, on the other hand, must have a different strategy to avoid predation. Brown et al. (2007) found that luna moth caterpillars make a clicking sound before regurgitating a substance that is likely distasteful to predators such as ants, mice and chicks. Furthermore, the clicking sound is transmitted within the optimal hearing range of bats, leading one to believe that this sound could be a bat deterrent. Under normal conditions, luna moths have the necessary defensive techniques to ensure a fair fight. However, when introducing an alien species such as a **European parasitic fly** (*Compsilura concinnata*), brought in to control the gypsy moth, it seems that luna moths and other members of its family, Saturniidae, are at a disadvantage. In a study conducted in Massachusetts, researchers found *C. concinnata* predation rates as high as 81 percent on one saturniid species (Boettner

From larva to adult: no two forms could be more dissimilar.

et al. 2000). In a similar study conducted in Virginia, researchers found predation rates as high as 78 percent in luna moths (Kellogg et al. 2003).

Delicate balances between predator and prey are dependent on habitat stability and are vulnerable to ecosystem disruptions, such as climate change and non-native species. Although this is just one species in the forested ecosystem, the luna moth story could be extrapolated out to other lepidoptera, which are a necessary component in the food chain. Lepidoptera success means success for higher trophic level species. While it is tempting to look to megafauna as sentinels for environmental changes, maybe it makes more sense to look to charismatic ubiquitous fauna to be bellwethers in our changing landscape, especially one as captivating as the luna moth. (*See* Bibliography for scientific references.)

— Melissa Duron

Mimicry and the Eastern Tiger Swallowtail Butterfly (and Others)

A swarm of **eastern tiger swallowtail butterflies** (*Pterourus glaucas* and subspecies *canadensis* and *glaucas*) "puddling" for moisture on the ground catches the eye and begs explanation. So does a rabble of **monarchs** (*Danaus plexippus*) or a flutter of **viceroys** (*Limenitis archippus*). Or any of the other colorful butterflies whose presence we enjoy here on the Midcoast. How can such visible and apparently defenseless creatures thrive in the presence of a thousand predators? They are so conspicuous and so slow in flight, how is it that they are not pounced upon? How is it that they are able to survive? The answer is that they are indeed preyed upon. They are in fact consumed with abandon by a host of sharp-eyed creatures, among them robins, cardinals, sparrows, grackles, squirrels, shrews and raccoons. But enough survive, and one reason for this is mimicry, which can occur for many of these butterflies during one or more of their life phases.

Many of us have experienced a momentary uncertainty when spotting a large orange butterfly. Is it a viceroy or a monarch? Viewed side-by-side the two are easy to tell apart but there's enough similarity to have sparked a discussion that went on for years. Lepidopterists presumed that this convergence favored the viceroys because they were aware that a predator that found the monarch to be unpalatable was then averse to the look-alike viceroys. According to that notion, they labeled the monarch as the model and the viceroy as the mimic. They theorized that the more a viceroy resembled a monarch, the better its chances of avoiding predation. (This is somewhat oversimplified: for one thing toxin levels vary from specimen to specimen depending on what that individual's larvae have eaten. Some predators learned to recognize this, while others can distinguish which parts of their prey are poisonous—which only confirms the truism that prey-predator relationships are often less than obvious.) It turns out that this is only half the story.

The connection between viceroy and monarch butterflies is complicated because the viceroy actually tastes worse than the monarch, i.e., contains more toxins and is less palatable to their shared predators. In other words a viceroy gains protection by resembling the foul-tasting monarch although it is foul tasting itself. This circumstance provides a window through which to appreciate how species survive and an opportunity for a quick introduction to mimicry. It's true that to oversimplify the subject is to risk inaccuracy, but it's a risk worth taking because mimicry is a phenomenon that is all around us.

Although predators use mimicry to avoid being seen by their prey, the technique is more often used by prey as a disguise against predators. The garden variety occurs when one species (the mimic) in one way or another emulates some aspect of another species (the model) in order to escape predation. The most widely recognized version of this is referred to as Batesian mimicry. The name honors Henry Walter Bates, the Englishman who traveled with Alfred

It is usually the young males that "puddle" or congregate to extract nutrients from ground moisture. The adults also sip liquid food such as nectar from flowers, using their proboscis, a long "tongue."

Russell Wallace to South America in the 1840s. Bates contributed greatly to Darwin's (and Wallace's) exploration of diversity and change, in no small way because his thoughts about mimicry dovetailed neatly with Darwin's theories. Effective mimicry, after all, is a means of survival that allows for evolution.

Batesian mimicry identifies the technique of hiding out in the open, i.e., visible and vulnerable, but safe because the look-alike model is unpalatable. The advantage is to the mimic rather than the model. A straightforward example of Batesian mimicry would exist if viceroys were tasty and monarchs were not. In that case the viceroy would be the mimic and the monarch would be the model. But this is not how it works because both species are unpalatable. This baffled Bates, and others, but was finally explained in 1878 by the brilliant and fascinating, German-born Brazilian polymath, Fritz Müller. Müller realized that when two unpalatable, look-alike species co-evolve the threat of predation is distributed over a larger number of individuals, i.e., both species benefit. Unlike Batesian mimicry, Müllerian offers an advantage to both model and mimic. The two are similar, but the distinction is worth recognizing.

With Batesian and Müllerian mimicry safety involves sheltering in plain sight: here I am, conspicuous as all get out, but you won't eat me because either I am bitter, poisonous, or dangerous, or I appear to be. According to Prudic et al. in *The Oxford Journal of Behavioral Ecology* (2007, Vol. 18), being conspicuous means, "...to signal their unpalatability to potential predators." Such an adaption is generally thought of as a means of defense, but there is a ripple of benefit that extends to the hunter. A warning signal to a predator redirects that creature to another target, and results in so-called "predator aversion." The use of such a warning signal, referred to by biologists as *aposematism*, is widespread—think skunk, whose contrasting stripes may even be seen at night. If your dog has learned to avoid skunks, then the usefulness of that animal's high visibility, i.e. aposematic coloration, not only saves his or her hide, and the dog's, it may even include you, the dog's owner. It is useful to think of aposematism as involving three roles: the model, the mimic, and the predator. Of course if your dog is reluctant to learn the lesson, he/she and you will pay the price. You can hardly blame the skunk that may have even raised its tail in a further aposematic suggestion—a kind of visual growl of warning.

If you turn aposematism (wanting to be seen) on its ear, you have crypsis, or protection through invisibility (wanting not to be seen). Crypsis includes camouflage, which occurs when a predator or prey remains unseen. Imagine a white snowshoe hare in the winter or an ermine that is all but invisible but for its distracting black tail: see the tail and miss the mouth. It's a mistake the weasel's prey will make only once. In aposematism the mimic is perceived but presumed to be something that it is not; with crypsis either the predator or the prey is not recognized for what it is.

Batesian mimicry may involve any of the senses. Some tasty moths are said to use the ultrasound signals of unpalatable species to protect themselves from marauding bats. Burrowing owls may vocalize like rattlesnakes from within ground squirrel burrows. Rowe et al. found that squirrels experienced with rattlers avoided those burrows, while squirrels that were unfamiliar with them entered the burrows. (*Ethology: The International Journal of Behavioral Biology, 1986*).

A larger, intriguing question, and one not easily answered, is to ask how mimicry evolved to be what it is today. How does a predator-prey relationship stabilize when it must constantly evolve to remain effective? Michael Schiff, author of *Why Copy? The Evolution of Mimicry*, has put forth a simple answer suggesting that the benefit of mimicking outweighs the cost of being more conspicuous. This is not very satisfying, but it points to a kind of equilibrium of design with which we must be satisfied.

Like the monarch, the eastern tiger swallowtail is a large and spectacular butterfly with a wingspan that can exceed six inches. Unlike the monarch, however, our eastern tiger swallowtail does not migrate.

The eastern tiger swallowtail lifecycle begins as a greenish-yellow oval, BB-sized egg that the female lays high in a tree: ash, red maple, aspen, basswood, birch, chokecherry, American elm, black cherry, black willow, sassafras or hornbeam. Irrespective of the species, within a few days the egg hatches into a caterpillar larva that morphs through five stages, or *instars*. The earliest ones are brown and white and resemble bird droppings (Batesian mimicry). The fourth instar is bright green with two well-named eyespots that to all appearances transform the green instar into a tiny snake with fierce eyes that signal the wherewithal to bite back. A pair of distended stalks that emit a foul odor, called osmeterium, complement this show of ferocity. The combination is an effective aposematic signal that communicates a strong "don't tread on me" message. For the fifth and final instar, the larva turns brown and grows to over two inches long. After 9-11 days, the caterpillar pupates and forms a cryptic chrysalis. In Maine this cycle is repeated twice yearly. On the third go *P. glaucas* overwinters as a chrysalis.

The larval and pupal stages of this butterfly offer examples of Batesian mimicry, first hiding as bird scat and, later, as a small snake. The adult female provides another illustration of mimicry. She has evolved into two versions. She is, in other words, dimorphic—has two phenotypes—the familiar yellow one and a dark morph. (In either case she can usually be distinguished from the male by the amount of blue on the trailing edges of the wings. The distinction is more easily made after you have seen several examples.)

The dark female eastern tiger swallowtail morph is no accident. She is a tasty butterfly who gains protection from her predators by mimicking the poisonous pipevine or blue swallowtail (*Battus philenor*). The larvae of this butterfly depend on plants belonging to the *Aristolochia* genus, which is toxic to most other animals, but not the blue swallowtail larvae. (The genus includes a large group of plants many of which are visually striking and whose appearance may be more familiar to us than the name. The common pipewort (*A. durior*), which can grow in Maine, has the curved shape of the meerschaum pipes favored by Sherlock Holmes, hence its common name, Dutchman's pipe. Another, birthwort (*A. clematitis*), resembles a vagina. These and other *Aristolochia* have a long history of medicinal application in many countries but, ironically, have recently been proven to be carcinogens.)

The blue swallowtail's larvae's tolerance for pipewort makes the adult butterfly undesirable to birds and other predators so that it then serves as a model for other species, notably our female eastern tiger swallowtail. Other mimics include the eastern black swallowtail (*Papilo polyxenes*), the spicebush or green-clouded swallowtail (*Papilio troilus*), and the red-spotted purple (*Limenitis arthemis*). The number of mimics points to the value of convergent evolution and the value of mimicry. Lepidopterists have noted a higher incidence of dark female eastern swallowtails where there is territorial overlap, which includes New England, with the blue swallowtail—confirmation, if not proof, of the complex effectiveness of mimicry.

—T. O.

◆ 5 ◆   Giant's Stairs and McIntosh Lot Preserve

"Pocket" tide pools harbor marine life adapted to daily strandings, yet able to withstand the fiercest of storm-driven surf.

WHAT FINER WAY TO END THE DRIVE DOWN BEAUTIFUL ORR'S AND BAILEY ISLANDS than to arrive at a grand show of geological glory looking out onto a wide stretch of sea. Perhaps the prettiest time to visit is in later June, when the beach roses that line the walkway are blooming and the bayberry and other shoreline shrubs are leafed out in their delicate early summer foliage. But any time during the warmer months is worthwhile, as this is a dramatic place at the tip of the peninsula, just right for a slow amble down the path with the primordial bedrock at your feet and the wide ocean studded with ledges and islands beyond.

Whatever aspect of nature you seek, it's here to explore: geology, birds, plants. And harbor seals may be seen swimming and basking, and possibly even the much larger gray seals that have become slightly more common of late (*see* p. 42). Among the many seabirds seen here in one season or another are common eiders. In June watch them as they shepherd convoys of recent hatchlings, diving for crustaceans and mollusks, especially mussels. Birders should also cover the McIntosh Lot at the southern end, an area of dense shrubbery, good for sparrows and other songbirds. Salt-tolerant plants grow along the path, including robust stands of poison ivy, wind-battered junipers, and various sedges and grasses.

Left: White quartz was once molten rock forced into cracks in the older metamorphic layers and "frozen in time." Right: Great slabs of rock lie tossed by winter storms amidst the uptilted sediments: what the earth creates, the sea seeks to break down.

Of course, it is the geology, the rocks, that make this site unique, particularly the feature for which the site is named (*see* p. 40), as well as the striking russet-colored metamorphic strata hundreds of millions of years old. If there are geology students from Bowdoin College or other institutions visiting, lend an ear to the professor's words for a thorough accounting of the earth's forces that have created this bold landscape. You'll long remember this special place.

Directions: Giant's Stairs and McIntosh Lot, Bailey's Island, 1 acre, Harpswell Heritage Land Trust

From the intersection of Mountain Road and Harpswell Islands Road (Route 24), follow Harpswell Islands Road south toward Orr's Island. Approximately 1.5 miles after crossing the Cribstone Bridge, turn left on Washington Avenue. Park at the Episcopal Chapel (when there are not services) or carefully along the street so as not to block traffic and emergency vehicles. Walk to the end of Ocean Street or south along Washington Avenue about ⅓ mile. Signs are posted at either end of the trail indicating access points. Dogs allowed on-leash.

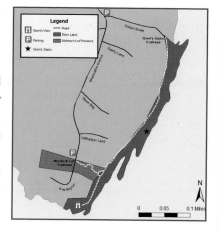

WebSource: http://hhltmaine.org/conserved-land/public-access/giants-stairs-mcintosh

(Ed. note: We wish to thank the Bowdoin College Daily Sun *and Ed Robinson of the Harpswell Heritage Land Trust for permission to reprint material that originally appeared on their websites.)*

Walking with Giants: A Geological Mystery

On the craggy coast at the southeast tip of Bailey Island, in the town of Harpswell, lies an unusual rock formation known, somewhat whimsically, as the Giant's Stairs. Large, black, blocky stones are laid on top of each other like a giant's staircase. They lead into the frothy sea, where on any given day one might see rafts of sea ducks, a pod of dolphins, foraging harbor seals or a lobster boat hauling pots.

The ¹/₃-mile trail to the shore can be accessed from either Ocean Street or Washington Avenue. Although it can be walked in as little as 10 minutes, better allow ample time to fully investigate and appreciate this intriguing geologic formation.

The smooth, dark stones are a visual anomaly against the flaky, rusty-gray metamorphic rock around them. Even more intriguing, the step formation doesn't follow the direction of the so-called "foliation," or repetitive layering, of the rock around it: rather, it runs counter to the layers of metamorphic rock. This has led geologists to believe that the rock forming the steps was created after the surrounding rock. While the Giant's Stairs are indeed a geologist's dream, the contrasting rock formations are so striking that even the casual observer will wonder what huge geologic forces shaped this piece of coastline eons ago.

The story of the Giant's Stairs began 400 to 500 million years ago, when this part of the world was made up of layers of mud, other sediments and mineral deposits that formed the

These stairs are indeed giant, as a class of Bowdoin geology students discovers firsthand.

Looking south past the point at Land's End and Jacquish Island.

shores of an ancient ocean. Approximately 300 million years ago, the ocean closed, and the land masses, or continents, came together to form Pangaea, the supercontinent. The layers of mud and sediments were buried. Subjected to high pressure and heat, they metamorphosed into a type of rock known as schist, while the minerals within the sediment crystallized into such stones as garnet and quartz. (These stones are visible today as translucent mineral "lenses" in the solid rock.)

When Pangaea began to break apart 200 million years ago, the tectonic plates that make up the Earth's crust both separated and collided. Pressure from the collisions pushed the sedimentary/metamorphic layers upward, causing massive buckling and cracking. The separating plates created additional fissures in the hard rock. On what would eventually become Bailey Island, a vertical crack opened up in the metamorphic rock, deep within the earth. Gradually, hot magma flowed into the crack. This material eventually hardened into basalt rock and formed a vertical seam known to scientists as an "intrusive volcanic dike." This seam of dark rock would become what is known today as the Giant's Stairs.

But there was one last geologic process that had to take place to create the "steps" as we see them. As the basalt solidified, and as the outer layers were removed by erosion over 200 million years, regular fractures, or joints, were formed. These joints, combined with nature's weathering, worked the rock into roughly the shape of a staircase.

While we understand the big picture of the geologic forces that created this unusual rock formation, gaps remain in our knowledge. Researchers continue to study the geological details recorded in the rocks to help us learn the complete story of the Giant's Stairs.

Gently sloping, smooth terraces of granite afford the residents of Seal Island a suitable hauling-out place with deep water all around. (photo: Peter Ralston / Ralston Gallery)

The Hooked-Nose Pig

There's no mistaking a large male **gray seal** (*Halichoerus grypus*). Hauled out on ledge or gravel beach, a male looks like a weathered erratic rock or a coarse-textured, half-empty, gray-brown partially collapsed balloon—until this huge animal raises its head, yawns, eyes his neighbors and resumes his nap. Look for the Roman nose, the separated nostrils and the square head. These field marks confirm that this animal is not its lesser cousin, the **harbor seal** (*Phoca vitulina*), and should leave no doubt as to why *H. grypus* is known as the horse-head seal, or why the Latin name means "hooked-nose pig"—a designation that slights its skill as a hunter. Though ungainly and awkward on shore, these animals embody swift grace in the water and are formidable predators, able to chase and kill even small whales.

Recent History. Until 1972 there was a bounty on gray seals in Maine and Massachusetts. That open season explains the near demise of the species in New England. Add other hazards—boat strikes, interaction with fishermen and their gear, entanglement with plastic debris, power plant entrapment, oil spills, subsistence hunting, harvesting for fur, or shooting the animals for sport—and it's a miracle that gray seals managed to survive at all. Their cousin, the **Atlantic walrus** (*Odobenus rosmarus rosmarus*) did not. Natural causes of mortality include predation by sharks, storms and disease. In addition, pups may be abandoned by their mothers, crushed by adults as they escape a threat by rushing to the water, or attacked by eagles. All in all it's a tough life, even for a "top dog" on the food chain.

By the late 1960s, gray seals in New England were confined to isolated colonies. In those days, seeing one was an event, akin to spotting a bald eagle or osprey. For the seals, the turnaround was the result of the 1972 Marine Mammal Protection Act (MMPA), which prohibited the killing, harassment or trade of marine mammals. Without it and subsequent amendments, there would be no gray seals in Maine today. (The MMPA parallels the Migratory Bird Treaty Act of 1918 in design and far-reaching significance.)

Following the MMPA, *H.grypus* slowly regained lost ground. By 2008 Green Island (near Petit Manan) had 59 pups, Seal Island (near Vinalhaven) had 466 and there were 2,620 in Nantucket Sound. The light-colored pups are easier to spot from the air, but the adults were counted as well: in 1993 there were 597 along the Maine coast. By 2001 that number had risen to 1,731. That's small potatoes when compared to Canada, where National Marine Fisheries data suggest a population approaching 350,000. It's safe to conclude that the "hooked-nose pig" is here to stay.

Lifeways. Gray seals breed and give birth at three known sites in Maine—Green Island, Seal Island and Matinicus Rock—and several locations in Massachusetts, principally Muskeget and Monomoy islands. Pupping at all these sites is increasing. Pups have also been found on Long Island beaches in New York, suggesting that their range is expanding southwards.

H. grypus as found in the western Atlantic, including Maine, differs from two other subspecies. *H. grypus grypus* are distributed around the British Isles, Iceland and the north coast of Norway. The Baltic seals, *H. grypus macrorhynchus,* live east of Denmark. These eastern Atlantic seals are on the IUCN Red List.

H. grypus is a "true" seal, a point that may be confusing to anyone who assumes that "a seal is a seal." But true seals are merely one group of three pinniped, or fin-footed, families. The walruses (Odobenidae) are hairless, toothy and notably larger: up to 4,000 pounds. The fur seals and sea lions (Otariidae) have external ears, fur and a rear end that curves forward, allowing them some mobility on land. The most familiar of these is the classic circus seal, actually a California sea lion *(Zalophus californianus)*. The true seals (Phocidae) are the most evolved for life in the water. They have no external ears, can retract their nipples, and the males have internal genitalia. In addition, their legs are attached directly to the pelvis, extend backwards and cannot be brought forward, making them very awkward on land.

Pinnipeds are members of a single ancestral line that began some 21 million years ago with a carnivorous, otter-like, freshwater creature called *Puijila darwini.* Some 50 extinct species are known through their fossil record, but 33 others can be found today, mostly in the polar waters of the northern and southern hemispheres. At one end of this monophylum is the huge southern elephant seal *(Mirounga leonina)*. Apart from the sperm whale, this is the largest carnivore on earth. It is a true seal, and a hunter that can dive down 3,000 feet and stay underwater for two hours. Its prey is squid, fish and smaller sharks. The largest southern elephant seal ever recorded was over 22 feet long and was estimated to weigh 11,000 pounds. At the other end of the spectrum is the fresh water Baikal seal *(Pusa sibirica)*, weighing a mere 145 pounds. (Intriguingly, both seals and whales descend from land creatures: seals from a hoofed ancestor, the

Adults keep a wary eye on human visitors.
(photo: Charles Altschul)

hippopotamus-like *Cetartiodactyla*; whales from the otter-like *P. darwini*.)

The gray seal is an omnivore who needs to eat four to six percent of its body weight daily, or around 40 pounds for an adult male. To this end the seal roams the water column searching for lobster and other crustaceans, sand eels, cod, herring, skate, squid, octopus, seabirds, and even the occasional **harbor porpoise** (*Phocoena phocoena*), a five-foot, 100-pound cetacean

Female and offspring rest on a thick carpet of rockweed, ready to slip into the water if need be. (photo: Charles Altschul)

that is a very fast swimmer. Gray seals usually consume their prey underwater, although larger animals may be brought to the surface to be torn apart and consumed piecemeal. They are capable of diving deep: 250 feet is not unusual, and they have been recorded at 1,560 feet. They can hold their breath for an hour. Gray seals are sexually dimorphic (physically different): a 900-pound bull may be 10 feet long, while a cow is smaller, but still weighs a quarter of a ton. Females may surpass the males' 25-year lifespan by a decade.

Seal Island. This is the capital city for gray seals in Maine and possibly the wildest location for miles around. The island is a fecund wellspring of coastal sea life that at last enjoys protection from the disruptive hand of human interference. A mile long by no more than 300 yards across, this glorified ledge is a harsh place—unless you belong there. Southeast of Rockland but closer to Vinalhaven island, it was historically a place to go for eggs, feathers or meat, a tradition that eventually led to the extirpation of seals and several kinds of nesting seabirds. As if that wasn't punishment enough, beginning during World War II and continuing until the 1960s, it was a target for military gunners and bombers, an activity that left a legacy of pockmarks in the granite and a scattering of unexploded ordnance.

In 1972, following passage of the MMPA, ownership was transferred to the Department of the Interior, where it subsequently became a part of the Maine Coastal Islands National Wildlife Refuge, now managed collaboratively by the US Fish and Wildlife Service and the National Audubon Society. Seabird restoration began in 1984 and became the life work of several scientists, notably Cornell University's Steve Kress. Gradually, the 65 acres of blasted granite were transformed into a garden of opportunity for seabirds. According to Project Puffin, in 2012, 737 pairs of puffins were nesting within the crannies, fissures and pockets of soil that crisscross the island, a phenomenon not seen since the nineteenth century. In addition, some 2,500 common and arctic terns, gone since 1936, began returning to breed. Other species have also come back: common murre (not nesting), roseate tern, guillemot, razorbill, laughing gull, Leach's storm petrel, double-crested and great cormorants, among others. There are bald eagles, too, which must view this island as a restaurant that opens for service when the gray seals begin to pup in January.

Approach Seal Island in dense fog from downwind on a June day and there's no mistaking the pungent odor of the rookery or the cries, croaks and groans of the birds or, when you're really close,

44

the sound of the foaming surf. The island lies in the water like a huge granite whale that a prudent mariner regards with wary fascination. On one hand there's the allure of this primordial dreamscape; on the other hand, given the rocky shore, the daunting prospect of an unexpected swell, or the untimely engine failure.

It is a frigid place in January, when the 35-pound gray seal pups are born into a world of freezing air and water, where even the sheltered nooks are exposed to high wind that can tear loose anything that can't adapt. But the gray seals do, and so they thrive, along with other winter residents: clusters of purple sandpipers, a few razorbills, long-tailed ducks, common eiders, the occasional Icelandic gull and as many as a dozen bald eagles that come over from the mainland to feast on seal placentas, or peck the eyes of an unprotected seal pup, leaving it sightless and vulnerable.

The white pelt of a baby seal is easy to recognize. This so-called lanugo (found also on human fetuses before birth) is thick, dense and long. The creamy-white color makes the newborn less notice-able against a background of ice or snow, and the fur is an effective insulator—necessary in the absence of body fat. By the time this coat is shed in two to three weeks, the young seal has gained six pounds per day and weighs nearly 100 pounds, all from its mother's milk. It then acquires the unique adult gray pelage that it will have for life and takes to the sea to hunt and forage on its own. This is a dangerous time for the juvenile: According to *A Field Guide to Whales, Porpoises and Seals* (Katona et al., 1983), first year mortality is around 50 percent.

Weaning is followed by mating. On Seal Island, where the colony is concentrated by the small size of the beach, gray seals are likely to be polygynous, with a dominant male breeding with "harems" of up to 10 females. However, where the colony can spread out, a sexually mature, three- to five-year-old male stands a chance of mating with a female. Breeding is followed by a 50-week gesta-tion, which includes a three-month delay, during which time the fertilized egg initially undergoes division, then halts development. The process allows the females opportunity to recover from calving and to synchronize the birth of the herd's pups the following year.

Because of toxic chemicals in the air and water, the future of *H. grypus* may not be as rosy as the increasing population suggests. Bio-accumulation (the concentration of persistent organic pollut-ants as they are passed along from prey to ever larger predator) reaches an endpoint within the largest and oldest species, such as gray seals.

Where can one see gray seals? They are not as easy to view as harbor seals, but diligence with binoculars can pay off, offering a glimpse of the large head that has earned the species the nickname "horse-head" seal. For that you need exposed ledges at low tide, common along the Harpswell peninsula and many other points along the Maine coast.

—T. O.

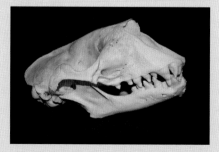

With 34–36 teeth and a stout skull, the species is well designed to pursue a carnivorous diet of various fish, crustaceans, squid and perhaps even small cetaceans. (photo: Barry Costa-Pierce)

♦ 6 ♦   Green Point Preserve

This pitch pine maintains a foothold on a rocky outcrop overlooking Winnegance Bay, against a backdrop of rockweed.

MIDCOAST MAINE IS PUNCTUATED BY MANY TIDAL RIVERS both long like the Kennebec or short like the New Meadows, an estuarine embayment of about 12 miles, draining 23 square miles. Fronting onto Winnegance Bay, an arm of the estuary jutting northeast into the Bath peninsula, this moderately sized site encompasses not only shoreline but a mixed spruce-pine forest on both sides of the ¾-mile trail that runs along a ridge out to the overlook on the bay. There are also vernal pools providing vital habitat for amphibians and the many other invertebrate species—including fairy shrimp, *see* sidebar p. 50—that inhabit these seasonal aquatic micro-worlds.

As with all preserves in the Midcoast area, Green Point's human history starts with the original people, the Abenaki who lived in northern New England and parts of the contiguous southern Canadian provinces, part of the Algonquian speakers that date from about 2,000 years B.P. (before present). In their language, Winnegance means "little portage," and it was here that they portaged canoes about 1 ½ miles across the peninsula to the Kennebec River. European colonists came early to this part of Maine with one of the first settlements being established at Popham in 1607. At this end of the timeline, in 2004 the owner of this land, Eastham Guild, Jr. (who "used his property as a place to keep in touch with nature," and who wished "to keep the land undeveloped for the locals to enjoy" according to the site brochure) conveyed this land to the Kennebec Estuary Land Trust. The Trust also provides public access to six other preserves in this region, including Bonyun Preserve, another seashore site (*see* chapter 11).

The shoreline here presents a rugged, rocky exposure described in a 2004 management plan for the estuary:

> The geology of the present-day New Meadows River includes a wide variety of formations from exposed and thinly covered bedrock on the terrestrial side to thick layers of glaciomarine mud deposits below the water. The interface between the land and the sea, or intertidal area, varies similarly from highly exposed, vertical bedrock walls to very soft mud in sheltered bays and

Directions: Green Point Preserve, West Bath, 45 acres, Kennebec Estuary Land Trust

Follow Rt. 209 from Bath 2.4 miles to the Winnegance Store. Take a right on High Street, which eventually becomes Campbell Pond Road. About 2.2 miles from the store take a right onto Birch Point. Parking is along the roadside 1 mile down on the left. Dogs allowed on leash.

WebSource: http://kennebecestuary.org/conserved-lands/green-point-west-bath

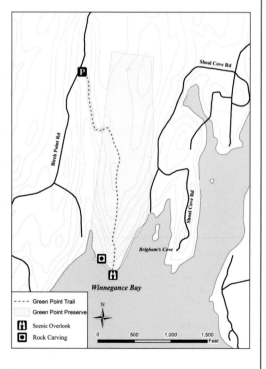

Along the trail to the shore, a grove of spruce saplings in the understory grows up beneath the canopy of pines and hardwoods.

coves. This varied geology provides a wide range of habitats and ecological niches, all of which combine to make the New Meadows River highly diverse and productive. (*see* "resources" at http://newmeadowspartnership.org)

It is the preservation of such "ecological niches" that will enable nature to maintain a tenable foothold in our development-fixated culture. Green Point Preserve is one more opportunity to appreciate the resident species of plants, animals and other biota that make up the ecosystem of Maine's shoreline. This is a destination that the curious traveler might take in along with the nearby Hamilton Preserve (Audubon) just to the north (covered in our previous *Best Nature Sites* book). Or visit on a trip down the peninsula to Popham State Park at land's end with its magnificent sand beach at the mouth of the Kennebec River.

Folded rock layers created ca. 400 million years ago form a sea cave above the thick layers of rockweed that dominate the intertidal area.

Goldthread (canker root) (Coptis trifolia) *contains berberine, a medicinal alkaloid found in many plants, and available as an herbal supplement. Humans through the ages have used the rootstock to treat a wide array of ailments. This hardy ground-creeping species grows through much of Canada south to North Carolina, and has a small star-like bloom.*

Looking like anything but the marine brown algae that it is, the **sea potato** (Leathesia diformis) *is blown ashore, to be seen among the tide wrack in deflated leathery looking bundles. It can be epiphytic, growing on other seaweeds or colonizing on rocks.*

Fairy Shrimp

Early spring is not everyone's favorite time of year to roam the woods; I've always thought differently. In addition to few biting insects, few leafed-out trees (allowing good visibility) and moderate temperatures, there's the excitement of getting outdoors after a long winter. Perhaps the biggest draw is the opportunity to explore vernal pools. This type of water body is a depression that holds water for at least the duration of its inhabitants' life cycles (usually two months or more in the growing season) and that has no permanent fish population. These pools have a number of values including flood storage, groundwater recharge and attenuation of pollutants, to name a few. For many naturalists, the most important point is that they are chock-full of strange and interesting creatures. These inhabitants are considered so essential that Maine environmental laws protect their special habitats. One of the most exotic looking, variable and interesting of them is the fairy shrimp.

In its season—usually from iceout to May—a single vernal pool in Maine may host from a few to thousands of these aquatic animals. There are more than 200 species of fairy shrimp crustaceans and their allies, including the little brine shrimp used as aquarium fish food. Most are short-lived backswimmers that filter bacteria, algae and small detritus from the water.

Although Maine is host to two and possibly three species, the one most often seen is *Eubranchipus vernalis,* the **eastern fairy shrimp,** sometimes called the "springtime fairy shrimp." It is slender, light orange or green, about an inch long, and swims on its back with wave-like pulsations of its eleven pairs of feathery, gill-supporting legs (phyllopods). It is found both in open water—which would not be possible if vernal pools had permanent fish populations—or sometimes hidden among the fallen leaves, especially on cloudy days. Because it is semi-transparent, its whitish forked tale may be most noticeable.

Telling males from females is fairly easy. During mating a male grabs his chosen female with a pair of modified antennae on his head, called *claspers* (reminiscent perhaps of a walrus). The female has no claspers but often has a bag-like egg sac behind her legs after mating. After the eggs develop somewhat, the female releases them, and they settle to the bottom where they estivate as cysts when the vernal pool dries. One might think they would hatch immediately, as soon as water refills the vernal pool in the fall, but they hatch only when given the "all clear" signal, described below. The new larvae then grow quickly, passing through several molts (as do all arthropods) to become adults by early ice-out in the spring. Sometimes they can be seen by the thousands in the narrow margin between the shore and the retreating ice.

The details of fairy shrimp reproductive "strategies" merit further discussion. The precise mechanism that triggers egg hatching is under dispute. Some observers speculate that a resting period of several months is necessary. Indeed, my own observations of shrimp-inhabited vernal pools that contain no shrimp in some years suggest this. On the other hand, experiments over the years suggest that freezing and/or desiccation, rather than a really long resting period, is what is needed. Also, it should be noted that winter eggs are quite hardy and can be carried

Male fairy shrimp. (photo: Leo P. Kenney, Vernal Pool Association)

to other vernal pools by either wind or animals, and they can remain viable for years. There is a distinction between these winter eggs and summer eggs, which hatch in the same season they are deposited, apparently when the male population is low.

Once mating has occurred, usually in April or May, the male dies; the female may live for the rest of that season. It is not known for sure if eggs, once laid, start to develop immediately or "rest" first. Since some vernal pools do not refill until mid-winter, this occurrence likely varies. Usually, the eggs hatch in mid-winter and the larvae grow to maturity in about 45 days. However, some pools that refill in fall have been recorded as having November hatches. Quickly drying pools may have quickly maturing fairy shrimp, with a life cycle as short as 16 days.

Fairy shrimp predators include just about any animal-eater in the pool: dragonfly and damsel fly larvae, back swimmer bugs, ducks, caddis fly larvae and water scorpions. However, it appears that their most fearsome (certainly one of the most interesting) predators are various diving beetles, especially their larvae. The larvae—aptly called "water tigers" and sometimes "toe biters" (although I know of no first-hand accounts)—are slender and slithery with long, pincer-like jaws with which to grab anything. I have placed a bunch of recently netted vernal pool creatures into a clear collecting jar and observed water tigers immediately attack fairy shrimp, tadpoles, mosquito wigglers—indeed any animal, even bigger than themselves, within reach.

Thus fairy shrimp are creatures well-adapted to, but wedded exclusively to vernal pools. It can change its egg type, its breeding period, its rate of growth—even the length of its life cycle. But it still needs those vernal pools.

— Ralph Perkins

Silence of the Whip-poor-will

The roses have faded, there's frost at my door
The birds in the morning don't sing anymore
The grass in the valley is starting to die
And out in the darkness the whippoorwills cry.
　　—Hank Williams, Sr.

Not so long ago the persistent call of the **eastern whip-poor-will** (*Antrostomus vociferus*) was commonplace—as much a part of the New England summer night as a loon's yodel or the emphatic grunt of a bullfrog. But today many Maine residents would not recognize that once familiar song. In fact, to hear one is to be startled. What led to its decline, and is there a conservation strategy to help bring them back? Why is its relative, the **common nighthawk** (*Chordeiles minor*), also disappearing from Maine? With these questions in mind, I began to query my birding friends for answers. I learned, not surprisingly, that there is no simple explanation. But there is a story. Actually, several.

Long ago shepherds believed that there was a bird that could extract milk from lactating goats. They could see them fluttering above their herds at night like huge brown moths with enormous open mouths. In time, early natural philosophers recognized the species, today called the **European Nightjar** (*Caprimulgus europaeus*, from Latin meaning goat-milking), named by the famous Swedish botanist Carl von Linné. During his life (1707–1778), he devised the taxonomic system and named thousands of plants and animals, latinizing even his own name to *Carolus Linnaeus*.

Today his principles of classification remain, but molecular phylogenetics has become the new driving force for understanding evolutionary relationships. This so-called cladistic approach has led to fundamental shifts in understanding how species are connected. An example among birds is the long-held presumption that owls are related to raptors, such as eagles and hawks, because of appearance and behavior. Their beaks, for example, have a similar shape: hooked and pointed for tearing meat. But genetic analysis reveals this morphological similarity developed independently (convergent evolution) rather than from genetic proximity. In fact, owls (order Strigiiformes) are more closely related to goatsuckers (Caprimulgiformes) than they are to raptors (Falconiformes). As an approach to understanding the deeper truths of evolution, genes trump morphology.

Caprimulgiformes, found nearly worldwide, includes several related nocturnal, insectivorous families. Our eastern U.S. summer residents are the common nighthawk, and the whip-poor-will and chuck-will's widow, formerly in the genus *Caprimulgus*, but now designated *Antrostomus*, which means cave mouth—a suitable description for these flying insect nets.

Given the small, hollow bones of most birds, it's no surprise that the fossil record of this group is thin, but recent genetic analysis confirms a progenitor that lived and spread

The eastern whip-poor-will is rarely seen either on the ground during day or flying at night, but it is still heard occasionally, intoning its unmistakable song, described in some guides as "clear and mellow." This incubating female sits on two eggs. (photo: Pamela Hunt, NH Audubon)

throughout the world in the late Eocene, around 40 million years ago—just when feathered flight was taking off. It's worth noting that this is about a hundred million years after *Archaeopteryx*, which, though feathered, had a sternum that was insufficiently crested for the attachment of strong flight muscles. Today, there are nearly 70 species of Caprimulgidae worldwide whose relationships remain incompletely defined. No doubt future research will reveal surprises and allow us to flesh out the comment in *The Audubon Society Encyclopedia of Birds* that they are "not songbirds, but somewhat owl-like." They are, indeed, an odd bunch of birds.

Goatsuckers in general and whip-poor-wills in particular are aerial insectivores whose large mouths are surrounded by a thatch of stiff, hair-like feathers called rictal bristles. These funnel insects into the gaping mouth, protect the owner's large eyes and presumably offer tactile feedback, just as they do on the smaller insectivorous birds such as warblers and flycatchers. A group of whip-poor-wills is known collectively as an "invisibility" or a "seek," an apt name when one considers that whip-poor-wills are one of the least studied birds in North America, according to the Cornell Lab of Ornithology.

Much of what is known is based on anecdote. According to New Hampshire Audubon, "This is a species of the edge, needing both forested areas for nesting and open areas for foraging." Within that territory each bird will have a singing post—a stonewall or horizontal tree branch on which they perch lengthwise, their short legs tucked out of sight—from which they fly forth into sudden visibility. They feed at night or as dusk is falling. When sitting on the ground, which is where they nest—although there is no actual structure—their cryptic coloration renders them difficult to spot. They prefer dry, mixed hardwoods relatively clear of undergrowth. Both parents incubate the two camouflaged eggs and care for the nearly invisible young. The chicks fledge about eight days after hatching, after which the female may leave them to lay a second clutch. In the autumn, our eastern whip-poor-will migrates to the southeastern United States and beyond to the eastern coast of Mexico and Central America.

I recall my childhood excitement whenever I found a sitting bird at dusk—and my surprise at their small size, which was at odds with the power of their song. Their wingspan rarely exceeds 19 inches, about the same as a northern flicker or two inches longer than a robin's. Approaching as close as I dared, I'd stretch out on the ground and wait for the magic of the singing to draw me into a spell that blotted out the stab and itch of mosquitoes. I never counted the repetitions, but they were often in the hundreds. The record is 1,088.

When they are not singing or resting or sitting on a nest, whip-poor-wills are dedicated predators. They fly low above the ground, trawling for flying insects, beetles and grasshoppers, occasionally surging straight up in pursuit of prey like a tiny baleen whale scooping zooplankton from a column of water. They may also pick and poke at rotten logs for ants and larvae. Or beat the canopy of a tree, scaring up moths, especially large ones such as the lime-green **luna** (*Actias luna*) or the eye-mimicking **cecropia** (*Hyalophora cecropia*). Any concentration of insects—such as around a flock of goats or sheep—attracts them, which is why they are associated with livestock.

Fortunate and observant the birder who spots a nightjar on the ground. And it takes some practice to distinguish an eastern whip-poor-will from its relative, the common nighthawk. Longer primary feathers that extend beyond the tail help identify the latter, as do the lack of rictal bristles, but these are of questionable value in the field. On the wing, however, the two are easier to distinguish: whip-poor-wills have relatively short, rounded wings and a smooth flight; nighthawks have a distinctive, erratic wing beat and pointed wings. They are likely to be seen in profile darting about high in the air, often in flocks, scooping and feasting on a variety of small animals including beetles, mosquitoes, moths, grasshoppers, lice, flies, locusts and ants. 2,175 such food items were found in one Maine bird's stomach. Nighthawks often

Chicks—this one probably less than a week old—are supremely camouflaged on the forest floor of pine needles and leaves. (photo: Pamela Hunt, NH Audubon)

take advantage of the bright lights that attract and reveal insects. They nest in open gravel and rock, burned-over areas and, famously, on the flat roofs of city buildings, where the female lays and incubates two eggs. Unlike the whip-poor-will, which breeds only in the northeast, this species breeds throughout the US and Canada, and winters from Mexico to Argentina. They may be the most studied nightjar in America, but much remains to be learned. As the Cornell Lab of Ornithology points out, the name nighthawk is not entirely appropriate as the bird hunts in the evening and morning, rather than at night, and is not a hawk. Another reminder that the naming of birds holds as many ambiguities as it does truths.

Data from the Banding Laboratory at Patuxent Wildlife Research Center in Maryland summarizes nightjar banding records for Maine arranged only by decade. The data are too sparse to be arranged annually.

	1960s	1970s	1980s	1990s	2000s	2010s (inc.)
whip-poor-will	13	7	6	0	0	0
common night-hawk	38	4	13	2	3	0
Chuck-will's-widow	0	0	0	1	1	1

My informant at the Center offered this caveat: "Keep in mind that banding records are basically random and the effort is in no way standardized. We have no way of knowing if the larger numbers in the early years are due to a targeted effort or not." He added anecdotally that when he moved to Maryland in 1988 he could hear five birds all summer. By 2000 there were none, but the number of barred owls had increased dramatically. The habitat, he said, had not altered in any way that could account for this change. Another Federal biologist confirmed this connection, noting that barred owls are aggressive nocturnal and crepuscular predators that are quite capable of killing a young or adult whip-poor-will.

Everyone that I asked agreed that the decline of whip-poor-wills and nighthawks in Maine and New England is a persistent reality. "The State of New Hampshire's Birds," published by Pamela Hunt, Ph.D., in 2009 quantifies the decline. New Hampshire is home to 19 species of aerial insectivores. These include not only whip-poor-wills and nighthawks, but several species of swallows, swifts and flycatchers, the majority of which are in decline. But why? Looking for that answer is like opening Pandora's box. Co-author Rebecca Suomala reports that the nighthawk population in North America is in long-term decline. In 40 years the number of these birds has plummeted by half, and the rate is accelerating. This gloomy picture applies to other insectivores in New England as well: 70% decline in bank swallows, barn swallows and chimney swifts. All these species rely on flying insects. Less flying food means fewer insectivores. But the familiarity of that answer does not mean the solution is any easier.

A naturalist with Maine Audubon, Stella Walsh, told me that "the reforestation of former agricultural land and development have certainly played a part in the decline of nightjars in

Prior to release from the bander's hand, this male individual shows the large eyes of the species that are essential for night vision. This trait has parallels among other nocturnal animals such as flying squirrels. (photo: Pamela Hunt, NH Audubon)

Maine and the rest of New England. The replacement of gravel with other roofing materials on flat roofed buildings may also have played a part in local situations. However, from the literature available, that does not appear to be the whole story."

A Canadian researcher, Carl Savignac, states that the main threat to nightjar populations in North America is "habitat and harvested forests, fire suppression, intensive agriculture and the gradual reduction of buildings with flat gravel covered rooftops. Other limiting factors may include a general decline in insect populations due to large-scale insecticide use, collisions with motor vehicles and climatic fluctuations at breeding sites and during migration."

Pamela Hunt identifies three generalized causes. The first is the presence of pesticides on the breeding and wintering grounds, as well as along the migratory route, that poison birds directly and reduce the food supply by killing insects. The second is climate destabilization. The increasing severity of spring and fall storms has a direct and obvious impact on migrants, blowing them off-course, delaying their journey, disrupting their food supply and otherwise stressing them. Also, early or late springs can put arriving birds out of sync with insect hatches resulting in potential starvation. The third is habitat loss: drained or filled-in marshes producing fewer mosquitoes.

She also mentions further threats to aerial insectivores: predation by domestic cats and skunks—lethal for any ground nesting birds—disease, acid rain and structures such as lighted buildings, communication towers and cars. Estimates suggest, for example, that between 300 million and one billion birds die each year by flying into buildings.

Habitat restoration, says Hunt, is key for these insectivores. Whip-poor-wills "appear to select disturbed/open habitat disproportionately greater than those habitats occur on the land-scape." The birds select this kind of landscape, be it agricultural, utility rights-of-way, forests that are timbered or subject to frequent disturbance, or fire in a pine-barrens. "Birds actually colonized a newly harvested area the spring immediately following the harvest." Create this habitat and whip-poor-wills will come. She adds that questions remain about patch size, location relative to other whip-poor-will populations and microhabitat features, but she is otherwise optimistic.

The chance of hearing a whip-poor-will in Maine is not what it once was. Ron Joseph, a retired US Fish and Wildlife Service biologist, recalls, "The song of a whip-poor-will today generates fond childhood memories of my grandparents' 105-acre dairy farm in Mercer, Maine. During summer evenings as a pre-teen and teenager from the late 1950s through the 1960s, my twin brother and I often sat on the screenless porch with my grandparents. July evening twilight is a magical time of day on a dairy farm with late-day chores complete: cows chewing their cud in their barn after pasturing all day, pigs lying on their side with full bellies of kitchen scraps and chickens clucking softly on roosting boards in the hen house. The whip-poor-wills were so numerous and loud after supper (dinner was the noon meal), we couldn't carry a porch conversation. Many summer evenings whip-poor-wills perched on the ridge pole of the 200-year old farmhouse and sang throughout the night. It was difficult falling asleep, even as tired as we were after working from sunup to sundown bailing hay and storing it in the barn."

But if you are fortunate to live in a likely location, don't give up hope. Listen for them on a summer night. Throw wide the sash and turn off the light. Better yet, step outside at 9:00 p.m. and walk slowly through the night with your ears and eyes open. If there's a whip-poor-will in song, there'll be no mistaking the call. Or maybe not. Listen carefully. As the Bird Banding Laboratory data suggest, and as birders along the coast of Maine have reported, **Chuck-will's widow** (*Caprimulgas carolinensis*) is an occasional visitor to Maine.

As the Latin name suggests, Chuck-will's widow is a southeastern relative to our whip-poor-will, but with several distinguishing characteristics. With a wingspan over 24 inches, it's the largest member of the genus in North America—big enough to swallow even small birds in one gulp as well as moths, beetles and other insects. If you have never heard a whip-poor-will or Chuck-will's widow, identification can be tricky, so compare the calls at the Cornell birding website www.allaboutbirds.org. The call is easier to recognize if you remember a couple of Chuck's other names, chick-a-willa and chip-fell-out-of-an-oak.

I asked Dr. Hunt about sightings of Chuck-will's widow in Maine because a friend had heard one. I wondered if climate change or other factors could explain a possible increase in their numbers. She replied that, to her knowledge, they are not increasing anywhere. She cited a tiny population on Cape Cod and Long Island that has remained largely unchanged for 20 years, while the population in the Southeast may be declining. As for Maine, their presence is minimal, even fewer than whip-poor-wills. One scientist from the Center For Ecological Research, in Richmond, stated that Maine has less than ten good records of this species. Clearly, a sighting here is unlikely. Chances are, if you hear a calling bird, it's a whip-poor-will. Either way it's a treat. Remember that the song of the whip-poor-will that our grandparents took for granted is now a privilege.

—T. O.

Nequasset Fish Ladder

The smokehouse has always been an adjunct to the harvesting of alewives, this one restored in recent years, with plans underway to upgrade the ladder as well. Fish are guided into the impoundment by an underwater berm of rocks, just visible in the photographs as a lighter streak.

FISH LADDERS ARE A WINDOW OF SORTS into the world of the fish species that use them, life forms we might not otherwise ever be able to witness, living most of their lives offshore, unseen in the ocean or inshore in bodies of freshwater. Despite their endangered status, **alewives** *(Alosa pseudoharengus)* in particular are still numerous enough in their spawning runs upstream to be readily visible on the Midcoast starting in the middle of May. And they come at about the same time that roadside shrubs such as shadbush and wild cherry are blooming: sure signs of the land and sea shrugging off the "cloak of winter." And so it is that we include this fish ladder in our offering of nature sites as a place to experience an extraordinary natural phenomenon.

Nequasset fish ladder, managed jointly by the Town of Woolwich and the Bath Water District, is right off Route 1 just north of Bath after crossing the Kennebec River, the main access of the fish returning from the sea. So even the busiest of curious travelers can make a quick stop to take in an event that has repeated annually for centuries and perhaps millennia. And it is through the efforts of municipal and non-profit agencies and the dedicated individuals thereof that such spawning runs of this and other species may continue. Alicia Heyburn, in coordination with the Kennebec Estuary Land Trust and other organizations, has participated in the ladder restoration efforts here and is author of the following article offering a closer look at this site and the larger issues of promoting the alewife run in the Kennebec River system of which Nequasset Brook and the upstream spawning lake by that name are a part.

Directions:

Nequasset Dam and Fish Ladder, Town of Woolwich

Parking for visitors is available nearby during off hours at the town office or at the adjoining recreational area. The site can be viewed after a short walk across George Wright Road. During the alewife migration the site is in commercial operation and visitors must respect the priority afforded to the fish harvest process. Planning is underway to replace the existing fish ladder and during the construction phase the site will be further restricted.

WebSources: http://kennebecestuary.org/resources/nequasset-fish-ladder-restoration
http://www.naturalhistorymag.com/perspectives/262286/restoration-of-the-alewife
http://www.maine.gov/dmr/searunfish/alewife/

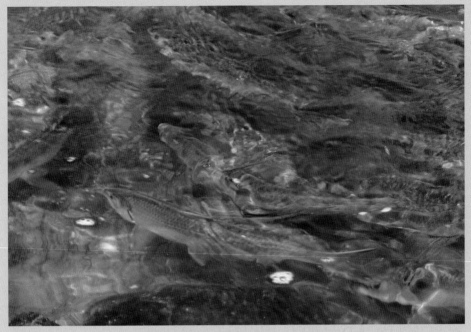

Returning alewives appear as a dark mass of undulating forms as they confront the currents leading to spawning grounds upstream. (photo: Theodore Willis)

Fostering the Run: An Overview

The Kennebec River currently has the largest run of alewives on the eastern seaboard, estimated at more than 3 million fish in 2012, with the potential to triple when alewives *regain* access to all the lakes that constitute their historic habitat in this drainage. In 2010, with support from the Gulf of Maine Council, the Kennebec Estuary Land Trust coordinated a survey of 400 road-stream crossings and dams in the lower Kennebec River watershed as part of a statewide effort to inventory fish passage barriers and prioritize habitat restoration projects. Thirteen barriers were identified in the watershed feeding Nequasset Lake. Because of the active community interest, the health and size of the current fish run, and amount of prime spawning habitat above the dam, the ladder at Nequasset Dam in Woolwich was seen as the top priority for improvement. This 1955-era fish ladder, weathered and aged, is being replaced with a new structure of similar design and more durable materials, ensuring passage for alewives and other migratory species, and the continuation of an ecological marvel and cultural tradition.

Nequasset Brook is part of the nationally significant Kennebec Estuary that drains one-third of the state into the Gulf of Maine. The dam impounds Nequasset Lake, a residential drinking water supply for four communities. The local alewife population is well documented in records dating back to the 1940s kept by the Woolwich Fish Commission, an elected body charged with managing the fish privileges held by the town. This well-administered site is one of only 18 in the state with a licensed harvest; it has been fished for generations, producing income for the town and desirable bait for lobstermen who eagerly wait to buy it directly from the harvesters.

Alewives are voyagers between salty ocean water and the freshwater of inland ponds and streams. Every spring from late April to early June, schools of adults, guided by their sense of smell, migrate by the millions from the sea into rivers, streams, and ultimately, lakes and ponds to spawn. To observe this is to witness one of the world's great migrations. It is a mesmerizing scene with masses of fish pointed into the current, their silvery sides flipping and twitching while navigating pools of dark water and rocky shallows toward the spot where they were born. At sea, alewives are a key food source for seals, whales, cod, haddock, striped bass and other important commercial and sport fisheries. As they migrate inland alewives feed bald eagle, osprey, great blue heron, gulls, otter, mink, fox, raccoon and turtles. During migration the predators are just as exciting to watch as the prey.

Members of the herring family, Clupeidae, alewives have slender bodies, grow to 10–11 inches in length, and weigh about half a pound. Their back is grayish green with flashy silver on their sides and belly, a forked tail and a single black spot just behind their eye. Their body style is streamlined and efficient, developed to push up through the current during migration.

The ten anadromous fish species native to Maine, in addition to alewives, are striped bass, Atlantic salmon, rainbow smelt, blueback herring, American shad, sea lamprey, Atlantic sturgeon, shortnose sturgeon and Atlantic tomcod. Many of these are found at Nequasset, along with the American Eel which is a *catadromous* species. These amazing creatures have a reverse migration, living most of their life high in the headwaters of streams and rivers and descending to the Atlantic Ocean once in their life to spawn. The inclusive term *diadromous* refers to all fishes that migrate between the sea and freshwater, generally termed sea-run fish.

Although alewives have co-evolved and co-existed with other native fish for thousands of years, the once common and prolific herald of spring has become a rare sight. Along with other marine fishes, Maine's historically thriving alewife population has plummeted during the last two centuries. Small wonder, as it is estimated that barriers along the migration route such as dams and culverts block 95% of prime spawning habitat for anadromous fish.

Many drivers are unaware of the number of times roads and even driveways cross streams, each crossing with a culvert or small bridge. Unfortunately, there are several common conditions at culverts that can create problems. Culverts are uniform in diameter and do not have the roughness and variability of natural stream beds; therefore they do not effectively dissipate energy. Thus, water velocities tend to be higher in a culvert than in the stream making it difficult for the fish to swim through this strong current. In addition, culverts are often narrower than the stream, constricting water flow at the inlet and creating turbulence. This can increase water speed in the culvert, and result in scour holes at the outlet, creating a waterfall that the fish cannot jump over. And if not properly maintained, culverts accumulate debris such as leaves and branches that can block access.

Surveys of barriers have resulted in coordinated efforts to restore fish passage along several of Maine's significant waterways such as the St. Croix, Penobscot, Sebasticook and Kennebec Rivers. The removal of the Edwards Dam from the Kennebec River in 1999, followed a decade later by removal of the Fort Halifax Dam at the mouth of the Sebasticook River, has led to the return of anadromous fish in those regions. Each time a culvert is replaced, a dam removed or fish passage built, it is a contribution to the restoration of the once prolific groundfish population, and historically lucrative fishery, in the Gulf of Maine. The alewife, a seemingly insignificant baitfish, actually plays a remarkable ecological, cultural and economic role as a voyager between marine and freshwater environments.

— Alicia Heyburn

In earlier times, dams such as this one were a necessary source of power for the production of goods and products in the New England economy, but presented insurmountable challenges to fish migrating upstream to spawn. Fish ladders have helped restore some spawning runs, as well as the removal of some major dams in Maine such as the Veazie dam on the Penobscot River in 2013. (*see* http://www.penobscotriver.org)

Roads Kill: Wildlife Mortality on the Byways

(Ed. note: The roads on which we travel are necessary for human enterprise but are hazards for wildlife. Those who are sensitive to the needs of wildlife must always be vigilant when traveling in our vehicles.)

"A few miles east of home in the Cascades I slow down and pull over for two raccoons, sprawled still as stones in the road. I carry them to the side and lay them in sun-shot, windblown grass in the barrow pit. . . . I carry each one away from the tarmac into a cover of grass or brush out of decency, I think. And worry. Who are these animals, their lights gone out? What journeys have fallen apart here?"

— Barry Lopez, *Apologia*

Who among us has not felt the thrill of having a wild animal cross the road in front of us at night while driving a country road? Maybe it's a big-eyed deer gracefully leaping across your path or a hunchbacked raccoon waiting for your car to speed by. It's a blessing: a reminder of another natural order that is always hungry and always attending to its own remote business. Equally, many or all of us have been brought down to earth by the terrible thud of a wild animal being hit by our car. The experience is uniquely human. It also magnifies the distance between our "civilized" world and the natural world that we so effortlessly impact.

An inevitable part of driving today is the occasional killing or injuring of wild animals. We all have been a part of this. If you drive, eventually you will hit or run over something: a turtle, squirrel, skunk or even a deer. With 190 million cars in the United States traveling our more than four million miles of roads and highways faster and more quietly than ever before, it is no wonder that, for some animals, automobiles are the main cause of death and injury—greater than any natural predators or man's other harmful behaviors.

It is estimated that each year hunters kill approximately 134 million wild animals for sport, food or as pests. Our cars, on the other hand, are said to kill on the order of a million animals a day, and this doesn't even include countless amphibians and insects. Of these deaths, there are some critters more vulnerable to our bumpers and tires than others. Some staggering annual numbers tally those most susceptible: 41 million squirrels; 22 million rats; 19 million opossums; 15 million raccoons; 350,000 deer; 60 million birds.

The number of wild animals that are injured by vehicles and crawl away to die or be preyed on later is impossible to estimate. Certainly it's many times the number that we kill outright with our cars and trucks. One of the inherent problems with animals being killed or injured on our roads is that dead or dying animals attract other carrion- and flesh-eating animals. These, in turn, are then at risk of being hit. This cycle is exacerbated by the nature of our roads, with mown grass on the sides that attracts grazing animals, while the sun-warmed tarmac brings in the heat-loving species after sundown.

Though some car-caused animal mortality is unavoidable, a little extra care while driving can potentially avoid some strikes. Mammals such as this woodchuck are especially vulnerable.

Despite the death we mete out with our vehicles, we—that is, all of us who drive—remain strangely absent from the act. As Mark Braunstein wrote in his report "U.S. Road Kills a Million a Day," "We don't call it car kills, as if we and our cars had nothing to do with it." Calling the problem "road kill" may be more about our obsession with cars than anything else, but that should not allow us to avoid a fuller understanding of the impacts and possible remedies. In time the rate of road kills will probably diminish even if we do nothing, but that will be because there will be fewer animals to run into. That is not a solution.

Maine's public roads occupy an area equal to about half the size of Baxter State Park. One of our most iconic animals, the moose—all 1,600 pounds of it—has to avoid this gauntlet of roadways as it goes about its business. With a total population of about 30,000 moose in Maine, we manage to hit more than 700 of them a year, or between two and three percent. In addition, Maine Audubon predicts that a number of Maine's endangered species are particularly at risk of extinction due to road collision. These are the Blanding and spotted turtles, black racer snake, and New England cottontail rabbit. Road collision also takes a toll on precious wildlife in other states. A report prepared for Congress found that collisions were a major source of mortality for 21 federally endangered or threatened species, such as the red wolf, Key deer and Florida panther.

So what can be done to reduce this deplorable carnage on our roadways? First, a great deal of effort should be put into designing our roads with wild animals in mind. Two mitigation measures, roadside fencing and carefully designed wildlife under- and over-passes, are the most effective but also, unfortunately, the most expensive. In the 2003 study "Road Ecology: Science and Solution," a quantitative look at various techniques offers a number of tools to reduce the carnage. But, as with many things, half measures can result in the opposite of what was intended. For example, if roadside fencing designed to keep wildlife out is not maintained, a breach can begin to function more as a trap for wildlife within the road corridor. The study further suggests other, less expensive strategies. Plantings of unpalatable vegetation may dissuade grazers from entering the roadsides. Creating more clear space along roadways would increase visibility to help drivers avoid collisions. Signage that identifies certain wildlife movement areas, particularly seasonally, is important. Even reconsidering our use of road salt in the winter would help, as it is often an attractant to mineral-loving critters.

However we design our many miles of roads, both here in Maine and elsewhere, the wildlife conservation goals of managing movement and diminishing mortality should be paramount.

Drivers—not innocents in this issue—need to be mindful of the wildlife we share these roadways with. We need to slow down to increase our ability to avoid collisions. We need to pay particular attention both at night and at the peak times of animal movement, early morning and dusk. We shouldn't throw food out our car windows, because even that apple core, while biodegradable, could bring any number of foragers closer to their destruction. And finally, as voting and tax-paying citizens, we can have a voice in how decisions about repairing old roads or building new ones are made.

—D. F.

Reptiles and amphibians frequently traverse roads as they move between water bodies. Snapping turtles seek out the sandy gravel along roads for egg-laying, putting this species at particular risk.

◆ 8 ◆   Reid State Park and Josephine Newman Sanctuary

A visit to Reid State Park in the early season lets you have the beach all to yourself. The top of the tidal range is evidenced by the dark line of "wrack" (dried seaweed and other flotsam) in the upper right. Grassy dunes, protecting the lagoon beyond, catch windblown sand.

T HESE TWO FINE PRESERVES WILL REWARD CURIOUS TRAVELERS who venture down the lengths of Arrowsic and Georgetown Islands, connected by bridges to the mainland and to each other, forming yet another of Maine's many fine peninsulas. And the drive down Route 127 from Route 1 affords some dandy views of the water especially at the bridges across the Back River channel and the upper reaches of Robin Hood Cove. And while we don't usually recommend lunch spots—even though there are most always good choices near our selected sites—you might try Five Islands Lobster Co. just past the turnoff for Reid State Park, a worthy stop after your nature walk not only for the seafood but for the beauty of the seascape that looks over five islands and east across lower Sheepscot Bay to the next peninsula formed by Southport Island.

Reid State Park

Sandy beaches dominate the lower coast of Maine where geological and geographical forces combine to move around large amounts of the tiny grains we so value on the seashore. The two rocky points that bound the shoreline of the Park (Griffith Head and Todd's Point) capture sand from the longshore currents to produce a stunning, mile-long beach, best visited during the shoulders of the season when fewer people are about. There is also a shorter sand beach to the south of Todd's Point. But there is much more to see here than just the beach.

The Park encompasses several different areas: the beach and dunes, behind which are the marshy tidal lagoon, and the woodlands and freshwater ponds. Each has its own biome, a "broad community of living organisms that characterizes a major habitat" as defined by Kenneth L. Gosner in his *Atlantic Seashores* guidebook. A good vantage point to start is at Griffith Head from where you can scan the ocean, the beach and the back waters of the lagoon. A tenacious grove of conifers growing just back from this headland is a favored foraging spot for warblers migrating up and down the coast in spring and fall. And eiders, scoters and other seabirds such as the striking northern gannet are to be seen on the broad ocean surface. Closer, in the intertidal zone, look for willets and other shorebirds prying crustaceans and marine worms from among the rocks. The lagoon will feature shorebirds and ducks, including mallards that are featured on p. 70.

As in all nature sites, it is ideal to visit perhaps once each season, to take in the changing aspects of the natural world, but definitely plan at least one trip here during the year if for nothing else than to stand in awe of its natural beauty.

Directions: Reid State Park, 800 acres, Georgetown, State of Maine, Division of Parks and Public Lands

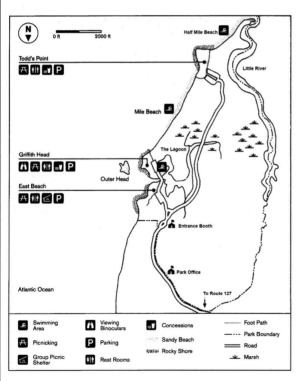

From Route 1 in Bath, turn onto Route 127 South in Woolwich. Continue for approximately 13 miles and follow signs for Reid State Park. No pets are allowed in beach areas.

(map: courtesy of Department of Agriculture, Conservation and Forestry, Bureau of Parks and Lands, www.parksand-lands.com)

WebSource: www.visitmaine.com/things-to-do/recreation-areas/reid-state-park/

Fringed polygala (Polygala paucifolia) *look like small orchids but belong to the Milkwort family that has about 50 species in the U.S. We found these growing along a sandy trail in the northern part of the Park. The function of the fringes may be as a landing platform for pollinators. The suffix "-gala" means milk, as it was thought that plants of this family promoted milk production in humans and cattle.*

Beach pea (Lathyrus maritimus) *helps stabilize the seaward front of the dunes.*

Dendritic drainage patterns branch like trees carved in the sand by water seeping from the upper beach at low tide.

Fierce northeast gales push driftwood far in-shore at the mouth of the tidal stream that drains the lagoon. Deposits of sand interlace the bedrock.

Migrating warblers and other songbirds favor coastal groves of spruce such as this one atop Griffith Head. The trees thrive despite direct exposure to ocean winds and salt spray.

*Look for sun-basking turtles around the Ice Pond, including the lesser known stinkpot or **musk turtle** (Sternotherus odoratus). If harassed it emits a strong odor (a hormone composed of fatty acids and proteins) from two glands on its underside, where the skin meets the plastron. The hormone may also serve in communication with other individuals, for instance in mating. Rarely found on land, except when females lay eggs, they are described as "bottom crawlers" for their ability to rest and walk under-water, but are also known to ascend overhanging shrubs up to six feet high, dropping directly back into the water if disturbed by predator or passing canoeist.*

69

(photo: David White)

The Mallard: A Commonplace Miracle

Five **mallards** *(Anas platyrhynchos)*—two green-headed drakes and three drab hens—splash down into an open stretch of Black Brook, not far from my house. It is late winter. They chuckle and shake and make quiet sounds, as if to say, "Aahh . . . We've made it. And now for a bit of shuteye." They scan the willows, melting snow and young skunk cabbage on the shore and then twist their necks, lay their heads on their backs and go to sleep. I'm less than ten feet away, motionless.

I've read that tucking the bill under their feathers allows ducks and other birds to inhale warm air, providing a tiny but significant caloric advantage. Also, because the bill itself is richly supplied with blood, tucking prevents convective heat loss. But falling asleep, and here? I, too, enjoy an occasional afternoon nap but, unlike the ducks, am not at risk from predatory mink, fox, raccoon, coyote, bobcat, fisher, skunk or large snapping turtles, all native to here. Bald eagles frequent this area, and any of them could kill a sleeping duck. And here I am: not a threat—but they don't know that.

Their orange legs scull underwater, keeping them a safe distance from the shore—while catching forty winks. This snoozing seems risky for a mallard, but they must be doing something right because they are the most numerous duck in North America. This has not always been the case. Ralph Palmer, in *Maine Birds* (1949), says that the mallard was never common in Maine. He tells us the first unquestionable reference in the state is by Audubon, who wrote in 1835 that they were rare east of Boston and never seen beyond Portland. Perhaps because of warmer winters, this is no longer the case. Today, around here, mallards may be seen year-round wherever there is open water—in harbors and tidal marshes. Whatever they are doing, it seems to be the right thing.

Courtship begins in autumn, extends into winter and ends in spring with copulation. This means there is good opportunity to see that behavior, even though some tidbits may last only a split second. Male displays include several moves and calls, including raising and arching that bright green neck and extending the neck and head low over the water, accompanied by a variety of grunts and whistles that are better heard than explained. Females display, too, occasionally provoking males to fight before submitting to copulation. But the most unusual display is the water-flick dance, occurring when a group of males surrounds a group of females. Males arch their necks, whistle, dip their broad bills under water and squirt water at their preferred consort. The moment is brief. To see it, you must be looking for it.

These displays call for explanation. There are many species of ducks, 148 in all, including geese and swans—all in the family *Anatidae*—of which 63 are currently found in North America. They range in size from the little buffleheads and teal weighing less than a pound to the 2-¾–pound mallard male—the female is slightly smaller—up to a trumpeter swan that may weigh over 30 pounds. The family divides into further phylogenetic categories but may also be segregated into groups by behavior. Maine examples include: perching ducks (wood duck), freshwater divers (mergansers), sea ducks (scoters), stiff-tailed ducks (ruddy duck), and the dabbling or surface feeders, such as our mallard and black duck. All are aquatic and have short legs and tails and long necks.

The *Anatidae* live on every continent except for Antarctica. Most have flattened bills with serrated edges through which they eject water and mud, retaining food. Mallards are the parent species for our domestic varieties, excepting muscovy ducks. They share a long association with humans and hybridize in captivity. But it's a different story in the wild. That's where courtship plays an important role.

Imagine a large, mixed flock of ducks congregated and ready to breed—a melee of shaking and dipping heads, wings in the air, arched necks, bodies upended, crowns raised and lowered: the possibilities are endless. Indeed, according to one source, male long-tailed ducks, alone, have a dozen distinct displays. Given all this sexual advertising, how is it that more hybridization in the wild doesn't occur?

One explanation, according to *The Birder's Handbook*, is that congestion "has created considerable evolutionary pressure for each species to develop distinctive displays, so that hybridization among different species displaying together will be minimized." The authors go on to say, "Thus, for example, the displays of Barrow's goldeneye are different from those of common goldeneye until the precopulatory stage is reached, but with nowhere near the frequency of hybrids between mallards and black ducks, which have very similar displays."

Courtship display serves to preserve the species. It triggers copulation with a same-species partner and reduces it with others. The more different the species, the less likely it is that copulation will occur. This is only a partial explanation for the myriad of courtship displays, but it is a starting point for closer observation of the ducks around us.

After copulation, the female mallard lays a single brood of eight to 10 eggs in a reed-grass nest near water. When all of them have been deposited, incubation begins. The male shares in this for about a week, after which he abandons his mate and joins other males. At that point his contribution to the next generation is over. Twenty-six to 30 days later the precocial chicks hatch. (*Precocial* means that chicks are feathered and able to move about and swim soon after hatching. The opposite is *altricial:* being unfeathered and blind at hatching, remaining in the nest as they complete maturation.)

With nesting season done, both adults molt, leaving them unable to fly for about a month. During this vulnerable period they avoid predation by hiding, diving or swimming. The male's bright breeding plumage is replaced, or eclipsed, by dull colors. During this time they continue to eat a variety of larvae, snails, agricultural crops and grains, acorns, insects, worms, and aquatic invertebrates.

According to banding records, mallards may live for as long as 29 years, although more commonly five to 10 years. U.S. Fish and Wildlife Service data state that 4,166,013 mallards were shot in 2010, about 28 percent of the total duck harvest of 14,867,000 for that same year. This figure takes into account about 25 other duck species, but not geese and brant. It combines the kill from the Atlantic, Mississippi, Central and Pacific flyways but excludes Alaska and Canada. Maine hunters seem to have a relatively light hand in this, being responsible for harvesting about 8,000 mallards in that year. Surprisingly, here in Maine mallards are not the most harvested species, nor are they in the rest of the Atlantic flyway.

Capable of flight speeds of 70 miles per hour, mallards are typically low, slow flyers powered by wings that are large relative to their weight. This allows them to spring instantly into flight, or drop quickly into a tiny body of water: hence the name "puddle ducks." And hence, too, their presence 10 or 12 feet away from me.

Not daring to move, I simply watch. After awhile I realize that the mallards' situation is more dangerous than I first thought. The one exposed eye, the one facing the sky, is actually closed most of the time. I can raise my hand very slowly without their noticing.

Science tells us certain birds—ducks, songbirds, falcons and gulls—can sleep with one eye open, as can whales, eared seals, manatees and, possibly, reptiles. Like humans, avian brains have two cerebral hemispheres, one of which can remain awake while the other sleeps. This *unihemispheric* sleep splits the difference between sleep and wakefulness in a way that has obvious survival value, so much so that one wonders why it is not more widespread among animals (although the expression "asleep at the wheel" suggests one explanation). Delving into the phenomenon using the tools of modern fieldwork and genetic research promises answers in the near future. But for now, scientists like Niels C. Rattenborg (Max Planck Institute of Ornithology) who study birds and sleep—with an eye, so to speak, on a deeper understanding—are only beginning to understand the process and elucidate the mechanisms of sleep not only in birds, but other species as well, including humans.

Current evidence suggests that unihemispheric sleep serves two functions. The first one applies to my dozing mallards. According to University of Sheffield Professor Tim Birkhead, FRS, and author of the engaging book *Bird Sense:*

> A study of mallard ducks showed that individuals sleeping in the center of a group (where it is relatively safe) spent much less time with an eye open than those on the edge (where they are more vulnerable to predators), and that ducks on the edge of the group were more likely to open the eye facing outwards from the group in the direction from which a predator might approach.

Sitting in the willows, I had not noticed this, possibly because five birds don't really have a center or a perimeter, but now with Birkhead's observation in mind, I have a mission to grab a spotting scope and take a closer look at a larger flock.

A second function of unihemispheric sleep is that it may allow birds to sleep while flying. Not long ago this notion was thought absurd. But today some scientists are not so sure. Discussion of this phenomenon centers around two species, European swifts *(Apus apus)* and glaucous gulls *(Larus hyperboreus)*, and is based on two observations. The first one that Birkhead brings to our attention is anecdotal:

> A French airman on a special nocturnal operation during the First World War reported that, as he glided down across enemy lines with his engine off, at an altitude of around 10,000 feet, "We suddenly found ourselves among a strange flight of birds which seemed to be motionless . . . they were widely scattered and only a few yards below the aircraft showing up against a white sea of cloud underneath." Remarkably, two birds were caught and identified as swifts.

Were the birds asleep? Birkhead admits not knowing, but "it is a possibility." But then he provides a contemporary, more convincing example: Glaucous gulls "have been seen flying to their roosts with only one eye open, suggesting that they are already sleeping before even reaching the roost." Given that knowledge is an expanding universe, we may soon know a lot more about this.

The alertness of my dozing mallards became obvious the very second I rose to my feet. They were in the air in an instant. Had their eyes been open, they could not have reacted more quickly. This was a testament to the survival value of this astonishing capacity by the familiar, yet miraculous, common mallard.

—T. O.

Dense mixed forest grows on the side of steep ridges right to the water's edge. This rocky point in the southeast part of the preserve offers nice views up and down the cove: a good stopping place for a backpack lunch.

Josephine Newman Audubon Sanctuary

Much of this site fronts the Y-shaped upper reaches of Robinhood Cove, one of those long, narrow, shallow water bodies characteristic of this part of the coast. Its proximity to Reid State Park makes this a natural "companion" site to tour on the same day. As with many nature sites that owe their existence to an abiding love of nature, this one was preserved by its former owner, Josephine Oliver Newman, a naturalist with a specialty in primitive plants and lichens.

The topography is quite rugged with many outcrops punctuating the pine-needle carpet of the forest floor. Several loop trails totaling 2 ½ miles skirt the shoreline or traverse the wooded interior with views through the treetops to the waters beyond. Near the trailhead look or listen for amphibians at the marshy pond lined with cattails.

The day we visited in later July, we were fortunate to come across a large cluster of monarch butterfly larvae feeding on their obligatory stand of milkweed in a field

---

Directions: Josephine Newman Audubon Sanctuary, 119 acres, Georgetown, Maine Audubon Society

From Route1 in Woolwich (across the Kennebec River from Bath) follow sign for Reid State Park and take Route 127 south just under 9 miles to the sanctuary access road on the right just after crossing a short bridge. No dogs allowed.

WebSource: http://maineaudubon.org/find-us/josephine-newman-audubon-sanctuary/

The aptly named Geology Trail winds by many such rock walls and outcroppings, following the contour of a north-south oriented ridge.

near the remnant foundation of the old farm. Thus we associate this site with this species (*see* next page) and know that such occurrences cannot necessarily be counted on, given the vagaries of monarch populations and the changing global climate.

Through the decades, many apples have grown and fallen from this old tree close to the remains of the homestead. Peonies, another sign of erstwhile human habitation, still grow nearby.

Young saplings mature in the "windfall" of sunlight, a natural clearing produced by blown-down spruce toppled in an easterly storm.

Some stones in this granite wall appear to have been worked by hand. Trees grow all around where sheep and cattle once grazed on pastureland.

Monarch Butterfly

Migration is one of nature's most important tools for survival. Animals around the world have adapted to conditions of extreme weather and cyclical food supply by moving. Of all those who travel distances to survive, the **monarch butterfly** *(Danaus plexippus)* seems to have stretched the limits of what is possible. The species elicits wonder. But its complex life strategy, in all of its adaptive elegance, comes with risk. Various interactions of weather, food and habitat over a wide expanse of this continent must "mesh" for this migration to continue year after year.

This large, three-inch butterfly has dark orange wings that are tiger-striped on top with duller camouflage underneath. Males are slightly larger than the females and can be identified by a dark spot in the center of each hind wing, called the *androconium*, which are specialized wing scales thought to produce chemicals attractive to females. (The monarch is sometimes confused with the smaller and darker viceroy butterfly that is no relation.)

The stages of its life cycle are characteristic of the order Lepidoptera (moths and butterflies): egg, caterpillar, pupa and then adult. The monarch has evolved four stages of growth given not only the insect's short life span, but also the need to travel long distances. It has done this by employing multiple generations that leapfrog each other as they make their way on the primary northern leg of their migration. And what a migration it is: some local eastern populations of this diminutive creature can cover distances in excess of 3,000 miles.

There are two distinct populations in North America, east and west of the continental divide. The eastern population, seen here in Maine, has the most dramatic migration, moving as

Female monarch lacks androconium spot on hind wing.

far north as southern Canada in the summer and then back to their wintering grounds in Mexico. The western population lives mostly in California and spends its winters in the more temperate evergreen or eucalyptus groves of the south coastal region of that state.

In the early spring, the eastern group breeds en masse in Mexico and then begins the migration north. On the way, females lay eggs at stopping points along the way. Their progeny will go through the four complete life stages of hatching, metamorphosis, reproduction and death. In this way, multiple generations will extend up the east coast until they reach their northerly limit. The first three generations that arrive in Maine have each lived no more than eight weeks, but the fourth and final generation has a different strategy.

This final summer generation, called the *diapause* stage, may live as long as eight months. Diapause refers to the insect phenomenon of storing lipids, proteins and carbohydrates to accommodate long periods of intense activity or semi-hibernation or both in the case of the monarch. We see this last generation congregating in early September, readying themselves for their titanic migration south. They have stored within their less-than-one-gram bodies the energy to migrate thousands of miles, to be semi-torpid for up to six months, to mate and then to start migration back north. This stage has to rank among the great migrations of the natural world, such as those of the salmon and the arctic tern. Some refer to this stage as the "Methuselah generation." Astoundingly, these butterflies can travel south 80 miles in a day. One tagged monarch was found 265 miles away the next day. This two-way migration, north and south, is not known in other butterfly species. In this respect, the species acts more like a bird than an insect.

Why would an animal evolve such a dramatic and risky life cycle? In part, the answer is that the monarch has developed a relationship with the lowly milkweed: both a strength and a weakness. Milkweed leaves, with toxic compounds called cardenolides, provide the butterflies with ample protection from predators but also limit the monarch to one food source.

Many plants like the milkweed have evolved methods to avoid predation. A common one is to taste badly, but what may be distasteful to one forager may be fine to another. The 140-plus species of milkweed all have sticky, toxic latex flowing through the veins of each leaf. Monarch caterpillars have adapted to the consumption of cardenolides, a steroid that acts in a similar way to the toxin digitalis found in foxglove. Because milkweed is the sole food source for the caterpillars, their bodies concentrate this toxin, making the monarch, in all its life stages, inedible by many of its natural predators. This toxicity is even passed along from the adult to the eggs and early hatched instar caterpillars. To avoid the sticky effects of the milkweed latex, monarch caterpillars will cut the veins serving a particular portion of a plant leaf and then eat the middle of that area, thus avoiding much of the latex altogether, evident in the circular patterns eaten from the leaves.

The four-step life cycle begins with several hundred eggs being laid individually on the underside of the milkweed's leathery leaves. These hatch after four days, and the young caterpillars begin eating milkweed leaves right away. With their bold yellow, black and white striping,

Monarch butterflies only eat milkweed in the caterpillar stage, but because they are able to store the plant's toxic cardenolides, they remain bitter and toxic to predators through the following stages of instar, pupa and adult butterfly. There are stories of predatory birds sampling adult monarchs in their wintering grounds and spitting out those that have high concentrations of this toxin, until they find ones that have more palatable, lower levels.

they advertise a stern warning of toxicity to predators. Over a two-week period, the caterpillars grow to some two thousand times their size at hatching. Fully grown, their body is up to two inches long, with two black feelers at the head end and two shorter black filaments towards the rear. During this meteoric growth they go through five molts of their skin; these stages are called *instars*. They then undergo metamorphosis, in which the last instars form a chrysalis in which they remain for another two weeks. The miracle is complete when the adults emerge and begin straight away to feed on nectar of flowering milkweed and other plants. If this is that last "Methuselah stage," these individuals will be slightly larger than previous generations, and will now have the capacity to travel like no other insect we know of.

It is estimated that a billion or more eastern monarchs make the long journey south to congregate in their over-wintering sites in Mexico, first discovered only in 1975. This makes the monarchs' winter gathering among the largest single aggregation of land animals. Some 30 sites in and around the evergreen oyamel forests of Michocacan, in central Mexico, are home for six to eight months. They feed only occasionally in the winter and then only on warm days. Amazingly, this last migrating generation will return to these ancestral winter staging areas without ever having been there: even, some believe, to the very tree that previous family generations spent their winters on. It has yet to be revealed how the monarch manages this.

Unfortunately, the story of the monarch is not complete without discussion of the plummeting numbers that are being recorded today. Monarchs are being affected by the lethal mix of habitat loss, increasing use of pesticides and the disruption of weather due to climate change. Monarchs' wintering populations are measured not in individuals but in numbers of acres of trees that they cover. Estimates in one of the primary over-wintering sites in Zitacuaro,

Mexico, suggest that at one time they covered as much as 50 acres. Winter 2013 estimates in the same region were 2.94 acres.

An unusually cold period in their winter quarters in 2002 may have reduced some localized populations by as much as 80 percent. Catastrophic winter storms in 2010 that produced rains of up to 15 inches in some areas

of Mexico have further reduced overwintering populations. (This is probably the primary cause of the apparent absence of monarchs in Maine in the summer of 2011.)

In 1986, the wintering grounds in Mexico received some protection in the form of a World Heritage Biosphere designation protecting slightly more than half the area. In 2008, the North American Monarch Conservation Plan detailed cooperation between the US, Canada and Mexico to help protect this valuable species. Government and non-government organizations have taken up the work of seeing this through; prominent among them is the Xerces Society. A March 2014 article by the Xerces Society reported a study showing that the wintering population has dropped for six of the last seven years and is now at one-fifteenth the population in 1997. The study further found that since 2000, Mexico has largely reduced logging within the protected wintering grounds. That suggests that impacts may be more from reduction in milkweed due to drought and herbicide use, as well as climatic variation in the wintering grounds. Chip Taylor, director of the conservation group Monarch Watch, believes that expansion of midwest farmland is also a cause of reduced numbers. The introduction of genetically modified soybeans and corn that are resistant to herbicides has allowed farmers to spray the areas between crop lands that once were prime habitat for milkweed with no fear of losing their crops, resulting in the loss of the primary feed for monarchs. Taylor estimates as much as 120 million acres of milkweed and, in turn, monarch habitat have been lost.

On the west coast, habitat loss in southern California is of primary concern. I visited one of the sites just south of Santa Barbara expecting it to be protected park land, and it turned out to be a median strip of eucalyptus trees between a housing development and a highway. Wintering sites have revealed population declines of 90 percent or more. In one site near Santa Cruz, 1997 winter population was estimated at 120,000 butterflies in residence; by 2009, only 480 remained.

— D. F.

Alphabet of Biological Terms: "A" is for What?...

English is a language said to have the richest lexicon of nouns, verbs, adjectives and adverbs. This holds particularly true for natural history terms—as in the preceding article on monarchs—mostly built upon the solid foundations of Greek and Latin that allow scientists to formulate new terms for anything, easily assembling the constituent word roots to create any meaning. (The older natural history guides often give the roots and their meanings making the species' Latin name easier to comprehend. For instance the Greek ανθοσ [anthos, flower] figures into Spiranthes, the genus of ladies' tresses, an orchid.) Thanks to *The Cambridge Illustrated Dictionary of Natural History,* and other sources, we have assembled a sample alphabet of this phenomenal vocabulary.

—K.S.

andromonoecious: having male and hermaphroditic flowers on the same stem.

apophallation: a technique used by some species of air-breathing land slugs.

biramous: having two branches as in the horned krill.

chasmocomophyte: plant growing on detritus in rock fissures.

diaphototropism: orientation at a right angle to the direction of incident light.

exdysis: shedding the outer skin or cuticle, chiefly among arthropods. (Hence, exdysiast: stripteaser, chiefly among humans.)

forbicolus: living on broad-leaved plants.

gonotheca: in some hydroids, a protective sac or capsule encasing the gonopore (sex bud).

helomochlophilous: thriving in meadow thicket habitats.

inquiline: inhabitant or lodger within another organism, such as microbes within a pitcher plant.

jactitation: dispersal of seeds by jostling motion of parent plant.

kinetofragminophora: class of free-living and endoparisitic ciliates (one-celled protozoans).

lepidophagous: feeding on scales, as in fish.

manubrium: in some hydromedusae (jellyfish), a pendulous, clapper-like projection beneath the umbrella containing part of the stomach.

myrmecochorous: dispersed by the agency of ants.

nyctigamous: having flowers that open at night and close during the day.

ornithocoprophilous: thriving in habitats rich in bird droppings.

pasculomorphosis: change in the structure of plants as a result of grazing.

quadrivoltine: having four broods per year or season.

rhizopleustohelophyte: plants rooted in the bank or bottom of shallow water with a floating stem and emergent leaf-bearing shoots.

syzgy: (1) close association between protozoans prior to gamete formation, but during which nuclear fusion does not occur. (2) time at which the sun and moon are in line relative to Earth.

thanatocoenosis: assemblage of organisms brought together after death by sedimentary processes.

ulmification: process of peat formation.

vitellogenous: yolk-producing.

welwitschia: large plants endemic to Namib desert living 1000 years or more.

xylophyte: plant living in or on wood.

ylespil: obsolete term for a hedgehog.

zymogenic: causing fermentation.

◆ 9 ◆ Steve Powell WMA on Swan Island

Forest, fields and marshland make up the varied habitats on the island. In this eagle-eye view from the north, the town of Richmond lies on the mainland to right. The main road from the landing (lower right) stretches the length of the island, with secondary trails to the east and west shores. (photo: courtesy of Maine Dept. of Inland Fisheries and Wildlife)

TIME STANDING STILL, A THROWBACK, PARK-LIKE, AN UNTOUCHED QUALITY: all these phrases come to mind within the first few minutes of setting foot on Swan Island, a Wildlife Management Area (WMA), one of many in the state. It is a place to come back to, as curious travelers are wont to do, for it is almost a world unto itself, and there is much to explore over its many hundreds of acres of woods and fields.

Even on one of the worst days in late spring, when the Maine weather had taken a turn for the worst, cold and wet, this gem of a preserve in the middle of the Kennebec River enchanted us as we walked through mature mixed forest and lush, expansive meadows. Among the Midcoast preserves cov-

Former residents buried in the Curtis Cemetery are listed on this sign, a testimony to the hard-working people who made their livelihoods on the island in the 18th, 19th and early 20th centuries.

Placid waters, disguising a strong current, between Swan and Little Swan Islands on the eastern side reflect a mirror image of the heavily forested banks. Nearby, archaeologists have uncovered evidence of Native Americans dating back 9,000 years.

ered in this book and our previous one, its statistics stand out: 1,750 acres of land and hundreds more of marsh; four and a half miles long by three-quarters wide embraced by one of Maine's major rivers. There is also an attractive campsite area on a gently sloping hill looking east to the morning sun, so welcomed when camping on the chilly Maine nights. And if you desire more of a bird's-eye perspective, there is a wildlife viewing tower with long vistas across the lush landscape.

The fields of yesteryear, relics of the island's pastoral past, are today a haven for grassland species of birds, mammals and all the supporting biota that form a natural community.

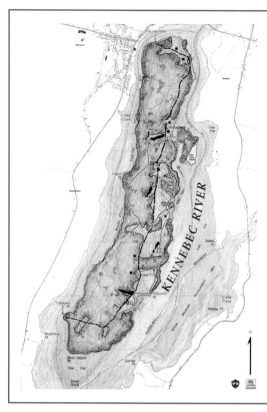

Directions: Swan Island Wildlife Management Area, 1755 acres, Town of Richmond, Maine Department of Inland Fisheries and Wildlife

Take Route I-295 to Exit 43 Richmond/ Litchfield. Follow Route 197 East for about 3 miles to Richmond Village. Turn left at the intersection of Routes 197 and 24. The parking lot is immediately on your right marked by a brown State of Maine sign. Dogs not allowed.

WebSource: http://maine.gov/IFW/ education/swanisland/main_content.htm

The marshland here is known as a tidal freshwater marsh where the salinity averages less than 1 part per thousand (1‰) as opposed to the ocean at 35‰. This is caused by a stalemate of sorts at a narrow, 800-foot constriction several miles downstream, known as the Chops. There the incoming seawater of the flood tide meets the fresh river water discharge of the Kennebec and five other rivers that join it just upstream in Merrymeeting Bay. The two opposing streams meet with very little admixture, raising a wall of water as if by an invisible dam, resulting in a five- to seven-foot tide of a brackish nature around Swan Island. This habitat is uncommon in nature, but has been colonized by specialized plant species that require daily submersion to thrive, here described by the Maine Natural Areas Program (www.maine. gov/dacf/mnap):

> Several hundred acres of tidal flats surround the island. The shoreline has a range of substrates—soft and firm mud, sand, gravel, cobble, and ledge— that provide suitable habitat for seven rare plant species. Wild rice dominates much of the marsh at the southern end of the island, joined by associated species such as **waterworts** (*Elatine spp.*), **three-square bulrush** (*Schoenoplectus pungens*), and **false pimpernel** (*Lindernia dubia*). Some of the wild rice may have originated from historic seeding efforts by MDIFW.

The road from the main landing winds over four miles, through fields and forest, passing historical houses along the way, terminating at Theobald Point on the island's southwestern tip.

In this modern age, Swan Island is a refuge for living things in an era of rapidly decreasing habitat and increasing pressure by human-produced hazards such as bright lights, glass buildings and introduced predators, principally domestic cats, fortunately absent from here (*see* p. 88). The natural history of Swan Island, like Maine's entire coast, starts with the reemergence of the land after the last glaciation and continues its 10,000-year existence to this day. The first humans documented by archaeologists were Native American arriving about 9,000 years ago, not just passing through as did the early paleo-hunters of large animals, but living here for about 5,000 years. European emigrants first arrived ca. 1600 and took up more or less permanent residence during the 1700s. In the 1800s the island became a town, Perkins, populated by farmers, fisherman, loggers, ice cutters and ship builders. It is striking to come across some of the old houses still on the island, the proverbial "mute testimony" to those times.

But now the only humans in this sanctuary are the small staff of dedicated state workers (managers, biologists, interns) who attend to the needs of the place. And of course there are the day visitors and overnight campers who come to savor this world apart from everyday 21st century life. Essentially this place "belongs" to the animals, plants, fungi and all the life forms that comprise the local ecosystem. Of note is the presence of at least two pairs of nesting eagles (*see* p. 86). We are lucky it has wound up in conservation.

The waterways around the island are sparsely traveled now in comparison to yesteryear when large sailing ships and all manner of working and passenger boats moved up and down the river, at that time a major concourse for humans, and the center of the state's economy. The short hop across the river from the landing in Richmond can be by the regularly scheduled runs of the state's boat; or ideally, bring your own small craft to reconnoiter the island's shoreline and perhaps paddle through the stands of wild rice growing in much of the shallow water on the west side. All access to this special place is by reservations with the Maine Department of Inland Fisheries and Wildlife office.

The extra bit of planning it may take to book a day pass or overnight camping permit is well worth the effort, for this site is a "first among equals." Put it to the top of the list of your curious-traveling itinerary.

With long vistas both to the east and west, the tower enables observation of wildlife from three stories up. We saw deer grazing in the distance as well as phoebes, tree swallows and rose-breasted grosbeaks close by. The cellar hole and stone-capped well of a vanished farm here signify life in an era gone by.

Wanderings of Maine's Bald Eagle Fledglings

In recent years, researchers from Biodiversity Research Institute (Gorham, Maine) set out to fill in some of the unknowns about subadult **bald eagles** (*Haliaeetus leucocephalus*). They climbed nest trees and fit prefledged nestlings with backpack-mounted satellite transmitters.

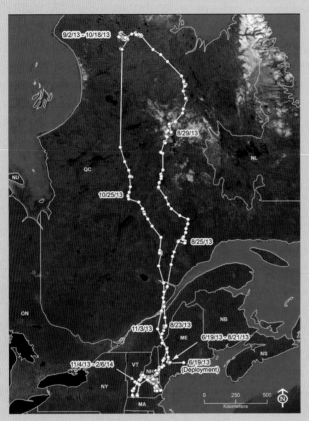

(Courtesy of Jeff Tash, Biodiversity Research Institute)

The units are harnessed to a thin, soft ribbon, which birds can wear without impeding their flight capability. Powered by solar panels, transmitters use passing satellites and onboard GPS units to provide accurate information on the birds' locations. The units can provide a daily log of subadult bald eagle movements for years, telling a story of their needs and lives that was once impossible to fathom.

The map shows movements of a satellite-tagged bald eagle fledgling fitted with a transmitter along the Androscoggin River in 2013. This individual wandered farther north than any other eagle tagged in the state— hundreds of miles into northern Quebec, well beyond treeline. Following its brief visit to Canada, the bird quickly trekked back down through Maine to New Hampshire in advance of the cold winter months ahead. With a little time and luck, birds like this one are helping us understand the patterns and needs of these mysterious, wandering young eagles.

Adult bald eagles may be the most widely recognized bird in North America. Throughout Maine, those spotting a notably large, powerful bird with a white head and tail contrasting a dark brown body have almost certainly seen an adult bald eagle. But as many know, not all bald eagles look like this. During their first year, bald eagles sport a dark brown beak, dark eye, and variably mottled chocolate brown feathers throughout their body and tail. Over the next four years, these young eagles—often referred to as subadults—will progress through a series of feather molts before achieving the characteristic white head and

tail many know as a bald eagle. Adulthood doesn't come quickly or easily for bald eagles. It represents a merit badge of sorts, achieved only after surviving the perilous early years of its life.

Subadult eagles represent the next generation of breeders, and their survival has a tremendous influence on the stability of the overall population. But in the absence of a mate, a territory or an

Fitted with a satellite transmitter and red leg bands before fledging in 2011, the subadult eagle "M/4" has beamed back a wealth of tracking data to scientists at the Biodiversity Research Institute as it traveled around the Northeast and southern Canada. (photo: Kristen Nicholas)

abundant year-round food resource, many subadults do what you might expect under such circumstances: they roam widely. Some of them travel for hundreds of miles. Over time, many of these young eagles will eventually settle down somewhere to attempt breeding themselves. But much of what happens to them between fledging and breeding has remained a mystery due to the sheer difficulty in studying them. Today, technological advances such as tracking devices are helping us understand bald eagle movements to aid in their conservation.

— Chris DeSorbo

It's a long way up to attach transmitters to young eagles well before they leave the nest to begin their wanderings. (photo: Chris Persico)

(Ed. note: Swan Island being essentially free of domestic cats—other than possible individuals crossing on winter ice—provides a level of protection to birds and small mammals not found on the mainland where the species is often part of the local predator/prey ecosystem. We offer this article in the spirit of public awareness.)

The Cat Can't Change Its Spots

The **domestic cat** *(Felis catus)* was first brought to this continent by early European settlers, and is now a thriving species that kills birds, reptiles, amphibians and small mammals. Be it pet or feral, it is an extremely successful, exquisitely evolved carnivore like other members of the Felidae, a family that includes 41 species worldwide, two of which—bobcat and lynx—exist in Maine. But unlike its wild relatives, *F. catus* flourishes despite poison, starvation, accidental trapping, disease, being hit by cars and being preyed upon by dogs and other animals. What sets the domestic cat apart? This dual nature of being both a house pet and wild predator explains why discussion of this species is often vitriolic. As Biblical Jeremiah noted long ago, "Can . . . the leopard [change] his spots?"

The Felidae are "obligate carnivores," dependent on meat for survival. Look in a cat's mouth for confirmation: small nipping incisors, interlocking canines, and cutting molars (carnassials). The large, flat, grinding molars of herbivorous/omnivorous animals (deer, pigs, humans) are absent.

Domestic cats, like dogs, enjoy human support. They generally sleep in human structures and eat human-provided food. Unlike dogs, which may kill livestock and wild mammals incidentally, some tame as well as all feral domestic cats hunt and kill inordinate numbers of birds and small mammals. They are, in effect, a subsidized predator but not a natural one, with an outsized impact on vulnerable species.

Recent estimates of bird and small animal mortality by domestic cats by S. R. Loss, T. Will and P. P. Marra (*Nature*, Jan., 2013) are alarming, as summarized in the abstract:

"Anthropogenic threats, such as collisions with man-made structures, vehicles, poisoning and predation by domestic pets, combine to kill billions of wildlife annually. Free-ranging domestic cats have been introduced globally and have contributed to multiple wildlife extinctions on islands. . . . We estimate that [in the U.S.] free-ranging domestic cats kill 1.4–3.7 billion birds and 6.9–20.7 billion mammals annually. Un-owned cats, as opposed to owned pets, cause the majority of this mortality. Our findings suggest that free-ranging cats . . . are likely the single greatest source of anthropogenic mortality for U.S. birds and mammals. Scientifically sound conservation and policy intervention is needed to reduce this impact."

Genus *Felis* includes small species occurring worldwide. Fossil evidence (see following sidebar) suggests that domestication goes back 10,000 years to Neolithic times. When humans began to grow grains, cats were drawn into a symbiotic association: they killed the rodents that ate the grain upon which settlements depended. Within 5,000 years the ancient Egyptians sealed the relationship, valuing cats for their ability to kill snakes and rodents. And they revered cats, mummifying them and celebrating them in art. The later Romans carried cats to Britain and elsewhere in their empire. Thereafter, wherever a ship sailed, there went a cat to keep the rats at bay. Whether cats served humans or we them is an open question, as in any domesticated animal or plant. It appears, however, that we now serve them to the detriment of vulnerable bird and small mammal species.

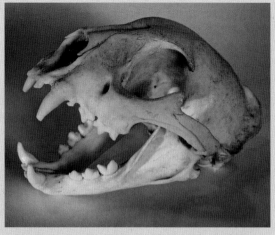

As carnivores, domestic cats have a dentition consisting of twelve incisors, four canines, ten premolars and four molars topped by large, forward-directed eyes and a generous nasal structure.

According to the American Pet Products Association, or APPA, in 1947 there were four million pet cats in America; by 1990 there were 58 million. By 2011 the population had risen to 86.4 million. How to explain this phenomenal evolutionary success? Jim Sterba, author of *Nature Wars*, points the way by reminding us of late twentieth century changes in pet keeping. Until well after World War II, the domestic cat served a real purpose in rural communities. Cats did what they have been doing since the Neolithic: catching mice and rats. Bringing one indoors as a pet was always possible, but the intense odor of cat feces and urine kept the practice under control. This changed with the discovery of the deodorizing benefits of kitty litter products. Suddenly, the species was re-identified: the cat's capacity for domesticity and the human need for companionship were a perfect fit. The pet cat was born. Today, fifty years later, the cat serves primarily as member of the family, which justifies spending about $1,000 per animal per year for veterinary services, food, litter, toys, etc. Pet cats have become big business.

This proliferation is only part of the story. Multiple researchers have calculated that the number of feral cats nearly matches the number of pet cats. The estimates hover around 80 million—about the same as the 86.4 million house cats. This means that there are between 146 and 186 million cats in the United States today. All indications are that this upward trend will continue.

F. catus has big eyes that are well suited for night vision, large ears that are sensitive to the high frequency sounds that small animals make, a capacity to smell that is complemented by cells in the roof of the mouth that allow the animal to taste odors in the air, whiskers that sense movement. And they are highly agile, capable of leaping five or more feet into the air to bring down a swallow, bunting or butterfly. Like their wild relatives, cats are successful predators. Supporting evidence makes it beyond debate that they are among the most ecologically damaging invasive species worldwide.

The International Union of Concerned Scientists' (IUCS) "Global Invasive Species Database" includes the domestic cat as "among the 100 worst of the world's invaders." "The most obvious impact of feral cats is the predatory impact they exert on native prey populations, this has resulted in the probable local or regional decline or extinction of many species." Imagine New Zealand, which has no native land mammals. Forty percent of native bird species became extinct after cats—along with dogs, ferrets and rats—were introduced to the island. Now, even the iconic kiwi is at risk.

Twenty years ago a procedure known as TNR (trap, neuter and release) gained popularity in Europe. It was thought to offer a solution to the soaring cat population. Sterilized (and vaccinated) cats could live out their natural lives without producing further offspring. Communities plagued by an overabundance of cats suddenly had a workable, non-lethal means of resolving their problem. TNR was a humane proposal that seemingly addressed the perceived shortcomings of traditional eradication methods. In time, so went the theory, the population would dwindle to a manageable level. TNR continues to have wide appeal—despite certain shortcomings.

There's the practical problem of dealing with the large cat population: if the 46,000 veterinarians in the U.S. were to neuter one feral cat per day, seven days a week, by the end of a year only 16 million cats would have been altered, less than 10% of the total population. Even doubling or tripling the number of neutered cats leaves millions of feral cats free to breed, which they do with abandon. Females exhibit a large reproductive potential: they can reproduce at nine months and can bear as many as three litters a year, each averaging four to five kittens. And unfortunately, abandoning cats in both urban and rural areas is common, exacerbating the problem.

However, the practice of TNR may be better than doing nothing according to those involved in such programs. They maintain its efficacy as a sensible and humane solution, especially when neutered cats are not released but placed in homes. The topic is hotly debated, as a quick internet search will reveal.

The International Union of Concerned Scientists offers a few simple suggestions. With respect to pet cats they advise neutering while the cat is young, keeping it in at night—it should really be full-time—and fitting it with a bell, which is said to reduce the number of bird kills. Most importantly they advise against owning cats and feeding birds, which seems obvious. To own a cat that is allowed out of doors and to have a bird feeder is blatantly irrational. It is up to cat owners—one of whom numbers among this book's coauthors—to confront this problem, ideally by maintaining pet cats solely indoors, a lifestyle to which they are easily habituated. Unlike many of the other sources of human-caused small animal mortality, the impact of domestic cats can be lessened with some simple changes on the part of their owners.

—T. O.

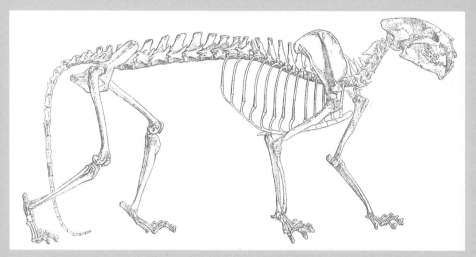

Dinictis, showing the flexible skeleton of modern cats, was over three feet long from head to base of tail and lived in North America about 36 million years ago. (from *Vertebrate Paleontology*, Alfred S. Romer)

Origin of a Species: Cat Evolution "101"

Cat-like animals and marsupial cats existed for millions of years before the antecedent of modern cats that lived in Eurasia 25 million years ago. That genus, *Proailurus* ("before the cats") weighed about 20 pounds, had binocular vision, retractable claws, carnassial teeth and the rounded skull and short muzzle that we would recognize today. Five million years later another cluster of boney fragments warrant a new designation that paleontologists call *Pseudaelurus*. "Pseudo-cat" was a larger, 50-pound animal that, over the next 10 million years, hunted its way around the world. It wandered south to Africa and east over Berengia, the thousand mile-wide land bridge that intermittently connected Asia and North America. This makes *Pseudaelurus* the first modern cat to enter the New World.

Pseudo-cat had a slender body with short, strong legs better suited to climbing than running, but unmistakably a cat, albeit a strange one. Although it required millions of years, the genus gradually morphed into two branches. One was the iconic sabertooths, or Machairodontinae, now extinct. The other is the Felidae, the various modern cats including *Felis catus*.

The process of this diversification has only recently been discovered. Genetics and the study of DNA have given researchers an ever-improving tool for unraveling the many old mysteries of feline evolution. Drs. Warren E. Johnson and Stephen J. O'Brien of the National Cancer Institute offer a case in point. By examining mitochondrial and nuclear DNA, they were able to divide the Felidae into two subfamilies: the Pantherinae (tigers, lions, jaguars and leopards); and the Felinae (cougars, cheetahs, lynxes, ocelots and domestic cats).

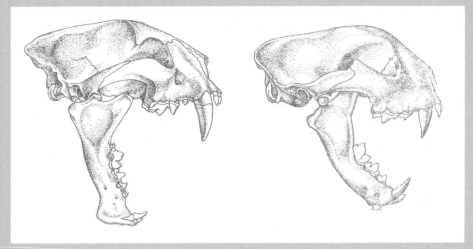

The skull of *Metailurus* (right), a relative of *Pseudaelurus*, shows the reduced upper canines and more rounded skull of modern cats, as compared with the skull of *Dinictis* (left); it lived in Asia and Africa about 25 million years ago. (from *Vertebrate Paleontology*, Alfred S. Romer)

Several species evolved in the North America, after which they spread out, occasionally back to Asia if the climate allowed. O'Brien's and Johnson's analysis has revealed when each of these species came into being. Cheetahs, for example, evolved in North America, expanded their range to Africa, then became extinct here. Lynx, too, began here before spreading to Eurasia, but unlike the cheetah did not vanish from this continent. There is reason to believe that 6.5 million years ago the iconic African leopard may also have originated in North America. It's hard to know what will be discovered in the next few years.

This ebb and flood of Felidae has come to an end. Berengia is now underwater and likely to remain so. And, aside from *F. catus*, all of the 41 species are at risk, many even at the threshold of extinction. None of them will ever again roam beyond their restricted, existing geographical distribution. Our single notable exception still has a shot at extending its range and may yet invade new territory, but as awareness of the domestic cat's ecological impact becomes accepted, even this may slow down.

—T.O.

◆ IO ◆   Pownalborough Courthouse Preserve

The elegant courthouse was at the center of Pownalborough, one of Maine's oldest colonial settlements. It would have appeared as a "beacon of civilization" in its day.

THIS PRESERVE FEATURES ONE OF THE MOST IMPORTANT HISTORICAL SITES in the state coupled with a 75-acre trail system that runs through old-growth pines along the banks of the Kennebec River as well as mixed hardwoods in the glacially sculpted uplands. This part of Maine, including nearby Swan Island (chapter 9), was at the heart of the earliest European settlements in the area. During years of deadly strife eventually all the land was wrested from the original settlers of Asian descent who had arrived in Maine thousands of years before. In the 1600s and 1700s, Maine was yet to become Maine, still subsumed within the power structure of Massachusetts, including the legal system (*see* p. 96). So, as you tour the courthouse and walk along the woodland paths here, you tread on ground with a long and complex human history.

Courthouse

Plan one of your visits here to take a tour of the fascinating interior of the building guided by one of the learned docents (check website for dates). Back in its day, the three floors, now furnished with actual or period pieces throughout, served as courthouse, tavern and inn—presumably in mixed order as court sessions were just quarterly, but settlers and soldiers lived in the area year round. Anyone with a passing interest in construction will marvel at the design, both outside and in, including an unusual truss system to carry and transfer the forces of the large roof. You will hear about famous people in history books: Benedict Arnold passing through on his ill-fated mission to capture Quebec, as well as John Adams—although there is great debate as to whether he slept here—and many others of national and regional import.

Trails

To feel that energy imparted by a large river flowing by, take the river trail amid tall pines with intimate views out to the waterway which connects downstream with the vitally important estuary of Merrymeeting Bay and ocean beyond. The 170-mile river is tidal up to Augusta upstream and flows out of Moosehead Lake, Maine's largest. As with all major rivers, in former days this was a major "highway" into the interior, and a large number of ships and boats—from canoes to freight barges (called gundalows) to tall ships—would have been passing by, or landing here in the cove on the north side.

An old-time sign portrays the dress of colonial days.

There is also a network of trails across the main road that cover the forested hillside. Stone walls and old roads (called rangeways in the day) evidence the settlement of Pownalborough that existed here starting in the 1760s.

Directions: Pownalborough Courthouse Preserve, 75 acres, Dresden, Lincoln County Historical Association

From Route I in Bath, turn left on Route 127 for approximately 12.6 miles. Turn left on Route 197 and follow for about 1.5 miles. Turn right on Route 128. After about 1.3 miles, turn left on Courthouse Road. At the end of this road there will be a parking lot and trailhead. Dogs allowed outside on leash.

WebSource: www.lincolncountyhistory.org/PCHAboutBuilding.html

Flanked by wife, Harriet, and daughter, Mary Helen, lies Wesley Hall (related to the founding Goodwin family) who died in 1888 aged 76. His stone reads, Dearest loved one, we have laid thee / In the peaceful grove's embrace, / But thy memory will be cherished, / Till we see thy heavenly face.

Flax (Linum usitatissimum), *growing here in a small garden on the left side of the building, was the cotton of its day. Tools of the process are on display. The plant is found in Paleolithic archaeological sites in Europe and was brought here by the Puritans.*

Along the Kennebec River—one of the five major watersheds in the state—a dead red oak decomposes slowly among the very alive old white pines.

Front façade sports nine 12-over-12-pane windows, topped by five of 8-over-8 panes. The façade's pleasing proportion of height to width is close to 1.618, the so-called "golden number" derived by the ancient Greeks, known by the Greek letter Φ (Phi).

Pownalborough Courthouse:
Foothold in the Wilderness

This magnificent building is the only remaining pre-revolutionary courthouse in Maine that survives in its original grandeur, nestled amidst 75 acres of broad lawns and mature forest. The height of the three-story post-and-beam structure competes with the towering white pines buffering the Kennebec River behind it. The simple white lines of its colonial design and balance of its Georgian symmetry stand out against the natural surroundings.

The sight of this Boston-style courthouse on the Maine frontier would have stood in greater contrast to travelers in the late 1700s. Founding father John Adams visited the courthouse early in his career and remarked that Pownalborough was "at almost the remotest verge of civilization." His difficult trip took him through "a wilderness incumbered [sic] with the greatest number of trees, of the largest size, the tallest height." Despite extensive logging efforts at the time of his visit, Maine still was a primitive pioneering community, a community that the original human inhabitants—the various New England tribes whose ancestors had arrived thousands of years before—fought unsuccessfully to prevent.

Because travel along forest trails promised a formidable undertaking, many accomplished the trip from Boston by horse and carriage and then by boat up the Kennebec River to

Pownalborough, taking as much as three days in all. In 1792, Robert Tree Paine, a signer of the Declaration of Independence and a prominent Boston judge who presided also at Pownalborough, started his trip to the courthouse on a Saturday, hoping to arrive by Tuesday to open court. However, his entire party, which included General James Sullivan and Increase Sumner, future governors of Massachusetts, was delayed not by dense forest but by a warden in Freeport. He arrested the elite group for violating a law prohibiting unnecessary travel on Sunday, ironically a law enacted by Paine himself.

The courthouse attracted Bostonian businessmen and lawyers, including many Harvard graduates, who would later become influential on the national level. Historian Henry Beerits noted that "no building east of Portsmouth accommodated so many gifted persons, and that it would be rare to find at any time, in so small a population, so many educated persons."

The settlement was part of a larger effort by the Kennebec Proprietors, an influential group of Boston merchant speculators, to develop a tract of land covering some 3,000 square miles along the Kennebec River. In addition to the courthouse, they fragmented Maine's wilderness with two forts along the river and dozens of towns with hundreds of families as well as creating land estates for themselves.

In 1760, the General Court of Massachusetts established two new counties in Maine: Cumberland County covered southern Maine and Lincoln County covered the Kennebec River valley, totaling three-fifths of the state. Pownalborough, named after Massachusetts Governor Thomas Pownall, became the county seat with great delight to the Kennebec Proprietors, who had the important town within their domain.

In 1761, The Kennebec Proprietors assumed the entire cost of constructing the nearly 7,000 square foot courthouse. Two chimneys served 12 fireplaces in 13 rooms, including the tongue-and-groove wood paneled courtroom, judge's quarters and jury room. Wide floorboards, exceeding 50 inches, may have purposely violated the King's law that reserved timber over 24 inches wide for His Majesty's Navy.

Boston architect Gershom Flagg, himself a Proprietor, was hired as glazier and, as Clerk of the Works, in turn hired his nephew, James Flagg, whose signature can be found on a ceiling beam. However, the site's history dates further back, as the building was constructed within the parade grounds of Fort Shirley. One of the Fort's blockhouses was converted into the courthouse prison and part of the barracks was used to house a prison guard. An archaeological survey conducted there found parts of the western and southern palisades of Fort Shirley.

The conversion of a defensive fort to a courthouse in service of peace and justice marked an important change in Maine's history. The capture of Quebec in 1759 put an end to the fear of the French in British New England and thus made the fort unnecessary. The courthouse was also Flagg's first project other than a fort, again signifying a turning point in the course of history.

As soon as the roof was finished, the courthouse became active. The majority of the proceedings in the second-story courtroom were relatively mundane. The Court of General

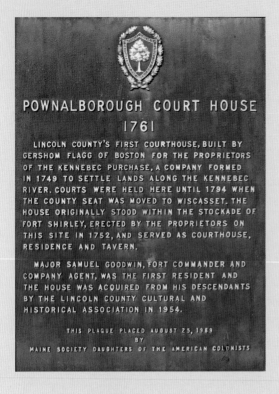

POWNALBOROUGH COURT HOUSE
1761

LINCOLN COUNTY'S FIRST COURTHOUSE, BUILT BY
GERSHOM FLAGG OF BOSTON FOR THE PROPRIETORS
OF THE KENNEBEC PURCHASE, A COMPANY FORMED
IN 1749 TO SETTLE LANDS ALONG THE KENNEBEC
RIVER. COURTS WERE HELD HERE UNTIL 1794 WHEN
THE COUNTY SEAT WAS MOVED TO WISCASSET. THE
HOUSE ORIGINALLY STOOD WITHIN THE STOCKADE OF
FORT SHIRLEY, ERECTED BY THE PROPRIETORS ON
THIS SITE IN 1752, AND SERVED AS COURTHOUSE,
RESIDENCE AND TAVERN.

MAJOR SAMUEL GOODWIN, FORT COMMANDER AND
COMPANY AGENT, WAS THE FIRST RESIDENT AND
THE HOUSE WAS ACQUIRED FROM HIS DESCENDANTS
BY THE LINCOLN COUNTY CULTURAL AND
HISTORICAL ASSOCIATION IN 1954.

THIS PLAQUE PLACED AUGUST 25, 1959
BY
MAINE SOCIETY DAUGHTERS OF THE AMERICAN COLONISTS

Sessions concerned itself with thievery, petty debts, and assault and battery. Professional lawyers and a jury convened to run the Inferior Court of Common Pleas, which handled land disputes, violent acts and larger debts. Judges wore robes and wigs and were well-respected community leaders with no formal legal training. Most punishments came in the form of fines, pillory, stocks or whipping post. (There is a facsimile pillory at the site to try on for size.) However, three severe sentences resulted in hangings on the site. One case made famous in the book *The Midwife's Tale* involved the raping of the minister's wife while he was out of town. Midwife Martha Ballard provided testimony on the victim's behalf but was ignored and the case dismissed, despite the woman giving birth nine months later.

The building also served as an inn and tavern, which was managed by Major Sam Goodwin, one of the Proprietors who had been a commander at Fort Shirley. Graffiti is still visible on the tavern walls dating back to 1775 when sailors from Machias passed through after a victorious naval battle resulting in the capture of the British sloop *Margarita*.

When the county seat and courthouse were transferred to Wiscasset in 1794, Goodwin acquired the property, which continued in his family until 1954 when it was sold to the Lincoln County Cultural and Historical Association. Goodwin's dining table still remains in the kitchen today. Over the years, Pownalborough has served as community center, tavern, auction hall, church, post office, dance school, private home, and now a public museum listed on the National Register of Historic Places.

— Ava Goodale

Roadside Plants: Unexpected Botanical Garden

When walking along a country road or looking out of the window of a car, we see plants along the roadside, in the ditch, up the bank and a little way into any bordering fields. Though to some such sights do not seem notable, this specialized habitat offers a distinct community of plants worth a second look, as diverse in its species as a botanical garden, existing on its own despite the harsh conditions.

Roadsides and fields might both be called "disturbed environments" because they are formed when humans disrupt the soil, drainage system and plants that are natural to the area. In making a road, we dig out some parts and build up other parts, dig drainage ditches along the side and make a hard, impermeable, heat-absorbing surface on the top. In making a field, we often do little more than cut down trees to let grasses grow in the sun. Or we plow and seed it for hay or crops, and even use herbicides to make sure that only the plants we want will grow there.

In both cases, the environment changes as a result; and the plants and animals that can live there also change. If we had done nothing there would still be mixed forest of leafy deciduous trees and needled coniferous trees because that is the kind of vegetation that naturally grows in the soils of coastal Maine's climate (cold, below-freezing winters with 40–50 inches average yearly rainfall). If we do nothing more, the mixed forest will slowly return, shading out the sun-loving field plants.

About half of the plants that live by our roadsides and fields are not native to North America. They followed the Europeans and their agriculture, adopted from its twelve-thou-

Blue flag iris *(Iris versicolor)* thrives in wet roadside ditches.

sand-year-old origins in the Near East. We tend to call these plants "weeds," because they spring up quickly in disturbed ground without being planted by us, and often interfere with our crops. European colonists brought some of these weed seeds unintentionally in their belongings, or intentionally as medicinals or potherbs. These plants are sun-loving and particularly tough. Their seeds germinate quickly in the trail of disturbed soil that we leave, and this is why we see them along the roadside. A short list of these European and Asian plants includes: witch grass, plantain (called "white man's footsteps" by Native Americans), Queen Anne's lace (wild carrot), dandelion, burdock, mullein, yarrow, oxeye daisy, sow thistle, St. Johnswort, hop clover, sweet clover, lupines (brought in by gardeners) and tansy.

Not all our wayside plants came across the ocean, and the farther back from the road you walk, the more native American plants you find: milkweed, goldenrods, most of the asters, sunflowers, black-eyed Susan, jewelweed, evening primrose. All these plants need sun, so when we cut back the forest, a huge variety of sun-loving plants spring up, many more kinds than grow in the forest.

The roadside has several different environments: dry, wet, fertile and sterile. On the *hard-packed, gravelly shoulder* you will see plants that can stand being walked on, driven over and parched by the extreme heat radiating from the blacktop. They must be resistant to road salt, exhaust fumes and oil spills. They must be able to get nourishment from poor soil. On the portion that is scraped by the snowplow, a tough, sparse grass spreads. Soft, fuzzy grey rabbit-foot clover lines the road in mid-July and is replaced by yellow hop clover by August. Other plants are plantain, pineapple weed, knotweed, cudweed, shepherd's purse, ragweed (because of the heat from the blacktop) and, sometimes wild strawberry.

In a *wet ditch* by the road, where all the runoff from the pavement goes, you see plants that like moist habitats or even marshes: jewelweed (in shadier places), sensitive fern, creeping buttercup, and blue flag (iris), and cattails in the wettest places, with rushes and sedges. (The golden jewelweed is being replaced by a giant Asian version, the pink Himalayan balsam [*see* sidebar, p. 173], and the cattail, so important to wildlife, is being pushed out by purple loosestrife.)

Up the *sunny bank* beside the road, masses of wildflowers grow if the bank is not mowed too often and not heavily eroded: lupines, dandelions, strawberries, oxeye daisies, daisy fleabane, cow vetch, red clover, day lilies, Queen Anne's lace, hawkweeds, milkweed, tansy, yarrow, evening primrose, mullein, goldenrod, sunflowers, asters and many different kinds of grasses. There are clumps of shrubs and young trees springing up: sumac, raspberry and blackberry brambles, wild rose, arrow wood, red-osier dogwood, young choke cherries and black cherries (often with black knot fungus), common elderberry and, sometimes, young poplar (quaking aspen) trees. Japanese knotweed, or Boston bamboo, can be seen spreading along the road edge and great tangles of Oriental bittersweet vine engulf

White sweet clover *(Melilotus albus)* grows to eight feet. If cut in a mid-summer road trimming, it can still regain its original height by autumn frosts before flowering and going to seed—all this in nutrient-poor, roadside gravel.

stands of trees and telephone poles. Hummocks of multiflora rose appear on abandoned fields. Here and there are old apple trees. On *shady banks,* overhung by woods, there are more ferns, mosses, woodland floor plants like bunchberry, patches of coltsfoot (in gravelly places), violets and poison ivy.

In the *fields,* back from the road, grow many of the "sunny bank" plants, the variety depending on how often the field is mowed or cut back and on what the soil and drainage are like. You might see masses of milkweed, sometimes dogbane, patches of wild strawberry, clumps of hardhack (steeplebush), tangles of bedstraw, of stitchwort (chickweed) and yellow rattle ("yellow rattle" because the seeds rattle in the dry pods).

— Beedy (E. C.) Parker (Adapted by the author from *A Natural History of Camden and Rockport* by E. C. Parker, Camden-Rockport Historical Society, 1984)

12 Rivers Initiative: Regional Conservation

(Ed. note: If progress "takes a Village," promoting land conservation "takes a Coastline," in this case the Midcoast and a collaborative initiative, here described by one of its participants.)

Conservation is about seeking balance: finding the best approach for preserving key landscapes with a growing population and demands on natural resources. Can we avoid irresponsible development, the introduction of invasive species, or the pollution of water? How shall we maintain the sustainability of our landscapes, local economies and communities? Here in the Midcoast, between the Kennebec and Georges Rivers, nine local land trusts and the Maine Coast Heritage Trust have started to answer these questions and to put forth a vision of a network of conserved lands that protects our ecosystems and ensures human benefits for generations to come. This is the 12 Rivers Initiative.

Midcoast Maine is at a crossroads of diverse terrestrial and marine ecosystems, with a coastline articulated by clean, relatively free-flowing rivers that run north to south. It has important habitats and species, including the world's southernmost Atlantic salmon runs and remnant groves of American chestnut. It is also at the northern end of the range for the Atlantic white cedar and swamp white oak. The region lies in close proximity to the densely developed coastline from Bath to Rockland, and is dependent upon fishing, marine trades and tourism. Behind the coast are smaller, interior towns from Dresden to Montville, defined by large, unfragmented habitat blocks, complex wetlands and farms. Maine's "Beginning with Habitat Program" has identified eight conservation focus areas within this part of the region. While distinct, these landscapes are stitched together, held apart and fed by its rivers: West branch of the Sheepscot, Dyer, Goose, Kennebec, Damariscotta, Pemaquid, Medomak, Georges, Oyster, Sheepscot, Back and Weskeag Rivers. Our work is imperative as we are losing species at an alarming rate across the globe, and alterations to our ecosystem through climate change are happening in ways we could not have predicted. Because of our interdependence with nature, it is prudent to conserve enough habitat for many species to survive. *Experts estimate that this should be at least 10% of a region's landscape; yet here in the Midcoast only 5% is conserved.*

In response, local land trusts recognize that by banding together there will be greater wisdom in identifying priorities, better avenues to share this important conservation story, and stronger outcomes in conserving what is meaningful and lasting. The 12 Rivers Initiative focuses on the larger landscape, while also ensuring that work continues at the local level, with each land trust functioning in its community with willing landowners. The ten land trusts in this initiative are Maine Coast Heritage Trust; Boothbay Region Land Trust; Kennebec Estuary Land Trust; Damariscotta River Association; Damariscotta Lake Watershed Association; Pemaquid Watershed Association; Sheepscot Valley Conservation Association; Sheepscot Wellspring Land Alliance; Medomak Valley Land Trust and Georges River Land Trust.

—Annette Naegel

◆ II ◆   Bonyun Preserve

Tall pines dominate much of this preserve, as close to "old growth" forest as you can get on the Maine coast. These trees started growing after logging ceased on this peninsula over a century ago.

N ESTLED BETWEEN TWO COVES ALONG THE SASANOA RIVER—part of the complex system of channels in the Kennebec/Androscoggin watershed—this is a "must-visit" destination for the curious traveler. Named for the family that generously donated the land and who has stewarded the land since 1947, it is a gem that has the feel of wildness and antiquity. Devote some time to wander among the impressive pines and other trees that thickly cover the site. Sit on the sun-warmed granite at Thomas Point and absorb the pulse of the estuary spread out before you; breathe in the salt air.

Situated about eleven miles off Route 1 on the

Remains of the tidal mill dam will persist for many years to come.

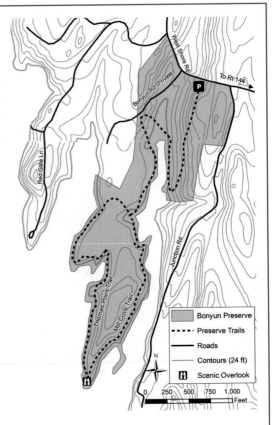

Directions: Bonyun Preserve, 120 acres, Westport Island, Kennebec Estuary Land Trust

From Route 1, take Route 144 south 10 miles to second intersection with West Shore Road. Turn right and continue 0.25 miles to parking lot and kiosk on left. No pets are allowed.

Bonyun Preserve

Preserve Trails

Roads

Contours (24 ft)

Scenic Overlook

0   250   500   750   1,000
Feet

WebSource: http://kennebecestuary.org/conserved-lands/bonyun-westport-island

southwest shoulder of Westport Island, it is of historical as well as ecological significance as it has the remnants of what was in the later 1800s a large tidal mill (*see* p. 107) straddling the cove mouth. Only the dam remains, constructed of boulders and large timbers, but a well-designed interpretive sign on the trail lets you visualize what was once a major commercial hub on this part of the coast.

We had the good fortune to have a guided tour from Archie Bonyun, who grew up here and lives nearby in the family homestead. With a deep sense of place, he enhanced our visit with an innate knowledge of the land, its natural and cultural history. But even without the benefit of someone in the know, it is abundantly clear that you are walking in a special place, where there are six different ecological zones represented. As described in the preserve brochure, they are tidal inlet, mixed old-growth woods, (*see* p. 108) freshwater marsh, estuary, riparian areas and pocket wetlands.

*Then and now: Thomas Point, originally settled by the family of that name in 1760, had a pier with a shingled "fish house," as shown in this 1850 photograph. (Courtesy of Archie Bonyun) Today on this southernmost tip of the preserve, **pitch pines** (Pinus rigida) thrive on the rocky prominence. Their tight cones take two years to mature.*

*Thick mats of moss with **polypody ferns** cover the granite bedrock outcrops on the side of the trails that hug the contours of the shoreline, from where the topography rises up a hundred or more feet to the central portions of the preserve.*

In the still waters of Mill Cove, a rising tide buoys up the rockweed, with its air-filled sacs.

Tidal Mills: Power in the Past

Then and now: Heal's Mill in 1850 and today. (Courtesy of Archie Bonyun.)

Tidal mills were a familiar site on Westport Island in the 1800s. Looking across Mill Cove you can see the remains of Heal's Lower Mill, which was used to saw logs into boards and to grind corn into flour (grist). This mill was built in 1830 by James and Moses Riggs and later operated by the Heal family. Production at the mill wound down by 1895 and most buildings disappeared by 1950.

On the west side of Westport Island, two mills were owned and operated by the Heal Family. The Upper Heal Mill was located by the causeway across Heal Pond on West Shore Road just to the north of here. Five tidal mills operated on Westport Island.

The site you see before you, Heal's Lower Mill, is sited just below the wharf where the steamer from Bath docked at "the Junction." The homes you see across the cove are on Junction Road which connected the steamer dock with Main Road.

Heal's Lower Mill was both a saw- and gristmill. When first constructed, the mill wheel powered an "up and down" saw to make planks and laths for building construction. The vertical wheel was replaced with a horizontal "tub wheel" and later equipped with two turbines of 20 horsepower each. The mill operated 12 hours each day, during maximum tidal flows, and could cut 700,000 feet of lumber and grind 5,000 bushels of grain each year. Corn was ground using two granite stones several feet in diameter and several inches thick mounted one above the other in a horizontal plane. The upper stone was rotated by a shaft fastened to its center. Adjustments to the distance between the stones governed the "fineness" of the flour.

— Dennis Dunbar

Old-Growth Forest in Maine: A Reverie

It wasn't until we were into our middle years that we realized if there is to be an old tree in our lives, it has to already be old now. It would have to have been old when we were born, and even long before that.

In Maine, old trees can be harder to find than you might think, given that in our state we have billions of trees in more than 17 million acres of forest. In Midcoast Maine, trees have been valued for shipbuilding, construction, firewood for cooking and heating, and fuel wood for lime kilns in the Rockport area. Midcoast Maine underwent deforestation starting with the early colonists and continuing until World War II. By the 1870s, Midcoast Maine was short of wood for the lime kilns, and fuel wood was imported by ship to Rockport from New Brunswick and Nova Scotia. The size of the average log harvested in the Maine woods went from 800 board feet in 1820 to 200 board feet in 1860. Photos from early times show many open, tree-less areas, which have long since grown back to dense forest. Most of the truly old trees are gone, their stumps rotted away completely. And one or two old trees alone do not make an old-growth stand.

Most tree species make good candidates for becoming an old tree. Red spruce can live to more than 300 years, and Northern white cedar can grow much older than that—more than 1,000 years. At least two trees, now dead, are known that lived for more than 1,500 years.

Yellow birch can be quite old, with a maximum age of more than 350 years, while eastern hemlock can be up to 550 years old.

People are enchanted by old-growth, where trees are left past their prime to die of natural causes and are not brought down by the sharp teeth of a chain saw. We enjoy walking among giant trees, contemplating life free of overwhelming human activities, where natural disturbance (ice storms, floods, microbursts, etc.), plants and animals—and not the interest rate—dictate the future of a stand of trees. Old-growth has many benefits, including superior fish habitat in brooks and streams, more diverse and more productive forest stands, more food within the food chain, more efficient storage of carbon, and buffering against flooding.

Some argue that "big trees" are the best criterion for defining old-growth, with a 16-inch diameter as the threshold at which a tree in a forest is "old." By that measure, there are indeed some wonderful old-growth places to visit in Midcoast Maine that offer the chance to appreciate the attributes of big trees in a natural environment. On a visit to such a place, one can enjoy a sense of solitude and peace while watching a patch of sunlight advance across the forest floor as the morning progresses.

Tree size, however, is not a precise indicator of old-growth. Most stands of large old trees in Maine have grown back after an earlier harvest but now contain both many more and considerably smaller trees than the original stand. Trees with ¼-inch per year ring widths are not uncommon in Maine's forests, and, depending on the species and some amount of luck, these might grow into 16-inch trees in less than 50 years. (A tree with a ring width of ¼ inch will grow ½ inch in diameter each year, or 16 inches in 32 years. Most trees will grow less than ¼ inch in diameter in the first five to 10 years.) On the other hand, old trees often grow on inaccessible or infertile sites, such as high up in the mountains, on or near ledges at any elevation, in wet and poorly drained soils, and in general on poor soil. Trees in old-growth stands often look deceptively small. The beautiful stand of trees with diameters of 16, 18 or 20 inches may not be old after all and, in fact, may be considerably younger than the stand next to it with trees not even half the size.

So, if size is a poor indicator, how can we recognize old-growth? At the sixth New England Old-Growth conference in 2004, scientists could not give a simple answer to the question, "What is old-growth?" They could readily list attributes that, while not exclusive to old-growth, are more abundant and/or of better quality in old-growth. Some of these include the presence of large logs, uneven ground due to falling of trees over centuries and absence of plowing, and depth of the humus layer on the ground.

There could be animals—including insects and other invertebrates—plus plants, mosses, lichens and fungi that are associated with old forest. Birds that associate with old forest include pileated and other woodpeckers, owls and goshawks. Mammals that frequent environments with large trees and large logs include fisher and pine marten. All these animals are not exclusive to old forest, but they might have inadequate habitat in young forests. Much study about this in recent decades has resulted in a relatively short list of such old forest associates, and it is difficult to say that such organisms *depend* on old forest. More likely, species of interest, such as an **old man's beard lichen,** *Usnea longissima,* need features like clean air, understory shade, moisture-rich environment and considerable time since latest disturbance. These features may continue to improve with time in the old forest habitat.

Stubble lichens, the Caliciales, are a group of tiny pinhead-like lichens that Dr. Steve Selva has demonstrated to be especially diverse on bark of genuinely old trees. Stubble lichens indicate forest continuity, meaning that disruption to the canopy has been minimal for many decades. While stubble lichens are among the best indicators of old growth, they are a challenge to study; it requires microscopy and considerable expertise to recognize the different species. However obscure, they are beautiful, mysterious and worth the effort.

People like to romanticize about a forest that shows no signs of ever having been harvested, a primeval forest. Perhaps we have a deep need to be among the trees. We can speculate about what the forest was like when the Abenaki people were in charge of everything here, before Captain George Weymouth landed near Monhegan on May 17, 1605. No one really knows, though. Typically an ancient forest can be hard to walk through, with lots of blowdown, or dense low branches such as in the krummholz near alpine summits. Unharvested old-growth forest in Maine is still present, but in small patches. Some stands are protected by land trusts, The Nature Conservancy or the state. These are an irreplaceable heritage, important in ways we are just beginning to understand.

If you own a woodlot and are interested in providing habitat features for plants and animals that use old forest, you might consider leaving a few of your largest trees to die naturally and remain standing until they collapse on their own. Leave some larger logs on the ground and create brush piles as habitat for wildlife. If your property includes a stream or shore, that is an ideal place for old forest to be left behind, because it protects water quality and is available to wildlife that move along riparian corridors. Support organizations that protect old forest, and get out and enjoy some of the places described in this guide. Bring kids along, because the next generation needs commitment and connection to the forest that we can provide. We'll see you out there!

—Alison C. Dibble and Jake Maier

◆ 12 ◆   Boothbay Region: Linekin, Porter and Ovens Mouth Preserves

Outgoing tide on the Back River at Ovens Mouth Preserve.

PUBLIC PRESERVES ABOUND ON THE BOOTHBAY PENINSULA thanks to the existence of the Boothbay Region Land Trust (BRLT). There are well over a dozen located all around this popular tourist area and on some of the outlying islands. We present a sample here of three that are seashore sites, each distinctive in its marine character. For a complete listing, *see* www.bbrlt.org.

Linekin-Burley Preserve

Located on the southeast portion of the Boothbay region, this densely forested site combines two tracts of land donated by conservation-minded families. Several interconnected loop trails traverse woodland and wetland areas in the interior as well as a section that runs along the coastline looking out onto the mouth of the Damariscotta River and several islands.

We toured the preserve on a placid mid-October day, a pleasant time for walking, if not the most productive time for bird watching, as by this point most fall migrants have passed through and the forest is descending into its winter dormancy. As in many of the BRLT sites, there are vistas marked on the trail map, with rustic benches upon which to sit and contemplate the surroundings. This one has two, one overlooking the water and the other along a stream colonized by beavers.

One aspect to think about as you take in the view of this rocky coastline is time. The geology of the coastline here is part of the Bucksport Formation (*see* p. 153), a strata of metamorphic and igneous rocks originating over 400 million year ago, when the area was part of a supercontinent that broke apart over a great expanse of time and before the Atlantic Ocean existed. For those with even a passing interest in this branch of science, an invaluable book is *Roadside Geology of Maine* (D. W. Caldwell, 1998), a well-written and illustrated paperback discussing many of the areas described in this book and our previous book, *Best Nature Sites: Midcoast Maine, Brunswick to Belfast.*

So visit this preserve as part of a swing through the other two BRLT sites in this chapter. It will reward you with sights and sounds in all seasons.

Directions: Linekin Preserve, 138 acres, Boothbay, Boothbay Region Land Trust

Proceed 3.8 miles on Route 96, starting from the traffic light at the intersection with Route 27. (You will pass through the town of East Boothbay). Soon after Alley Road on the right look for the Linekin Preserve parking lot on the left. Dogs allowed on-leash.

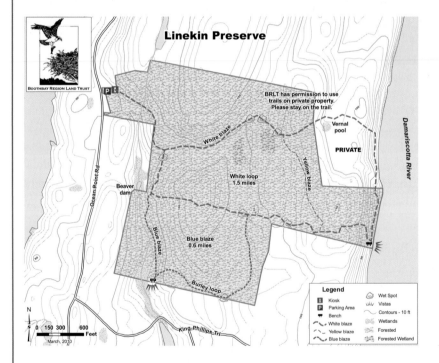

WebSource: www.bbrlt.org/documents/LinekinBurleyGuide.pdf

Note: As the BRLT manages their preserves for specific conditions, trails in some preserves are sometimes changed or eliminated; check the website or call land trust for the most up-to-date information.

The steep shoreline, with the characteristic striations of the Bucksport Formation, runs north-south and is indented in places with fractures in the rock.

Mid-October was not too late to find a young **eastern milk snake** (Lampropeltis triangulum) along the path. Food includes invertebrates such as insects and slugs as well as vertebrates such as amphibians, other snakes and small mammals. It suffocates prey within its constricting coils and swallows it whole. Rock crevices afford hibernation sites for the cold months. Among other characteristics, the V-shaped white marking atop the head behind the red patch is diagnostic. This species is intolerant of human intrusion and should not be handled.

A spruce sapling grows atop a large slab broken off from the nearby rock outcrop. Rock walls in the preserve attest to former days of pasture and grazing sheep; the land has been untouched for many years and presents a mature growth of mixed forest.

Porter Preserve

Not "far from the madding crowd" of downtown Boothbay, where in July and August a parking spot is rarer than a whooping crane, is this small but picturesque piece of the natural world in which to take refuge from the tourist world. These 19 acres of woodland with a loop trail following the shorefront harbor an old gravesite and remnants of a cellar hole reminding us that many generations have gone before. Most recently, this southern tip of Barters Island belonged to the family that eschewed development pressure and placed easements on the land. The preserve also has a working waterfront, the Robert's Wharf where local lobstermen ply their trade.

The mile-long trail has numerous vistas with the "trademark" benches from which to take in the sights and sounds of the surroundings. There is a pocket "beach" midway that exhibits the characteristic muddy sediments of the Maine coast, a habitat suited for marine invertebrates if not for human beachcombers. At the northern end, you'll come to the Memorial Grove and the wharf. A botanical inventory posted at the kiosk lists 16 species of wildflowers, 15 trees, 20 shrubs, 6 ferns and 7 mosses and lichens; so, there's much to meet the eye of the curious traveler interested in plants. "See" how many you can find on the trail.

One of the many overlooks here, this one perches on the iconic granite bedrock of Maine's coast and takes in the lower Sheepscot River.

Directions: Porter Preserve, 19 acres, Barters Island, Boothbay Region Land Trust

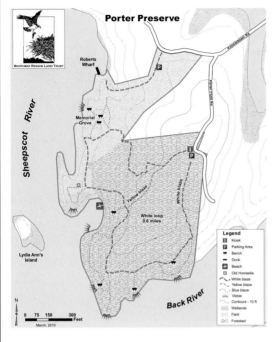

From Boothbay Harbor travel north on Route 27; take a left at the monument in Boothbay Center onto Corey Lane. Proceed 0.3 miles. Turn right onto Barters Island Road and travel 2.2 miles, crossing two bridges. Turn left on Kimballtown Road. Proceed 0.5 miles and turn left onto a dirt road. Proceed 0.1 miles to a small parking lot on your right just beyond the cemetery. Please do not park along road. Additional parking is available at the end of Kimballtown Road near the stacked lobster traps. Dogs allowed on leash.

WebSource: www.bbrlt.org/documents/PorterPreserveGuide.pdf

Note: As the BRLT manages their preserves for specific conditions, trails in some preserves are sometimes changed or eliminated; check the website or call land trust for the most up-to-date information.

A white "ring" rimming the shoreline represents an ancient intrusion of igneous rock that occurred hundreds of millions of years in the past.

115

In olden days, small coves such as this were perfect for boat-building sites and impromptu landing places.

At the start of the trail is the cemetery of the Caswell family and others. According to The History of Boothbay, Southport and Boothbay Harbor, *Samuel and Hepsibah Caswell lived at the southern end of Barters Island and had eight children from 1818–37. This headstone of one son (Alfred Caswell who died in 1886 at age 52) is cradled by the overgrowth of a red oak, signifying the nature of time.*

Ovens Mouth Preserve

This preserve looks interesting on the map, but wait until you actually visit: it ranks among one of the "best" on the coast for its unique character. According to the site brochure, the name comes from the fact that European colonists saw a resemblance to an oven—the sense of which is not immediately apparent—but it may refer to the narrow opening of the central cove that divides the preserve into eastern and western portions.

Several miles of trails in an extensive network of primary and secondary loops cover both portions of the preserve, most of which is forested in mixed growth that dates to the 1930s when pasturing ceased on the land. There is salt- and freshwater marshland, but the main attraction are the loop trails that hug the shoreline with many vistas onto the deepwater channels and coves so favored by the original human inhabitants and later European settlers. It's pleasant to indulge in a bit of "time travel" on visits to nature sites, imagining Native American birch bark canoes paddling by, or perhaps a smuggler's sloop at anchor, well out of sight of British navy patrols out on the wider coastal waters.

Vestiges of cultural history remain, notably the remains of a dam that once blocked the central cove to form an ice pond, formerly a major export resource from this state. This spot is also notable for the modern, impressively engineered footbridge that spans nearly 100 feet in an unsupported arch. Other hints of history are the stone walls of former pastures and an old house site, marked on the map, on the high ground of the eastern peninsula.

The vista on the eastern peninsula is a good stopping place to enjoy the serenity of these tidal waters. On a placid autumn day, we saw loons and seals feeding in the strong currents.

But nature sites are, after all, about natural history, and these many acres, along with other BRLT preserves, provide an essential refuge on the Boothbay peninsula to both the macro- and microspecies that collectively comprise the local ecology. Visits here at various times of the year will reveal different aspects of nature. As always, the spring and fall bird migrations offer opportune times to witness species in action, and all during the warm months you may see bald eagles and ospreys plying the waters. For those with an eye for the botanical world, the hundreds of plant species are there for the seeking. And as you gaze at the channels here or any other of the tidal rivers in Maine, think of the many fish species, unseen beneath the surface waters, including the eel (*see*, p. 121). So, if you have to pick one site for exploration in the Boothbay region, come here and spend some time.

Directions: Ovens Mouth Preserve, 146 acres, Boothbay, Boothbay Region Land Trust

From the monument at Boothbay Center, travel north on Route 27 for 1.6 miles. Take a left onto Adams Pond Road. Proceed 0.1 miles. Turn right onto Dover Road. Continue 2.4 miles to the dead end. Parking is on the left. Dogs allowed on leash.

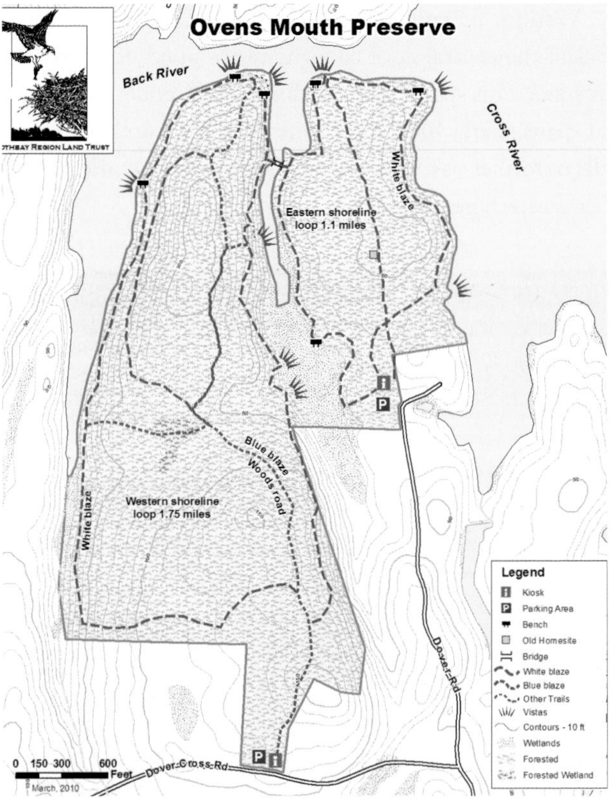

WebSource:
www.bbrlt.org/documents/
OvensMouthGuide.pdf

Note: *As the BRLT manages their preserves for specific conditions, trails in some preserves are sometimes changed or eliminated; check the website or call land trust for the most up-to-date information.*

At various points on the trail, it's hard not to think of the cliché "still waters run deep."

The bridge, at the center of the preserve, employs laminated beams to span almost 100 feet. From here you can scan both sides of the cove to the north and south. The old dam is visible below.

Like a river flowing around an island, this maple trunk has bifurcated and rejoined.

Rotting stumps are habitat for mosses and arthropods such as ants and pill bugs.

Shelf fungi, such as this **red-belted polyphore** *(Fomitopsis pinacola)* on white pine, rot wood and so aid woodpeckers and other cavity nesters in their excavation of trees.*

Glass Eels

Maturation stages of the eel (clockwise): the larval leptocephalus; immature elver, or glass eel; the yellow form, during which time differentiation into male and female occurs, and the final silver spawning form. Adult eels are imprinted to their natural spawning location somewhere in the Sargasso Sea. Both European and American eels gather there to spawn. The Gulf Stream pulls tiny eggs and hatched larva in a northerly clockwise direction. Eels do not necessarily return to the rivers their parents came from. (Illustrations courtesy of Ethan Nedeau, Biodrawversity)

There's a strange confluence of fishermen and fish along Maine's coast at night from the third week of March to the end of May. There you'll find lamp-lit fishermen bent over a handheld dip net or a fixed net called a fyke catching baby eels, or elvers, as they make their way to freshwater rivers and lakes. The **American eel** (*Anguilla rostrata*) shares virtually all the same characteristics as its European cousin *Anguilla anguilla* but for a few vertebrae. They are in fact so closely allied that both species end their long ocean migration as adults in the same general proximity of the Sargasso Sea. American eels from Brazil to Canada all congregate as adults and mate there. This "panmixia" behavior is wrapped in mystery. It has never been observed and sets the imagination loose to think of millions of these snakelike shapes, wrapped in the warm waters of the Atlantic south of Bermuda, writhing in giant silver clusters like spaghetti in a pot.

Once born, the young eels are carried back towards the Atlantic coast by the Gulf Stream and randomly released to move towards the nearest freshwater source. How this life strategy allows for a healthy dispersal of populations from river to river is, like much of this creature's behavior, not yet known. The difficulty with identifying the river origins of local adult populations is that eels imprint on their natal origin in the Sargasso Sea, not to the rivers in which they mature and live until returning to the Sargasso to spawn. The migration north of glass eels is at the mercy of the Gulf Stream and random distribution back to the rivers.

It's no wonder that there is still confusion over this fish. In 1653, Isaac Walton of *The Complete Angler* fame wrote that he believed eels were generated from horsehair that dropped into puddles of dew at certain times of year. And in 1876, a young Austrian science student named Sigmund Freud dissected hundreds of adult male eels in an attempt to find their sex organs. His failure to identify any, after much effort, caused him to abandon this line of inquiry and follow another path.

So little was known about the American eel that the earliest larval stage was thought to be a different species. Born from a pelagic egg that develops into a larva shaped like an elongated leaf, scientists early on named this animal *Leptocephalus*. This larval eel form will drift north and west with the strong ocean currents of the Gulf Stream for up to a year until it has matured to the glass-eel stage, so called because of its transparency. These gin-clear juveniles, less than two and a half inches long, are what bring Maine fishermen to the shoreline on the cold nights of early spring. The fishermen are here because nobody has yet to figure out how to mimic this complex reproductive behavior. Therefore, the farms in Asia that raise eels for the worldwide sushi trade must import the baby glass eels and grow them in captivity.

Those glass eels that are fortunate enough to have made it through this long ocean journey and then through a crib work of nets will move into Maine's rivers or lakes to grow to four feet in length, in the case of the larger females, and only half that size for males, who often will stay behind in brackish waters. Eels can live as adults in freshwater as "yellow eels" for up to 30 years before they change color and shape and return to sea as "silver eels" to travel back to their home spawning grounds in the Sargasso and their life's final act.

The peculiar strategy of the American eel that causes it to spend the majority of its life in freshwater and breed in salt water is called *catadromous* and is the opposite of Maine's most famous fish resident, the *anadramous* Atlantic salmon. The eels' return to freshwater is eagerly anticipated by the more than 400 Maine license holders who are allowed to fish for glass eels. In 2012, a convergence of a European eel disease outbreak, a tsunami in Japan and plummeting populations of American eels in their native habitats left Maine and South Carolina as the only viable sources of supply worldwide. That made for historically high prices for glass eels that pushed values as high as $2,600 per pound. Mind you, this is all paid in cash, often late at night, and the stories from this 10-week season were many. There was the couple who made $150,000 on the first night of the season and then a "disappointing"—for them—$75,000 the second night. And a buyer who spent over $240,000 in cash in one hour on one night of buying baby eels. At approximately 2,400 to the pound, each of these babies was valued at about a dollar a piece. In just 10 weeks this fishery was the second highest dollar-value seafood landing in Maine, second only to lobster.

The story of the glass eel is a global tale that has all of the bizarre world market extremes brought to bear on this resilient fish. The pattern of scarcity spiking the perceived value for the remaining few that we foolishly use up repeats the human history with the buffalo, the whale and the turtle. It is also a story of a fish that migrates great distances, only to be harvested as a juvenile and shipped an even greater distance from Maine to Asia to be raised, harvested again and then often shipped back to the Atlantic coast where it finally is eaten.

—D. F.

Don't Blame the Dutch: Good News for the American Elm?

You see them standing tall along roads and in overgrown meadows: remnant monarchs next to tumbled-in stone foundations, living proof that someone with a name once lived here. Sometimes they are accompanied by lesser acolytes—untended fruit trees, a thicket of sumac or an abandoned well—but the **American elm** *(Ulmus americana)* is often the most prominent living gravestone of a departed family. In other settings— along the streets of New England towns, for example—a few resistant specimens remain as graceful icons of another century, but for the most part, they are as absent today as horse-drawn carriages, bedside candles, outhouses and outdoor wells. What was once America's favorite ornamental tree has suffered insult and injury beyond measure, yet survives here and there. It seems improbable that our elms will ever reassert their celebrated splendor and stippled shade, at least in our lifetimes, but it's not impossible. There just may be an end to Dutch elm disease.

A Dutch plant pathologist, Marie Beatrice Schwartz, is credited with identifying the cause of the disease in 1921. A few years later another Dutch scientist, Christine Johanna Buisman, familiar with the symptoms of the disease from her native country, recognized it in Ohio. Unfortunately, these two well-intended scientists irretrievably associated their country with a disease whose origin has nothing to do with northern Europe and everything to do with the Himalayas. One may as well fault Daniel Gabriel Fahrenheit, another Dutchman, for the weather simply because he standardized the measurement of temperature. A further irony is that the disease had previously been reported in France, but for some unknown Francophobic— or Francophilic—reason, that country did not receive credit. Be that as it may, it seems only slightly less unjust to hold accountable the two primary vectors of the disease, the European **bark beetle** *(Scolytus multistriatus)* and the native **bark beetle** *(Hylurgopinus rufipes)*. (Elms growing within twenty feet of each other—in effect a roadside monoculture—can pass on the infection through their roots without the help of a third party. This underground embrace is a near certain kiss of death.) The point is that the beetles do not cause the disease by them-selves. They merely fly from tree to tree doing their thing, seeking healthy young elm tissue and doing little damage—so long as they fly from one healthy tree to another.

The trouble begins when a female beetle lands on an infected tree or log and moves from there to a new host, bringing with her thousands of tiny spores from the **vascular wilt fungus** *(Ophiostoma ulmi)*. These spores are the culprits that are responsible for Dutch elm disease. When the female beetle arrives at her new residence, she drills through the bark, eats her way into the wood and deposits eggs. When these hatch as larvae they chew their way out of the maternal den, leaving behind a signature gallery and system of tiny tunnels. After the larvae pupate, they emerge as adults, and fly off, blissfully unaware of their impact.

Those tunnels bored by the female beetle and her larvae provide a congenial home for the *Ophiostoma* fungi that she introduced. They care not a whit whether the surrounding tissue is living or dead. So whether parasite or saprophyte, they nourish themselves, germinate with enthusiasm, and contentedly produce both spores and mycelium—the filamentous, vegetative component of a fungus that absorbs nutrients. (The mycelium of a mushroom is the part we don't see and is typically underground or out of sight within the tree trunk.) As the spores and mycelium grow, they increase in volume, not only within the passages created by the larvae, but within the xylem of the tree as well. This is how the infection spreads to other parts of the tree.

A healthy elm counters the intrusion by producing tylose, a cellular growth that is a built-in defense mechanism. Tylose blocks the vascular system, cutting off the supply of nutrients to the offending part, i.e., sacrificing the part to save the whole. Under other circumstances this might work, but with *O. ulni* it doesn't. Starved of sap, the leaves in the crown of the tree show the first symptoms of the disease. They turn yellow, wilt and die. Eventually, the entire limb will gradually give up the ghost. Seasons may pass before the rest of the tree is dead, but die it will, from the top down—a phenomenon that is visible to the naked eye but is not obvious until you know what to look for. (Elms infected via the roots of another tree present differently.)

A little dendrological history before the bad news: having devastated the elms of Europe, *Ophiostoma ulmi* arrived in this country in 1928, most likely having enjoyed a free ride across

124

the Atlantic on a ship transporting elm logs intended for use as veneer. By the early 1940s, the European pandemic had run its course, but was still active in North America. Then, in the 1960s, a second outbreak occurred, this one caused by a different, more potent kind of fungus, *O. novo-ulmi*. According to C. M. Braisier and K. W. Buck in a study published by *Biological Invasions* in the Netherlands (2001), *O. novo-ulmi* spreads as two distinct, competitive subspecies, *O. novo-ulmi* and *O. americana*. Irrespective of the complexity that suggests, within ten years the preponderance of elms that had survived the earlier epidemic had succumbed to *O. novo-ulmi*. Again, just for the record, *Ophiostoma* comes not from Holland, but from the Far East. (If there is any small justice to this, it's that the disease is now occasionally referred to as DED, an abbreviation that at least avoids naming the country—no small thing as over forty million elm trees have died from DED in the United States alone.) There is, according to most sources, no reason to anticipate a cure. But there may be a remedy.

Most of us blithely refer to elms as if the species with which we are familiar exists by itself, but this does not do justice to the *Ulmus* genus that emerged some twenty million years ago in Asia and dispersed its papery-winged samaras, or seeds, around the Northern Hemisphere and southwards across the Equator, all the while evolving into twenty to forty deciduous species that are now scattered worldwide. Because of hybridization, the exact number is uncertain, but *The Sibley Guide to Trees* states that six of these are now native to North America, and that, additionally, five naturalized cultivars are also present. That said, the dominant species here in Maine is *Ulmus americana*, which, under historical conditions, grew as one of the normal, leaf-shedding hardwood species of the eastern North American forest. Many, if not, most specimens were cut down for a variety of purposes unrelated to landscape architecture.

Elm's interlocking grain resists splitting, as anyone trying to knock a bolt in half quickly discovers, and it is notably resistant to decay, hence its widespread application as piping to transport water. Because of its strength and because the trunk is long and straight, elm served admirably for the keels of wooden ships—which by itself is a consignment to extirpation for mature trees growing anywhere near a shipyard. Elm is also pliant and can be molded to a curve. As a result, it was selected for longbows when yew was not available, at least when these were a tool of war in olden Europe. Both here and in Europe it was, and is, chosen for use as wheel hubs—no small thing before the invention of the automobile. Today, its commercial value is diminished, but it is still sought for its strength and elegance of grain, especially by cabinetmakers.

Give an elm tree a couple of centuries and individual specimens take on their own identity. One of the oldest known examples was named "Herbie" in Yarmouth, Maine. Herbie was the tallest American elm in New England and possibly the only one with a personal caretaker. When Frank Knight, who became the town's tree warden in 1956, realized that he couldn't save all the trees in town, he concentrated on one and orchestrated heroic measures: pruning, fungicides and pesticides, sparing no reasonable effort. Frank and Herbie became legends—and Herbie survived for over 50 more years under Frank's care.

Having survived 14 attacks of *Ophiostoma*, Herbie ultimately succumbed to systematic disease. In January, 2010, Herbie was cut down. Tree rings indicate that he was 217 years old, but because he was a seedling that grew in the wild, shaded by other trees for ten or twenty years before he was transplanted, there is a possibility that the tree was older even than that. Seed, sprout or seedling, Herbie was around during the American Revolution.

Two years later, in 2012, Frank Knight, Herbie's long-term warden, followed Herbie into the ground. At 103, Frank was as venerable as his tree. He was buried in a casket made from the Herbie's wood. This event was at the heart of what came to be called the Herbie Project. According to Jan Ames Santerre of the Maine Forest Service (and author of "Herbie: The Reincarnation of an American Elm Tree in Maine"), there is a new concentration in the field of urban forestry: the utilization and marketing of urban street trees. Municipalities face a considerable expense removing the dead or dying trees that line their streets, *U. americana* among them. There is, too, another potential value to these ancients. They hold information of interest to dendroclimatologists. But that's another story.

So what is the good news, the light at the end of the tunnel? According to a study by C.J. D'Arcy published by the American Phytopathological Society in 2001, there are three ways to approach DED management. The first is cultural. This means avoiding monocultural stands (rows along streets). In those cases, the best procedure is to quickly remove all dead and dying limbs that may harbor the fungus, and to complement this by severing any grafted connection between adjacent trees. This is a labor intensive treatment, and is at best no more than a delaying tactic, but one that may just possibly add two or even three decades to the life of a tree.

The second is chemical and requires injecting a fungicide into an infected tree. This carries no guarantee and is also expensive, hence is most often used only for high value trees—for example, those lining the Washington D.C. Mall.

The third approach is favored by many phytopathologists and involves two remedies. The first is the development of disease-resistant cultivars. These have been grown in Europe and the United States and hybridized with the native *U. americana*. Time will tell, but this approach offers some promise, at least for our grandchildren.

The second is cloning resistant specimens, a technique that is also enjoying some success. It's no accident that Herbie's cells are being cultivated and are now generating sprouts. Other hybridized and cloned trees are available, each with their own historical names, "Valley Forge," for example, was developed by the Agricultural Research Service in Maryland, and for nearly two decades promises a reasonable level of resistance to that Far Eastern disease with the northern European name.

—T. O.

◆ I 3 ◆ Griggs and Marsh River Preserves: *On the Riverfront*

Salt marshes are the "heartland" of the coastal ecosystem.

THESE TWO PRESERVES, BOTH PART OF THE SHEEPSCOT RIVER WATERSHED, are a window into the "back channel" marine environment of spartina saltmarsh, a quieter environment that contrasts with the high-energy rocky coast of Maine. But this type of area is the proverbial nursery to life in the ocean and along the shore, from the visible macro animals and plants (fish, crustaceans, vascular plants and algae) to the microscopic phytoplankton (photosynthetic-like plants) and zooplanktonic animals that feed upon them. Both sites are thickly wooded with interesting hillside topography to enliven a nature hike. As they are close together and moderate in size, consider doing both on the same day. The Sheepscot Valley Conservation Association owns these preserves and many others upstream along the river. *See* their website for a complete listing.

Griggs Preserve

Situated on a bucolic neck of land along the eastern bank of the Sheepscot River upstream from Wiscasset and downstream from the reversing falls, the mile and a half trail network features old pines among second growth woods and a boggy area. Stone walls mark former fields, where sheep grazed in past centuries. The landscape has changed over the years allowing a renewal of wildlife; such refuges are ever more crucial to the continuation of the natural world. On the way in from Route 1 you'll see Straw's Farm, a great example of sustainable farming as practiced in modern-day Maine, growing local food for this area of the Midcoast. Such farms play a similar role in maintaining non-chemical-based food production that wildlife refuges do for the natural world.

Midway on the top trail is a winter den for **porcupines** *(Erethizon dorsatum)*. This mammal, belonging to a South American rodent family, stays active all winter, becoming colonial for group warmth as opposed to its solitary summer lifestyle.

The chance to observe this and other species promotes an awareness of the biologic life that exists side by side with our human world. On the lower trail, be sure to enjoy the river view and check for waterbirds such as ducks, herons and shorebirds.

Directions: Griggs Preserve, Newcastle, 56 acres, Sheepscot Valley Conservation Association

From Wiscasset, take Route 1 North about 2 miles and take a left at the top of the hill onto Cochran Road (look for Skip Cahill's Tires/Sunoco Station). Proceed about one mile and take left onto Trails End Road (marked with a private driveway sign). The parking lot and kiosk will be on your left. Please keep all cars in the parking lot. Dogs allowed on leash.

WebSource: www.sheepscot.org/griggs-preserve-newcastle

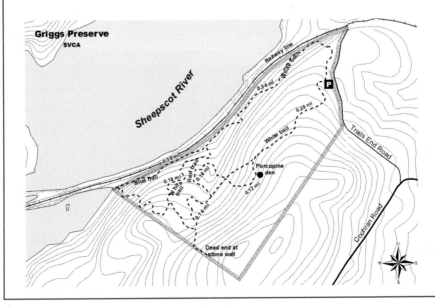

*According to mushroom expert Greg Marley (see Bibliography), these spore cases are the persistent remains of one of our most common forest puffballs, the **pear-shaped puffball** (Lycoperdon pyriforme), often found fruiting in number on dead wood. This species is edible and good when collected young, firm and pure white on the inside.*

Eastern red columbine *(Aquilegia canadensis) blooms in later May near the overlook of the river and offers its nectar only to long-tongued insects and hummingbirds. This is a host plant to **Columbine Duskywing** (Erynnis lucilius), a butterfly presently found only in southern New England, and the Great Lakes states plus southern Canada.*

*Even before the flower has fully emerged, the **pink lady's-slipper** (Cypripedium acaule) is a showy plant. This is the most common of Maine's four lady's-slipper species.*

129

Marsh River Preserve

Just downstream from the restored Sherman Marsh (*see* next page) this slightly larger preserve is similarly situated on a hillside neck of land bounded by the Marsh River as it yazoos its way down to joining the Sheepscot just north of Griggs Preserve. An interpretive trail map available at the kiosk or online describes points of interest at ten stations throughout the site. If you like big erratic boulders—those chunks of rocks dropped on the

*Glacial erratic lies where dropped thousands of years ago. Such boulder tops support plant life such as **common polypody**, or rockcap ferns* (Polypodium vulgare), *growing in a substrate gradually built up by lichens, mosses and leaves.*

land as the glaciers melted—you'll be able to add one to the life list by walking the upper loop to station #10. We see smaller glacial boulders everywhere in New England in the form of stone walls and piles, also to be seen here, the product of untold hours of labor during the agrarian years of the 1800s and before.

At another interpretive station you will find **witch hazel** (*Hamamelis virginiana*), that unusual medicinal plant that blooms in the fall and winter. The buds and leaves have the distinctive, pungent smell familiar to those who have used the astringent lotion made from the bark. Two overlooks on opposite ends of the trail afford a chance to sit and observe river life: birds, fish, maybe a mink patrolling the shoreline. Unseen, traveling upstream to spawn may be Atlantic salmon, a small population of which exists in the Sheepscot (*see* p. 134). Or just watch the river flow by.

Directions: Marsh River Preserve, 70 acres, Newcastle, Sheepscot Valley Conservation Association

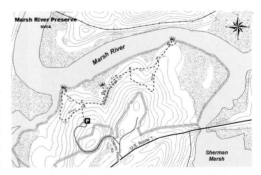

From Wiscasset take Route 1 North for 4.5 miles and turn left onto Osprey Point Road. Bear left onto Eagle Point Road and follow to cul-de-sac and park. From the North, take Rt. 1 South into Newcastle and take a right onto Osprey Point Road which is just past the Sherman Lake Rest Area. Bear left onto Eagle Point Road and follow to cul-de-sac and park. Dogs allowed on leash.

WebSource: www.sheepscot.org/marsh-river-preserve-newcastle

Salt Marsh Restoration: How to Define Success?

Salt marsh restoration returns habitat degraded by human endeavors to a more natural condition.

Many salt marshes along the New England coast have been degraded over the past two centuries by ditching and draining in an effort to convert the marshes to dry land that is suitable for agriculture. (The marsh at the Marsh River Preserve shows signs of ditching for mosquito control.) Other marshes, such at Sherman Marsh just upstream, have been dammed in such a way that flooding transforms the marshes into shallow, freshwater lakes. The modified marshes have served as brickyards, roadways and disposal sites for dredged sediments. Some marshes may have suffered less obvious changes due to human activity, including invasion by non-native species and reduced tidal flow resulting from undersized culverts. Since the middle of the twentieth century, ecologists have studied the impacts of these modifications on salt marsh functioning.

It turns out that salt marshes provide a wide range of functions that benefit people and ecosystems. Salt marshes serve as breeding areas for invertebrates, fish and migrating birds, including the secretive **saltmarsh sparrow** *(Ammodramus caudacutus)*, whose nesting is tied closely with natural tide cycles. Marshes provide storm buffering and water filtration, as well as carbon and nutrient cycling. Many of these functions are hard to measure, which makes it difficult to quantify damage from human development. While describing the extent of impacts on salt marshes is difficult, defining restoration success is even more of a challenge.

Traditionally, restoration has been defined as human intervention that leads to a series of changes that result in "turning back an ecological clock" so as to recreate a resilient site that mimics an ideal, past (usually pre-colonial), unimpacted state. In the absence of historical data, ecologists often choose a representative "reference" site to serve as a standard to which the restoring marsh should be compared. Success is measured by a series of indicators; hydrology and salinity are the most basic measures, sometimes accompanied by plant community composition and water quality parameters. Some studies go as far as to include surveys of fish and bird populations. These measures describe the structural components of the ecosystem well.

However, rapid global change has created additional pressures that influence the interactions between the physical and biological components of the marsh.

Of course, ecosystems of all types have never been static; they are dynamic systems that constantly respond to pressures and changes. One of the key attributes of a healthy ecosystem is that it is resilient to change. However, the changes that are resulting from climate change are unprecedented in both rate and severity. Since the last ice age, salt marshes have slowly accreted sediments on the surface of the marsh that allow the system to keep up with natural changes in sea level. The extraordinary rate at which sea level is rising as a result of climate change may cause salt marshes to flood.

With so many uncertainties surrounding the ecological impacts of climate change on salt marsh ecology, restorationists must assess restoration with an eye to the future. In some sites, increasing sea levels could change the hydrology of a marsh such that it can no longer support the same plant and animal communities as it did in the past. Decreased ice accumulation during the winters could interfere with cyclical changes in plant communities. Warmer temperatures could increase the salinity in pools on the surface of the marsh that served as sanctuaries for young fish. Increased carbon dioxide has the potential to alter competition between plants, leading to changes in the plant community. With all of these new pressures, it may be unrealistic to expect a salt marsh to "return" to a familiar state. As a result, ecologists may need to change the way in which they evaluate restoration.

It is clear at this point that some marshes will experience structural changes (or have already shown some changes) in regards to hydrology and community composition because of climate change. What is not clear is how even small structural changes might lead to cascading changes in the functioning of the marsh (e.g., nutrient and carbon cycling). For instance, increased flooding could favor an introduced species of herbivorous insect, which then outcompetes other herbivores on the marsh. Changes to the insect community could then impact the fish and birds that consume those insects, and so on. When these cascading effects are affecting those marshes that had served as "reference" marshes in the past, to what standard should we hold restoration projects? Should restoring sites mimic pre-climate change conditions, or should they be held to a new standard?

One angle might be to assess restoration in terms of functionality, rather than relying solely on structural measures. Sherman Marsh, in Newcastle, Maine, has undergone a dramatic series of changes over the past 80 years. The salt marsh was dammed in the 1930s, such that it became a shallow, freshwater lake until the dam washed out in 2005. Since the dam breach, ecologists have monitored the plant species composition of the marsh so as to describe the structure of the marsh, but also monitored how that plant biomass travels through the food chain as a measure of functionality. In this way, ecologists can assess the project's success in terms of what species are there (structure) and how they perform (function). While many of the insects and spiders typical of a New England salt marsh have returned to Sherman

Marsh, there are interesting exceptions. For instance, a different species of insect is feeding on the **cordgrass** (*Spartina alterniflora*) in Sherman Marsh than in the nearby, relatively unimpacted reference marsh. While the herbivore in Sherman Marsh may be performing the same function as the herbivore in the reference marsh, it is unclear what that means for the marsh in the long term. Will one of those insects be prepared better for impacts from climate change? Ecologists may just have to wait to find out.

— Abby O. Pearson

Work began in 1932 to replace the 1920s-era swing bridge with a concrete bridge and dam across the outlet of the marsh, blocking tidal flow and forming a freshwater lake. (Courtesy of Maine Dept. of Transportation)

The current steel bridge was constructed in 1962 over the concrete dam. In October, 2005, the dam washed out in a storm; tidal flow returned to the marsh restoring the habitat over the ensuing years. (photo: Abby O. Pearson)

DMR biologists Jake Overlock and Toby Bonney plant eggs along the upper reaches of the river where salmon would naturally spawn in nests made in gravel beds called "redds." (photo: Jason Bartlett)

Atlantic Salmon: Holding on in the Sheepscot River

The 58-mile Sheepscot River is unique for many reasons, including its reversing falls in Sheepscot Village, tidal mud flats that support rare mussel and plant species, and the highest water quality rating in the State. But one feature stands out with national, perhaps even international, significance: the Sheepscot River supports a remnant wild population of the endangered **Atlantic salmon** (*Salmo salar*), known as "The Great Leaper."

Atlantic salmon are one of Maine's ten native anadromous fish, meaning they migrate from ocean to freshwater to reproduce in their natal streams. Historically, salmon were abundant in all of Maine's major rivers and tributaries with suitable spawning grounds. With the advent of dams and changing land use patterns, salmon populations declined throughout Maine and were extirpated from much of southern New England's waterways by the mid-1850s. Found in 14 Maine rivers, their presence is an indictor of ecosystem health; salmon seek clear, clean, cold waters with relatively unhindered access to the ocean and spawn in areas that offer coarse gravel bottoms with well-oxygenated waters of a specific velocity and depth.

Stocking efforts to supplement the wild population began around 1890 with the establishment in East Orland, Maine, of the Craig Brook Hatchery on Alamoosook Lake in the Penobscot River drainage. Since then, 96 million salmon have been released, but despite stocking efforts, populations declined dramatically in the mid-1990s and prompted their endangered species listing in eight Maine rivers. Each year, the Maine Department of Marine Resources (MDMR) stocks over

3.5 million salmon at different stages of juvenile development. However, these efforts have not permanently increased wild salmon populations. 2011 saw record numbers of returning adult salmon in the Sheepscot with a total statewide count of 3,500 individuals, although the following year this number dropped to 700. (By comparison early 1800s estimates were 100,000 adults in the Penobscot River alone.) This dip is thought to be related to mortality at sea, resulting from changing ocean conditions, such as temperature, currents and prey availability.

MDMR fisheries biologist Paul Christman has an idea on how to reverse this trend and has developed a new approach for restoring this emblematic species. "Our goal is to have fish be born as wild as possible," he says. His innovative method centers on hatching eggs in the wild rather than using hatcheries to rear and release fish before their adult phase. The approach is not necessarily new, but he has employed new technology to increase the scale so it can be used for population supplementation.

Christman and his team visited the Sheepscot River in the winter of 2011–2012 to insert about 120,000 pinkish-orange salmon eggs into the gravel substrate and returned again the following winter with 119,000 eggs. Overall 1.4 million eggs were embedded throughout three key watersheds. The specific DNA of these eggs was not new to the river, as the eggs originated from adult salmon taken from the Sheepscot as juveniles and raised in a hatchery. Because salmon return to their stream of origin, they evolve into distinct populations genetically tuned to the river's distinctive conditions. These unique genetic traits affect growth rate, disease resistance, migration patterns and spawning *phenology*. (Phenology is the study of the relation between recurrent natural phenomena—e.g., migration or flowering—and climate.) Maintaining genetic diversity and integrity is crucial for individual fish to combat the riverine ecosystem's selective pressures and ultimately variable ocean conditions. Because of this, MDMR manages each river as a separate stock, making sure not to cross populations.

After the planted eggs hatch, the fish (now known as *alevins*) stay in the gravel through roughly the second week in April, getting nutrients from their yolk sac. After 4–6 weeks they emerge as fry. The exact timing is temperature dependent: warmer weather triggers earlier emergence. Biologists estimate emergence rates using a fry trap at specific planting sites and typically find that sur-

Facing upstream, the smolt trap captures enough departing fish for biologists to estimate spawning success. (photo: courtesy MDMR)

Fry taken from traps are evaluated and released. (photo: courtesy MDMR)

vival is similar to the natural rate of about 10%. In a hatchery setting, over 90% of eggs would reach the fry stage and be released into the wild. However, Christman is leery of such high numbers and points to data that show lower long-term survival, pointing out that in the controlled hatchery environment "there is no process of responding to natural conditions, so in the wild the young die off because they are not prepared to respond." Christman's fry show greater resilience, as they have been answering to the river's patterns and cycles since day one.

After about a month, the fry develop vertical striations and are now called parr. They feed and grow over the course of 1–3 years before undergoing physiological changes to prepare for the marine ecosystem. Now called *smolts*, they imprint on the river through scent as they travel downstream. Biologists continue their monitoring effort on the Sheepscot by trapping the departing smolts each spring. The fish enter an aluminum trap about the size of a car, positioned at narrow points below Head Tide Dam. Fish are counted, given a small punch in their tail fin and released upstream to see if they'll be recaptured. The number of recaptured fish allows researchers to estimate how many fish are missing the trap, giving an estimate of the river's overall population. Data that have been collected in the Sheepscot for the last four years reveal a healthy, stable population. Each fall, biologists have one more opportunity to conduct counts in the river through a method called electrofishing that stuns fish temporarily. Before an Atlantic salmon breaks out into the coastal waters, it could potentially have been handled up to four times by MDMR biologists.

After entering the open waters of the Atlantic, salmon travel north, as far as Greenland and return home after 1–3 years. Although Christman is confident, he has to wait patiently for the salmon to complete their five-year life cycle to see the full results of his efforts. Only over the next decade will it become apparent if egg planting can successfully supplement the overall population and even replace fry stocking. The longer-term goal is to discontinue stocking. His vision is to "leave the river to its own devices" in hopes that future generations of Atlantic salmon are better suited to meet the challenges of the changing oceans.

— Ava Goodale

◆ I 4 ◆   Hidden Valley Nature Center: *Boardwalk on the Bog and Much More*

Hidden Valley is about nature, and people seeking nature, such as this group visiting "the wall" near North Head. (photo: Gary Hayward)

T HANKS TO THE VISION of wife-and-husband team Bambi Jones and Tracy Moskovitz, Hidden Valley Nature Center (HVNC) offers a thousand-acre tract featuring 30 miles of trails through second-growth forest, a small lake, vernal pools and a fabulous bog accessible by boardwalk. Since 2007 the preserve has developed family-based and educational activities funded in part through a sustainable forestry program. (In 2014, the American Tree Farm System recognized the couple and HVNC as Maine Outstanding Tree Farmers.) And this is one of the few preserves where you can book cabins or even a yurt for over-nighting among the nocturnal residents such as owls, foxes and coyotes.

The center's mission in its own words has three parts: (1) To offer premier opportunities for outdoor, non-motorized recreation; (2) To offer educational opportunities related to the natural world, ecological literacy and sustainable communities; and (3) To model innovative and sustainable forestry practices. The network of people associated with the preserve is clearly meeting these goals as a look at their website will show. There are regular events—cross-country skiing on groomed trails, vernal pool walks, "owl prowls" and forestry management, for example—in all seasons that are a good way to get to know the preserve and all it has to offer. Other notable events include biathlons and half-marathons, and timber framing and chainsaw classes: all in support of the preserve.

The Bog

Recently, the center has erected a boardwalk to take visitors into the heart of this botanical gem with its resplendent mat of sphagnum moss, sheep laurel, Labrador tea, orchids and literally hundreds of other species. Of particular note is the "star" species: the **northern pitcher plant** (*see* p. 140) joined by two other "carnivorous" plants, sundews and the less visible bladderwort. The sphagnum moss is a foundation plant of the bog and is aptly described by Beedy (E. C.) Parker in her *Natural History of Camden and Rockport:*

> Sphagnum moss *(Sphagnum sp.)* lives and grows in acid conditions. Moss plants, which have large chamber cells to absorb water like a sponge, make a springy waterlogged mat over the surface of the bog, partially floating on the water. Dead material falls off the bottom of the mat and accumulates in thick layers of peat on the bottom. Eventually the whole bog is filled with compressed, undecomposed plant bodies.

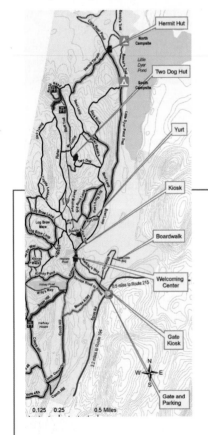

Visits to the bog in successive warm months reveal an ever-changing panoply of blooming flora inhabiting the thick mat of floating sphagnum that is the substrate of the bog. Go starting in May to see swamp azalea, followed by various pink orchid species (arethusa, pogonia and grass-pink), and the various species of heath

---

Directions: Hidden Valley Nature Center, 1,000 acres, Jefferson

From Route. 1 in Wiscasset, turn north onto Route. 218 North. Go 6 miles and bear right onto Dock Road at the Alna Store. At the end of Dock Road turn right onto Route 194 East, and take the first left in .25 miles onto Egypt Road. Continue north on the Egypt Road for 3.5 miles. Gravel parking lot on the left. Dogs allowed on leash.

WebSource: http://hvnc.org

Plant expert Wanda Garland leads frequent walks at HVNC and other preserves on the Midcoast. (photo: Bambi Jones)

plants such as blueberries and sheep laurel. Fall is colorful here not only for the tree foliage but also for the pitcher plants and sphagnum that turn the richest of deep reds. See how many of the forty bog plant species listed on the Naturalist's Corner pages of the HVNC website you can find on your trip to this exciting part of the preserve.

The boardwalk affords a portal to view the more visible animals that live in or visit the bog, such as the arthropods (insects and spiders), amphibians, reptiles, birds and mammals. You may witness the activities of beaver (*see* p. 143) or dragonflies or even perhaps a coyote.

Upland Trails

The varied topography of the preserve affords a great experience "through hill and dale," with any number of loops and side-loops threading through the forest. The detailed trail map grades these as easy, moderate and difficult, so you can plan your route according to your needs. Take a lunch with you to enjoy at the picnic tables placed at various points. Rather than naming the trails red, green, blue, etc., some thought has gone into the nomenclature here, such as Low Brow Loop, Coyote Lookout, Warbler's Way and Two Dog. The tops of the knolls are a good spot to scan for spring migrants before the dense deciduous foliage makes birding mostly an auditory experience. Small ponds and several vernal pools are there for those who like the natural history of aquatic habitats, and for a truly "vernal" experience, sign up for the annual spring egg count of the pools, usually toward the end of April.

And if you care to go for a paddle, by prior arrangement canoes are available on the 109-acre Little Dyer Pond. Because it has no public access and very little development or human activity, the fishing is great; and at the northern end beavers are busy. Though this book focuses on seashore sites, HVNC should be a "required" detour inland.

Sitting among tufts of cottongrass (the sedge Eriophorum sp.) and alert to the rustling of a rodent on the edge of the bog, this coyote shows the not-often-seen sienna color of the back of the ears. (photo: Sheryl Bickel)

Cobra Plant: Belle of the Bog

Sarracenia purpurea with sphagnum moss. Early autumn at the bog is a colorful time as the green pitcher plants acquire a distinctive red-veined appearance. This plant has captured a spider. (photo: Jill Metcoff)

The *Cambridge Illustrated Dictionary of Natural History* tells us that the beautiful pitcher plant of the bog community is alternatively named for its viper-like resemblance. And like a cobra, and snakes as a whole, its nutrition is in part carnivorously based. Within the liquid of the pitcher, alternately called the hood, it can trap and digest arthropods; the decomposed tissue of such insects and spiders is its nitrogen source. The downward pointing hairs—shaped almost like tiny fangs—of the hood's entry force prey in a one-way direction—again, the cobra metaphor.

It is a most aesthetically pleasing plant species, the three-dimensional leaf a striking evolutionary departure from the two-dimensionality of most leaf forms. It lives among all the surrounding species on the sphagnum mat, including two other species of animal-eating plants, the sundew and the bladderwort.

This species of bogs ranges from northern Canada to Florida as two subspecies, our northern *purpurea* and the southern *venosa*. Extraordinarily, it is a plant that practices both photosynthesis to assimilate carbon dioxide, and carnivory to oxidize proteins through the breakdown of prey. During a 30–50-year life span, an individual *purpurea* thrives within the complex bog ecology, the basis of which, as opposed to the soil on land, is the sphagnum mat, the substrate for animals, plants, fungus and other phyla of life forms. It is a floating, two-foot-thick vegetative layer, with water beneath.

It lives also with species inhabiting the liquid of the hood: microbiota, such as microscopic rotifers (a little known but common class of microbe) and protozoans, as well as larger animals visible to the unaided eye, such as larval insects, including mosquitoes and midges. This is an *inquilinous* community, an inquiline being in the ecological sense a "lodger" species living in or on a larger host, broadly covered under the term commensalism, literally, sharing the same table. In this case the aquatic inquilines in the pitcher do the work of digestion, producing nutrition for the plant and for themselves.

For more on this unusual plant and associated plants in the bog, go to the excellent writeup by Robert Zottoli in the Naturalist's Corner section of the preserve's website.

—K.S.

Green frogs (*Rana clamitans*) hunt insects (such as the **bog grasshopper**, *Appalachia arcane*) and spiders on fall-reddened sphagnum. This species spends the winter in torpor below the frost line in moist soil or in the sediments of pond and stream beds.

Vegetation will in time close off the visible surface water as organic debris accumulates on the bottom and the plant community creeps ever inward.

Life on the bog's surface warrants close inspection. This specialized botanical community thrives in conditions of high acidity, supporting an ecosystem adapted to this unique microenvironment.

Round-leaved sundews *(Drosera rotundifolia)* attract small invertebrates such as ants and flies to the sugary droplets exuded at the ends of spicules that then envelop and eventually digest the animal.

Pitcher-plant flowers develop seed heads suspended beneath the bracts. As with the plants' leaves (hoods) the flowers turn from green to a rich red in autumn.

The Inherited Environment of a Beaver

The surface of the pond is black, and smooth as mercury. The herons have retired to their rookery. The least flycatcher and hermit thrush are both quiet. The elusive female hooded merganser has disappeared; even the loons are silent. A vee-shaped wake cuts straight across the darkening pond and returns a few minutes later, purposeful and efficient: a **beaver** (*Castor canadensis*) at work.

The creature throws a rippling bow wave like a tiny tugboat. These are powerful animals that occasionally weigh over a hundred pounds, although these days that's way above average. It is not, however, as large as its Pleistocene forbearer, *Castorides ohioensis*. That animal weighed over two hundred pounds and was eight feet long. It became extinct, as did other North American megafauna, toward the end of the most recent ice age 12,000 years ago, having survived some 130,000 years. Today, our beaver is the only extant member of the family *Castoridae* and one of only two members of its genus, *Castor*. The other, *C. fiber*, is Eurasian and has a similar appearance, but a different number of chromosomes. Attempts to hybridize the two have failed. *C. fiber* was extirpated from most of its former range, in part because it enjoyed a unique status in medieval Europe.

Pliny's *Natural History*, published a.d. 77–79, recognized beavers as a kind of fish because of their hairless tails. This allowed the faithful to consume them on the many days when the Catholic Church required abstinence from red meat—a kiss of death for the luckless beaver.

The fossil record for rodents—that includes squirrels, rats and mice, lemmings, voles, porcupines, paca, capybara, guinea pigs, and hamsters—goes back at least 30 million years and reveals a variety of species. Some 40 percent of all mammals—over 2,200 species worldwide—are rodents, of which beavers are but a small subset that migrated to North America from Eurasia between 2.5 million and 5 million years ago. By the time Europeans arrived here, *C. canadensis* likely numbered anywhere from 60 to 400 million animals. Even the lowest estimate suggests just how successful beavers are at survival. Their impact on the landscape, then as now, was significant. Hence they are often referenced as an example of "niche construction," an interesting concept in which an organism shapes its own environment and hence its genetic destiny. This concept, which will be discussed at greater length below, has recently provoked discussion among evolutionary scientists.

The primary raw material that the New World beaver provided for the Old World market was the unsheared, waterproof pelt. This was turned into men's hats, coats and gloves, as well as women's hand-muffs. In addition, secretion from the anal gland served as a base for perfume and medicines, and the meat, of course, including the fatty tail, was also consumed, though principally in the Americas. As is and was the case with so many other species, human greed for a natural resource led swiftly to local extirpation. Fortunately for *C. canadensis*, a changing fashion market rescued the beaver from near extinction.

Adult and yearling emerge through skim ice on the bog. Beavers are the largest North American rodent, weighing 30–60 lbs. and larger. Offspring disperse from the family unit in their second year, establishing new territories in the same or neighboring watersheds. (photo: Sherrie Tucker)

Today, according to the International Union for Conservation of Nature (IUCN), protection and re-introduction has successfully returned the beaver to much of its historical range, where they now number a healthy 6 to 12 million individuals that exist without any major threats. There is every reason to imagine a rosy future for the species. In fact, one well-documented experiment demonstrates just how successful beaver can be when they are placed beyond the reach of their normal predators: coyote, wolf, lion, bear, fisher and wolverine.

In the 1940s, beavers were brought to Tierra del Fuego for a commercial fur venture. When the enterprise failed, the Argentine government released 25 pairs into the wild. A 2011 report aired on National Public Radio stated that those few animals had increased to an esti- mated 200,000 animals, which had chewed and dammed their way over nearly 40 million acres, devastating the indigenous forest ecology. Tree species that have not co-evolved with beavers cannot regenerate from their roots and, as a result, simply die when they are gnawed down. A dominant native tree species, the Lena beech, has been particularly decimated. Abandoned beaver ponds have become bogs that invite non-native species. Scientists now fear that the animals will spread north into continental South America where they will further dam- age roads and cattle grazing land through erosion and flooding. Through their combined efforts, both Argentine and Chilean agencies are learning that eradication is both unlikely and controversial, and that even control is very challenging.

The hallmark of the order Rodentia is their incisors, which never stop growing, and which are kept in check only by regular use: Hence the expression "busy as a beaver" is based on the necessity to keep chewing. A walk around a Maine beaver pond will reveal a willingness to select several different kinds of trees, either to eat the inner bark (cambium), or to drag the entire trunk away for dam and/or lodge construction. My impression is that poplar is the preferred species, at least in this part of Maine, but willow, beech, birch and red oak may also fall victim to these industrious herbivores. One morning I discovered that they had preyed upon a large serviceberry shrub that was growing immediately below my open bedroom window. Overnight the beaver had reduced a healthy 10-foot bush to a few four-inch stubs. I searched for the evidence near their lodge a half-mile away, but without success. I concluded that they had placed the branches in long-term underwater food storage, where the stems would be available during the winter.

We associate beavers—their dams and their lodges—with washed-out roads, blocked culverts and drowned trees. Most of us think it wonderful that they are "there," but relieved that they are not "here." This is understandable, especially if they invade your front lawn to eat ornamental shrubbery and trees. But there is another, positive side to their activities that often goes unappreciated.

In a series of interviews on Maine community radio station WERU, Jake Maier, a Maine forestry consultant, mentioned some of the many benefits that beavers provide to the environment. The trademark dams that we are quick to complain about also create wetlands that reduce and moderate downstream flooding. These ponds allow silt and other fine sediments to settle out so that the downstream water is cleaner. Furthermore, the ponds can serve as sink traps for fecal coliform and streptococci bacteria that get into streams from grazing livestock and other quadrupeds. Organic matter that flows over the dam—leaves and pollen, for exam-

"Illicit" logging on Little Dyer Pond. (photo: Chuck Dinsmore)

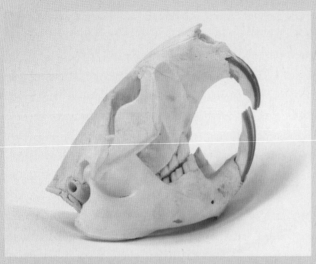

Beavers have 20 teeth, with 16 opposable grinding teeth (premolars and molars) and four prominent incisors that originate deep in the bone of the skull and jaw and grow constantly throughout life. The outer, pigmented portion of rodent incisors is hardened by dietary iron and thus wear's more slowly than the inner side.

ple—feeds insects, which in turn support fish, birds and mammals. Additionally, these impoundments create habitat that sustains certain species, including native trout, during periods of drought. And after the beavers have abandoned a site and the dam falls apart, the former bottom of the pond is a nutrient rich, shallow basin that may sustain different plant and animal communities.

Many people consider the association between Giardia, which is both an organism and the disease it causes, and beavers to be an unfair burden on the latter, because the parasite lives within the intestines of many other species: deer, moose and otter, for example, as well as humans. Contact with water, soil or food contaminated by the feces of any of these hosts may result in an infection, which may also occur through poor personal hygiene on the part of the victim. It is therefore not the exclusive "fault" of the carrier. Once the parasite is ingested, it lives in the intestine of its new host, from which it passes into the soil or water. To single out beavers as the only, or even the prime, culprit is therefore unmerited. In fact, studies in Europe have shown the presence of Giardia in the absence of beavers.

A dam, the beaver's signature stick and mud structure, can range in length from a few feet to a half-mile, large enough to be seen from space. According to EcoInformatics International Inc., the longest beaver dam in the world is in northern Alberta, Canada. The dam is 2,790 feet long and has been over a quarter-century in the making. It's unclear how high this example is, but a somewhat shorter, 2,140-foot dam in Montana is 14 feet high. Such long-lived modifications to the landscape are necessarily inherited by successive generations of local beavers, whose in-the-wild lifespan averages just six years. This example of an organism-driven change to the environment may influence the process of natural selection and the dynamics of evolution—no small thing. This is the essence of niche construction theory, a new, refined interpretation of adaptation and natural selection that was introduced by Richard Lewontin, a Harvard evolutionary biologist, in the 1980s.

According to niche construction advocates, adaption, as it is usually defined, is "a process by which natural selection effectively moulds organisms to fit pre-established environmental templates." In other words, the organism that is best equipped to respond to the challenges of the environment has the best chance to leave offspring. To this, Lewontin and other niche constructionists add a new wrinkle. They ask: What happens when the organism itself is the agent of change? How does this influence the progression of events? They suggest that standard evolutionary analysis does not give this question sufficient attention. It's this unconsidered impact on evolutionary analysis that makes niche construction theoretically significant and provides the rest of us with a new lens through which to appreciate natural history. And beavers provide a perfect illustration.

The authors of *Niche Construction: The Neglected Process in Evolution*, provide this context: "Organisms, through their metabolisms, activities and choices, define and partly create their own niches. They may also partly destroy them. This process of organism-driven environmental modification is called niche construction. Niche construction regularly modifies both biotic and abiotic sources of natural selection and, in doing so, generates forms of feedback that change the dynamics of the evolutionary process."

For example: "When a beaver builds a dam and lodge, creating a lake and influencing river flow, it not only affects the propagation of dam-building genes but it dramatically changes its local environment, affecting nutrient cycling, decomposition dynamics, the structure of the riparian zone, and plant and community composition and diversity."

The phenomenon can be exceedingly visible, a beaver dam being the obvious example, but hardly the only one. Other animals nest, burrow, dig, weave, spin pupal cases, create mounds or what have you. "Earthworms," say niche theory writers, "have the anatomy and physiology of freshwater animals, yet live in the soil. They are able to survive because they modify the soil to suit their physiology, through activities such as choosing the optimal soil horizon, tunneling, exuding mucus, eliminating calcite, and dragging leaf litter below ground." The results of this activity include enhanced plant yields; diminished surface litter; more topsoil; more organic carbon, nitrogen and polysaccharides; and enhanced porosity, aeration and drainage.

Similarly, plants impact their environment by emitting atmospheric gases, bacteria fix nutrients, and both fungi and bacteria decompose organic matter.

One criticism of niche construction is that it can be taken to extremes. A falling leaf, a footprint in the damp soil or decomposing animal droppings are in themselves trivial events with little evolutionary significance. On the other hand, a dam and the impounding of water, along with the subsequent cascade of environmental modifications, may well affect not only the beavers of that community but also other organisms in both time and/or space and thus ultimately may affect natural selection. Under these circumstances, proponents of niche theory would suggest that their perspective has useful relevance. It's worth thinking about. (*See* www.nicheconstruction.com)

—T. O.

◆ I 5 ◆   La Verna:
Heritage of the Ages

440 million-year-old geology waits patiently at the shoreline of Muscongus Bay. (See also front cover photo.)

THREE WORDS FOR THIS SITE: Don't miss it. Not many places on the Midcoast offer such a striking landscape on its seaward periphery, as well as diverse backlands including freshwater wetland and a variety of forest types. Though beauty is subjective ("in the eyes of the beholder"), few will not be impressed with La Verna, where 2½ miles of trails through various wooded and riparian habitats come out to the coast with its remarkable geologic formations thrusting upward at the edge of the sea. In the course of fieldwork for two books of Midcoast nature sites, we consider this one of the best "coast-scapes." Upon first seeing the multi-colored outcrops against the backdrop of the sea, the sweet-sounding Latin phrase *mirabile dictu* ("wonderful to relate") comes to mind.

And though the stratified sediments, called the Bucksport Formation, are visible at other locales along the coast, nowhere do they erupt in such dynamic angular splendor jutting skyward toward the east and the island-studded Muscongus Bay. Tilted and uplifted by tectonic forces so long ago, layer upon layer of ancient sea sediments have metamorphosed through time to their present condition, along with intrusions of molten rocks hardened into the light-colored igneous quartz and granite visible today.

Spider webs on spruce trees near the shoreline are highlighted by the dew on a foggy summer day.

From the parking area, a half-mile right-of-way trail traverses private land and connects with the north and south loop trails of the 120-acre preserve. Along this access, new conifers are growing up among an area of dead trees, the forest regenerating from some past mortality event. If you want marine nature head to the shoreline at low tide when hanging tide pools (*see* next page) are left ensconced at different levels in the rock strata. Ospreys nest nearby on the southern trail loop in a dead pine.

Directions: La Verna Preserve, 120 acres, Bristol, Pemaquid Watershed Association

Take Route 32 south from Round Pond. Go 3.5 miles south of the Round Pond Post Office (which is the same as 3 miles north of New Harbor Center). Notice Ocean Hill cemetery on your right. Soon after the cemetery, there is a parking area for the preserve on the right (west side of road). Preserve access is gained by following a trail located directly across Route 32 from the parking lot. Dogs allowed on-leash

WebSource: http://pemaquidwatershed.org/Documents/LaVerna_brochure.pdf

For Geology: www.maine.gov/doc/nrimc/mgs/explore/bedrock/sites/sep11.htm

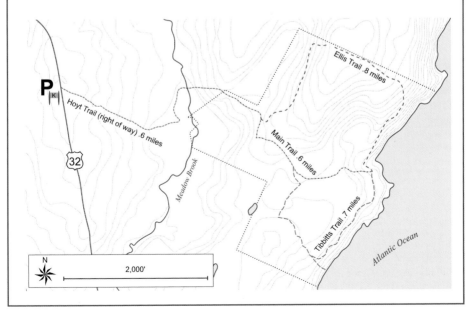

Tale of a Tide Pool

The first surface waters—fresh and then salt as minerals leached in—started to emerge on Earth beginning possibly about 3.8–4.2 billion years ago. This essential molecule of two hydrogen atoms bonded to an oxygen enabled life on this planet. Liquid water gradually produced the first unicellular life forms that evolved into multicellular life, such as blue-green alga

Chondrus crispus

Ralfsia

Hildenbrandtia

Agardhiella

Ulva

Midday with the sun high overhead is the best time to peer into tide pools. Spend a few minutes or more watching the residents—fish, crabs, snails and marine algae—as they swim, walk, crawl and grow in this specialized niche environment. Marine algae, commonly called seaweeds, have complex life histories and divide into green, brown and red groups. This pool, photographed shortly after the vernal equinox, will develop rapidly as the season comes on. The rich hues give this pool an almost tropical appearance.

(Cyanobacteria), followed by green and red alga that led to true plants. Then evolved a plant-animal common ancestor, giving rise to ancient phyla of invertebrate wormlike animals, and so on up through past eons of geologic time. Tide pools are where much of early evolution took place: where we came from.

Race forward in time to the tide pool shown opposite, a multicolored tableau that includes algae, mollusks, crustaceans and other life forms. (Brief descriptions of the labeled alga species appear below.) This pool sits nestled in Devonian age metamorphic rock, highly layered, fractured and wave worn. And some of the species in this pool were just beginning their evolutionary journey—the *Immense Journey* as the scientist Loren Eisley called it—back in those days of 440 million years ago. As on land, the foundation of aquatic ecosystems is the plants, starting with microscopic phytoplankton that bloom in the warm months that feed the equally small animals called zooplankton, that in turn feed larger invertebrate animals that feed larval fish, and so on up through the food chain to the largest fish and marine mammals.

Seaweeds comprise three main phyla generally growing from highest to lowest in the intertidal zone: the greens (Chlorophyta) need the most sunlight to photosynthesize, followed by the browns (Phaeophyta) and the reds (Rhodophyta), requiring the least light.

The red alga **Irish moss** (*Chondrus crispus*, see photo) is ecologically important in forming an intertidal zone midway between the rockweeds of higher levels, and kelps and deeper water algae on the lowest zones; and it is economically important, harvested to make carrageenin used as a thickener in food and industrial products. Another red species is a **crustose alga** (*Hildenbrandtia prototypus*) that grows slowly on the substrate in thin reddish to orange films. Also in the red family is **Aghard's red weed** (*Agardhiella*) growing here at the northern extent of its range.

The two green seaweeds shown are very different in form. **Sea lettuce** (*Ulva lactuca*) is just beginning its annual growth in this pool, later forming large green sheets that are edible. The species is tolerant of many local conditions, even polluted areas. The green **crustose alga** (*Ralfsia sp.*) has the same morphology as the above red form, over which it appears to be growing.

Also living in this pool are two familiar mollusks. In the Class Bivalvia is the filter-feeding **blue mussel** (*Mytilus edulis*); and in the Class Gastropoda (*see* p. 162) is the grazing **common periwinkle** (*Littorina littorea*). Both species are prevalent animals living in a range of habitats from rocky shores to tidal marshes. Both are important food species for other animals, including humans.

— K. S.

Eelgrass *(Zostera marina)*, here growing in a tide pool outflow, is a true seed plant (phylum Spermatophyta) unlike the seaweeds that are algae. The species had a troubled 20th C. on the eastern seaboard, experiencing mass dieoffs from disease, and after recovering somewhat in previous decades, is now in sharp decline due to consequences of global warming: acidification, sea temperature rise and a population explosion of green crabs.

We usually see marine algae (here the **hollow green weed,** *Enteromorpha,* and brown **rockweed,** *Fucus)* out of the water, but when immersed at high tide, they are buoyed upright in the water column, resembling a land plant. "The chemical composition of seaweeds is markedly different from land plants. In general, land plants owe their rigidity to cellulose, whereas seaweeds contain only about five percent cellulose and owe their mechanical strength to alginic acid." (from: *Encyclopedia of Organic Gardening,* J. I. Rodale et al., 1975)

La Verna's Long Geologic History, in Brief

The layered bedrock originated as sediment in a marine basin during the Silurian Period of geologic time, approximately 430 million years ago. This particular set of deposits has been mapped as the Bucksport Formation, which extends from the Boothbay-Pemaquid region northeastward to the town of Bucksport. The time of subsequent metamorphism and the formation of the igneous rocks is not known precisely, but research in the surrounding region suggests it was probably in the Devonian Period, between about 420 and 370 million years ago.

In contrast, a continental ice sheet last modified the New England landscape during the last Ice Age, from about 25,000 to 14,000 years ago. Notice that we're now talking about thousands of years rather than hundreds of millions. And the current shoreline is even younger, having moved and changed significantly as sea level has risen in Maine approximately 150 feet in the past 11,000 years. So while the rocks are very old, the surface exposure is quite new.

— Henry Berry IV

(from: www.maine.gov/doc/nrimc/mgs/explore/bedrock/sites/sep11.htm)

While in the area . . .

Osborn Finch Preserve, 11 acres,
Waldoboro, Pemaquid Watershed Association

Directions: From Damariscotta, take the Biscay Road to Route 32. Travel north on Route 32 for 6.3 miles and turn right on to Dutch Neck Road. At the fork, go left for 2.5 miles. Preserve sign and grass parking area are on the left. Dogs allowed on leash.

About 12 miles to the north of La Verna on Dutch Neck (named for the German colonists), this intimate preserve is distinctive for its aesthetic woodland trail to the water, where you'll find a wide view out onto the Medomak River with its comings and goings of birds, seals and lobster boats. Stone walls dating back to those first Europeans in the area are now covered with a luxuriant mat of moss in the cool shade cast by large pine, red spruce and hemlock trees. Tide pools are there for visitors who like these enclosed worlds of marine plants and animals. The shoreline tree cover with mixed hardwoods sees good traffic of spring and fall warblers and other migrants. And, like Hidden Valley Nature Preserve (chapter 14), there's an opportunity for an overnight stay in a well-designed cabin for four, perched on a rocky escarpment right on the water, usually booked for the season well in advance (*see* the website for information).

WebSource:

www.pemaquidwatershed.org/Documents/Osborn_Finch_brochure.pdf

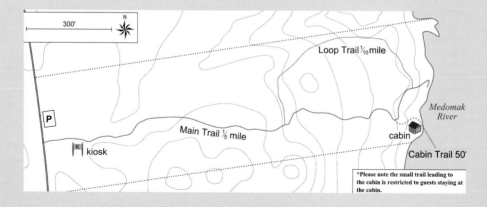

154

Shoreline at Osborn Finch Preserve with cabin, and rock face on the side-loop trail.

Pemaquid Point Lighthouse Park, 7 acres, Town of Bristol
Directions: From Route 1 in Damariscotta, take Route 130 South for 14 miles to the end of the Pemaquid Peninsula. Dogs allowed on leash; $2 admission fee per person during summer and fall seasons.

WebSource: http://www.bristolparks.org/lighthouse.htm

Lighthouse seekers will want to visit the point to admire another of Maine's historic beacons, this one located at land's end on this peninsula, a dramatic site of bedrock stretching into the sea. When the swell of the ocean is up either from local winds or storms far offshore, the roar of the surf is humbling. Looking out to the south from here is an unbroken expanse of ocean, with the curvature of the earth defining the horizon. Birders can set up spotting scopes here or scan with binoculars for sea birds and perhaps even a spouting whale (*see* www.mainebirdingtrail.com/Brochure.pdf). During the season there is a small charge for entry to the park, or you can park at the abutting restaurant for lunch or ice cream and stroll down on the lawn and steps to the shore. Low tide is an opportunity to scan tide pools.

Seashore springtails (Anurida maritima) *form dense, blue-gray aggregations on the surface of tide pools. They are members of a primitive order of insects, Protura, that includes the familiar* **snow flea** (Achorutes nivicolus) *that dot the surface of the snow, and* **silverfish** (Lepisma saccharina) *that seek out sources of starch, such as in book bindings. Proturans hatch as small adults, undergoing no metamorphosis other than adding segments to the abdomen.*

The lighthouse sits atop a spectacular point, with beautiful and complex rock formations of the same age as those at La Verna Preserve not far to the north. The former lighthouse keeper's dwelling to the left now houses a small museum devoted to the history of the site.

◆ 16 ◆ Fort Point and Town Forest, St. George

Oak trees line the riverbank where a blockhouse fort formerly stood with earthworks protecting the cannons, a strategic defensive position that was nevertheless overwhelmed by British raiders in 1814. This site is a good place to scan for winter sea ducks.

IF YOU WANT A HISTORICAL POINT OF LAND with beautiful views both up and down the Georges River, drive south from Thomaston to enjoy this short walk down the trail, bordered by **blackberries** (*Rubus* spp.) and shaded by tall aspen trees among other mixed hard and softwoods. Visiting recently on a late summer day, we found the ripe blackberries plentiful and sweet. A marshy stream with thick cover, a haven for birds and other animals, complements all this.

The trail emerges onto a meadow at the point with the old fort's semicircular earthworks still guarding a lovely sweep of the river. The fort, situated on a "thumb" of land jutting to the west, would have controlled the entire mile-long stretch of river—if not flanked to the rear where two coves punctuate the topography on this eastern shore. Action was seen here during the War of 1812 between the Americans and British:

> During the War of 1812 there were two noted engagements with the British. British raiders rowed up the river in dense fog in June 1814 and captured the fort which had been erected by the U.S. government in 1809

Directions: Fort Point Trail, 2 acres, Town of St. George

From Route 1 in Thomaston, head south for ca. 5 miles. Take right onto Wiley's Corner Rd. and quick right onto Spring Lane to parking area near to the spring.

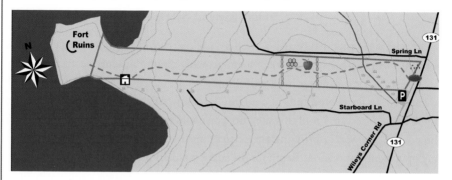

Dogs allowed on leash. The Historic Fort Point Trail is a collaboration between the St. George Conservation Commission and the St. George Historical Society, maintained by volunteer efforts.

WebSources: www.stgeorgemaine.com/about_history.html
www.stgeorgemaine.com/documents/Parks%20and%20Recreation/Fort_Point_Trail.pdf

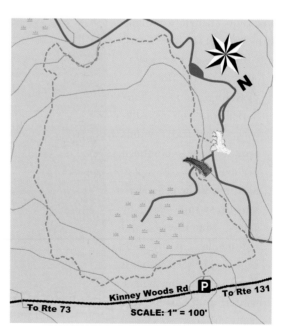

Directions: Town Forest Trail, 58 acres, St. George

From Route 1 in Thomaston, take Route 131 toward the town of St. George. After approximately 4 miles, turn left on Kinney Woods Road. Continue 0.8 miles and park on the south side of the road in the designated parking area.

WebSource:
www.stgeorgemaine.com/documents/Parks%20and%20Recreation/Forest_Trail.pdf

to protect the growing commerce at Warren and Thomaston. The raiders then retreated down the river. In August of 1813 the local militia turned out and repelled raiders from the ship *Bream*. Two vessels belonging to Hart and Watts were destroyed or taken.

—James Skoglund, St. George Historical Society

Late summer visits will reveal, as well as blackberries, the bright orange berries of a **mountain ash** (*Sorbus* spp.), a shrub form growing along the southwestern tip of the point. These berries growing in plentiful bunches are eaten by animals and formerly were jammed or fermented into liqueurs by humans, especially in Europe where the common name is rowan. From this site, too, you could have seen the fictional sloop *Sally* of the novel *Come Spring* bringing the settlers upriver on their way to founding their colony in present-day Union. Remnant foundation stones along the trail echo history.

In the parking area there is a spring still used as drinking water by those who bring jugs to fill, with health department test data prominently displayed near the spring head, a water source for centuries to be sure, perhaps for millennia. So, bring your canteen and fill up on water and all the richness that this unassuming preserve offers.

Nearby this site is another Town-owned preserve, the 58-acre **Town Forest,** incorporating a pleasant woodland loop trail, meandering ¾ of a mile through mixed second growth. Jones Brook, an enchanting, shaded woodland stream bordered by ferns, drains the area. The town's brochure says of the flora:

> Traveling along a half-buried corduroy log walkway, the trail winds around the northern perimeter of a mossy northern white cedar/balsam fir swamp edged by alders, winterberries and red maples. Skunk cabbage may be seen amongst these wet areas in the late winter and spring, and many different species of mosses may be found within.

*Fruiting body of **Jack-in-the-pulpit** (Arisaema triphyllum), still green in early September, turns red, with each berry producing several seeds that will germinate the following spring. Plants need three years to flower.*

Mountain ash berries ripen in late summer sun and remain on the plant into winter providing food for a variety of birds and mammals, such as grosbeaks, waxwings, squirrels and deer.

Scaly cap *(Pholiota sp.) growing on a decaying stump along the trail. Mushroom expert Greg Marley describes one of the genus,* P. squarrosa, *as mild to moderately toxic to some, producing gastrointestinal symptoms. The family in general is not recommended for eating; some species are poisonous.*

*Although both are called "popple" in Maine, the leaf on the left is from a **quaking aspen** (Populus tremuloides). A stand of these is likely to share a single, extensive, interconnected, water-hungry system of roots. The right hand leaf is from a **bigtooth aspen** (Populus grandidentata). Members of the genus hybridize readily, which can make species identification a challenge.*

St. George Town Forest offers a trail that threads through the woods along a quiet stream. The Town is collaborating with George's River Land Trust to link the existing trail in the Town Forest to Fort Point.

161

Thinking about Slugs

If you spend time on the Maine coast during the summer, you will surely encounter a slug, either in the garden, or wherever there's shade and moisture. Walk around barefoot at night on wet grass and you will confirm just how squishy and sticky a six- or seven-inch **leopard slug** (*Limax maximus*) can feel as it dies under your toes with an audible pop. In that moment of arrest and dismay, you just may wonder how this largest of our local slugs came to its end under your foot—that is, if you dare look.

Slugs and their shelled cousins, snails, belong to that diverse and shifting phylum of invertebrates known as Mollusca, which is Latin for soft—as you are already aware from your recent experience of scraping one off. Mainers are familiar with many of these—bivalve oysters, clams and mussels are among the more familiar examples. In recent summers, as the water temperature of Penobscot Bay and others has warmed, we have begun to enjoy increasing numbers of squid as well. These, like their close relatives, octopus, and cuttlefish, are cephalopods (Greek for head-footed) and have gills, as does our intertidal resident, the **common periwinkle** (*Littorina littorea*). But these marine mollusks are in the minority within the phylum. The majority of mollusks are terrestrial gastropods (Greek for belly-footed). These, the slugs and snails, are adapted to life on land—sort of.

There are 60,000–80,000 of them scattered about the world, and they have neither gills nor developed lungs. Instead, respiration occurs within primitive lung-like chambers, the presence of which has recently placed these creatures among the Pulmonata, a designation that is slightly confusing because the word means lung in Latin. Currently, six pulmonate orders are recognized, two of which are comprised exclusively of slugs, but taxonomic revision is ongoing and likely to remain unsettled until DNA analysis moves the research forward. (As a result of constantly evolving knowledge, the applicative phrase here should be, "the truth for now is....") All the same, what distinguishes a slug from a snail at a basic level is the absence of the snail's signature mobile home. Whether it resembles a tiny upside down ice-cream cone or a ping-pong ball–sized brown spiral, the shell affords the snail a degree of protection from predation and desiccation that is not enjoyed by a slug.

Slugs exchange air through a *pneumostome*, an opening located usually on the right-hand side of its mantle. This is the unmistakable raised feature that dominates the forward section of their body and that contains a tiny internal plate corresponding to the snail's shell. Another unusual anatomical feature is the location of the animal's anus, which is somewhat unexpectedly located within the pneumostome. Adjacent to that multitasking aperture, but forward of the mantle and conveniently positioned on the creature's head, is the genital orifice, or *gonopore*. That immediate vicinity is further distinguished by two pairs of tentacles above the animal's mouth. The longer ones are the eyestalks, which are sensitive to movement and light. The shorter pair can detect chemicals. All four can retract when the slug senses danger. In other words, there's a lot going on in that little head.

These two species of slugs—spotted or leopard and gray garden slug—show the key to their land-based existence, the pneumostome, through which they breathe, unlike their aquatic relatives—both marine and freshwater— that have gills. The eyes of terrestrial gastropods are at the end of the tentacles.

Of the 765 known terrestrial gastropods crawling around North America, approximately 50 are exotic slugs, 16 of which are in Maine. Of these, five are native. The other 11 are uninvited European immigrants whose means of arrival and subsequent dispersion is a matter of informed conjecture.

The accepted explanation is that most arrived as stowaways onboard vessels carrying plants, soils, logs or other slug-friendly material, including ballast. The **leopard slug**, *L. maximus*, for example, was first noticed on this side of the Atlantic in a Philadelphia cellar in 1867, presumably having survived a transoceanic passage. From there, it "made its way" further afield, once again likely being transported without any effort on its part to wherever opportunity provided an opening. A year-round greenhouse or commercial garden would have been perfect. From there a single slug might have been passed on to a smaller garden, and then to a kitchen. Because so many people prefer not to squash them, they often make it back to the outside via the garbage or compost bin. Presto. They are on their way to establishing a community.

Some of the smallest snails such as the tiny **ice thorn** (*Carychium exile*), a mere 0.07 inches long, can hitch a ride within the feathers of a bird or be carried in nesting material. This may explain the presence of these snails at the top of steeples or other unlikely locations. There is wind, as well, which is thought to explain the presence of small land snails on some isolated Pacific islands. James. D. Harwood, a researcher at the University of Kentucky, has estimated that within a recent five-year period as many as 5,000 gastropods from 100 countries have been intercepted at our borders.

Slug movement has been aptly described as "sliding on slime." They can even crawl over razor blades without injury. Several barriers to slug infestation are commercially available, but slugs are also restrained by their own limited ability to generate mucus. When a surface is dry

This **amber snail** (*Succinea* sp.) is a relatively recent arrival on the Midcoast.

and scratchy, they can manage only a short distance before their capacity for mucus production is exhausted. When that happens, they dehydrate and are injured —which leads to death. This clearly limits the size of their home territory and their ability to migrate.

When they do move about, generally at night, evidence of their nocturnal peregrination is easy to spot. Where they wander, they leave a silvery, iridescent trace that marks their progression over the landscape. This visible trail, mostly water and mucoprotein, informs others of the same species of their presence. This makes finding a mate easier, but it also opens the door to attack by predators, among which is its carnivorous relative, *L. maximus*, a creature that, in attack mode, is capable of charging in for the kill at a neck-snapping velocity of six inches per minute.

This begs a question about gastronomy: if slugs are snails without protective shells, and snails are dished out in restaurants irresistibly smothered in warm garlic butter, might not slugs also be on a fine-dining menu? Somewhat to my relief, I could find no recipes for *L. maximus*, although possibilities do exist for the yellow, West Coast **banana slug** (*Ariolimax californicus*). The "escargot" that we commonly enjoy in restaurants is generally one of two species, either the **brown garden snail** (*Helix aspersa*) or the European **Burgundy snail** (*Helix pomatia*). Savory as a plate of *H. aspersa* might be, experimenting with other belly-footed slime sliders leaves me cold. So, if we don't eat leopard slugs, who does?

The list of predators is extensive and includes, but is not limited to, starlings, ducks, owls, moles, foxes, toads, snakes (especially garter snakes), shrews, fish and carnivorous beetles. In addition, some flies and nematodes may parasitize them. Of these, in my experience, the **American toad** (*Bufo americanus*) should be at the top of the list.

Snails, in turn, eat extensively. The term detrivore, i.e., consuming detritus, does not do them justice. Some prefer carrion. Others are carnivores. Still others are generalists. It's safe to say that if you grow it, they may eat it, be it a flower, vegetable, fruit or mushroom, and will do so with surprising voracity. As if that wasn't enough, slugs can also be vectors of disease, including downy mildew. And, they can carry the fecal bacteria, *Escherichia coli*, from garden to salad to your own gut: all the more reason to wash your organic produce. Some of the little ones are hard to spot. There are, of course, ecological benefits to the little, and not so little, dears: soils are aerated and nutrients released. They consume dead and rotting matter, much as worms do, and hence there is much to say in their favor. So we may want them around—just not in our own gardens.

What, therefore, keeps slugs away from where we don't want them has been a focus of agriculturalists for centuries. The following are a few recommended measures pooled from various sources:

- Remove places where slugs can shelter. Surround garden with close-cropped ground cover or a slug-unfriendly surface such as lime, cinders, coarse sawdust, gravel, etc.
- Provide oat bran. Once ingested, the bran swells, with fatal consequences. This has the advantage of being benign to humans and pets, but it is made useless by rain.
- Soot/ash and coarse diatomaceous earth (made from diatoms). Distributed around a garden, these absorb mucus, causing the slug to dry out. Desiccation is fatal. Must be renewed after rain.
- Copper barriers (Snail-Barr). Slugs die from the electrical charge. Effective for raised beds.
- Beer traps. Attract slugs, which drown in the liquid.
- Handpicking. Done daily, then weekly, can be quite effective.
- Water in the evening. Pick them off at night using a flashlight.
- Certain plants, such as basil, hosta, beans, lettuce, marigolds and strawberries, are slug magnets. Either don't grow them, or use them to attract slugs. When the slugs are feasting, they can be eradicated.
- Other plants, such as geraniums, impatiens, nasturtiums, rosemary and sage, repel slugs.
- Non-metaldehyde (Sluggo). An organic product that immobilizes and leads to desiccation.
- **Nematodes** (*Phasmarhabditis hermaphrodita*) offer a biological control for organic gardeners.

Scott M. Martin is the author of "Terrestrial Snails and Slugs (Mollusca: Gastropoda) of Maine," (*Northeastern Naturalist*, 2000, 33–88). This historical compilation touches on virtually all that has been written about the topic up to the date of publication and includes some of the beautiful black-on-white drawings by Edward S. Morse that were first published in *American Naturalist* in 1867. Martin's article reflects the higher relative number of snail species in our state, but snails are, after all, only slugs with shells, so in a larger sense that distinction is unimportant—particularly so as much of Martin's taxonomic data is outdated anyway. But the overview he provides is a pleasure to read—and a window into earlier science and some of the traditional names for some species. When it comes to old names, snails shine.

Who would not stop to examine a creature called a "toothless column," or fail to be mesmerized by a "white-lip dagger," or the ghastly named "armed snaggletooth"? (It should be noted that a few of these have only occasionally been seen on this side of the Atlantic: **Black arion** (*Arion ater*), for example, has been spotted only three times in North America, and then in scattered locations—once in Bay Bulls, Newfoundland, once in Detroit, Michigan, and once on Vinalhaven Island, Maine—and that was in the 1920s. This means that even if a species has been positively identified, a viable population may not exist.)

As for our 16 resident Maine slugs, malacologists, i.e., those who study slugs, continue to rearrange their taxonomy as genetic analysis reveals new truths about them. However, one method, based on traditional and now possibly flawed information, classifies them into three convenient families. The first is the seven round-backed, rounded-tailed Arionidae, all of which come from Europe, share a vestigial shell that is buried within their mantle and range in size up to eight or even ten inches. The second family is the four fungus loving, pointed-tailed, native Phylomycidae, whose dorsum is entirely covered by a mantle and which can be four inches long. And the third family is the five keel-backed, pointed-tailed Limacidae, including *L. maximus*. These may grow to seven inches. You might hope that these hotdog-sized slugs are the largest in the world; they're not. That prize is held by its northern European cousin, the **black keel-backed slug** (*Limax cinereoniger*), a species that has not yet made it to North America. If and when that happens, it will be hard to miss: it's dark to the point of being black, has a striped ventral surface and is nearly twelve inches long. The consequences of not seeing that on the footpath are bound to be memorable.

One source suggests that the number of slugs that reside in one acre may collectively weigh as much as 70 pounds—a disconcerting thought when you're strolling about at night,

The shells of land snails, like their marine relatives, exhibit many variations on the spiral theme. (photo: Alison C. Dibble)

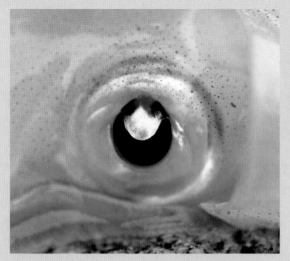

The cephalopod eye—this one belonging to a **long-finned squid,** *Loligo pealei*—is a textbook example of convergent evolution with the vertebrate eye: a functionally similar anatomical structure derived independently over millions of years of change through time. In some recent summers, as average water temperatures of Penobscot and other bays have warmed, large numbers of this usually more southern species have been present inshore.

and a nagging one even during the day. Having consumed several times their own body weight in your garden, where do they go to recover from a night of binging? They avoid a dehydrating breeze, and they prefer a narrow temperature range in the low 60s, being sensitive to changes above or below that. When it's hot, they seek moist, shady refuges. When it's cold, they find underground shelter and become less active. If you look consistently for them in one area, you'll find their preferred haunts. One favorite hideaway in my garden is beneath an overgrown rhubarb plant where the leaves hide them from sunlight and predators. I can be pretty sure of finding them there, or under a nearby rotting plank. Damp cellar holes are also fertile ground for a slug hunter/enthusiast. Unlike the little salamanders you might also expect to see in that sort of environment, slugs appear to have a real preference for a neighborhood inhabited by humans. Even though their primary threat is dry weather, which may kill up to 90 percent of the eggs and young per year, in Maine they must also escape winter. But survive they do.

One explanation is that slugs are hermaphrodites, meaning that a single slug can be both male and female, i.e., have the sexual organs of both genders. Can a slug fertilize itself? Yes, of course. That's a primary value of being a hermaphrodite. This circumstance allows a single specimen or one that finds itself without a like-minded partner to colonize new territory—but this is the exception rather than the rule. The more typical procedure is called reciprocal outcrossing and, as the term suggests, involves two consenting adults.

The sexual act begins on the ground and then moves swiftly upward into the air, becoming something of a high-wire act. The couple climbs a handy tree or wall that offers enough overhang from which one of them will exude a cord of mucus down which, in a frenzy of anticipation, the two slugs rappel. Suspended from this thin, glistening rope, they dangle in a full-bodied embrace. Each slug's penis emerges from the gonopore in its head and is inserted into the gonopore of the other. The two penises entwine, expand and eject sperm, which is absorbed by the other and stored by both. Alas, sometimes this clinch is costly: think two corkscrews that are wound up tightly and won't pull apart. If you're a slug, you exercise a bizarre procedure politely referred to as *apophallation*, which is as gruesome as it sounds. It means that one or both of them chews off either their own or the other's penis. This is no doubt preceded by an interesting discussion—one that has not yet been recorded. One wonders what, exactly, the conversation of who does what to whom might sound like. In any event, there is a consolation prize: The diminished slug can still mate, but solely as a female.

Irrespective of apophallation, ten to 30 eggs are laid in the ground a few days later. Those that survive the winter will hatch the following spring. In two years the little hermaphrodites will achieve sexual maturity. The capacity to self-fertilize that is enjoyed by hermaphrodites clearly allows individual animals to establish a beachhead in virgin territory, but what about apophallation? How does this not lead to smaller penises? Researchers have addressed this but without arriving at clear answers.

L. maximus was assigned its current name by Linnaeus in 1758 but was previously referred to by the first-century Roman naturalist Pliny the Elder. He was probably interested in slugs in their own right, but he was allegedly also curious about their tiny—¼-inch by ½-inch—internal, calcium carbonate shell. Whether he ground it up to use as an antacid or for other purposes is unclear. What is certain, however, is that these shells provide a scant and elusive fossil record. Unfortunately, even a shell in hand, or under a microscope, does not reveal its species, so without DNA analysis, at present it seems that the evolution of the pulmonates cannot be traced back beyond 12,000 years ago, although the phylum extends back 65 million years. This murky past is complicated by convergence, a circumstance wherein unrelated organisms evolve toward a common design that has been selected for within a shared ecological niche. For us today, this means that terrestrial slugs are not necessarily related, even though their appearance might suggest otherwise. The scientific shorthand for this is polyphylly, i.e., evolved independently from unrelated taxons. What was scientific truth only a decade ago may no longer be the case. DNA analysis is turning a lot of data on its head, confirming the truth of the old proverb, "The more you learn, the more you realize how little you know."

At a glance slugs may seem off-putting, but a magnifying glass and a little curiosity will change this attitude. They are a colorful and engaging window through which to see much of what we take for granted.

—T. O.

◆ 17 ◆   Owls Head (Lighthouse) State Park

Spartina cordgrass, a foundation plant of the tidal marsh, has taken hold in the quieter waters on the north side of the park, in the lee of the rocky islets connected by a stony bar.

LIGHTHOUSES ATTRACT THEIR OWN CURIOUS TRAVELERS seeking the history, the seascape and the aesthetics of the structure itself. This one also has a significant preserve to go with it for curious travelers seeking fauna and flora along the Maine Coast. Situated on the eponymous point of land at the southern end of Penobscot Bay, Owls Head Light has guided mariners to Rockland Harbor since ca. 1825, commissioned by then-President John Quincy Adams. Walk out to the overlook at the base of the light. It's a good vantage point to watch the commercial and recreational marine traffic making its way to and from nearby Rockland Harbor, and a strategic spot to scan the waters for marine birds. And to the northeast, you'll see Vinalhaven's three wind turbines in the distance, about ten miles away.

From the spacious parking area with picnic tables affording views of Owls Head Bay, the trail immediately forks leading right to the lighthouse and left to several rocky beaches with wave-worn stones separated by wooded headlands and a trail along the shoreline. For the sheer magnificence of the views near and far, take the lighthouse fork, a high trail looking down on pocket beaches on the short way to the point; but for a good view of nature along the tidal shoreline with the Camden Hills in the distance, choose the left fork with its shaded path to the shore. Really, as the park is relatively compact, you can easily survey both areas with time for a picnic lunch along the way.

169

Lighthouses have an abundance of associated lore, including dog stories. "Spot" was a springer spaniel in residence during the 1930s, who assisted in lighthouse duties, and who is said to have warned the mailboat away from the rocks with timely barking on a fog-bound day. (photo: Des FitzGerald)

If you enjoy knowing the origin of place names, the Town website offers this:

> When Owls Head was visited by Champlain in 1605, it was called Bedabedec Point the Indian word meaning, "Cape of the Winds." Some historians claim the name is of Indian origin and is expressed in their language by the word, "Mecadacut," meaning "Owls Head."

Most visitors to the state will certainly "do" the Rockland/Camden area, so Owls Head is a must for any grand tour of the Midcoast, whether it's for the natural history of the preserve, the cultural history of the lighthouse and its attendant lore or simply for the beauty of this lower Penobscot Bay seascape.

Climbing to the base of the light affords an expansive view of lower Penobscot Bay, good for boat and bird spotting. This is also a good vantage point to see many different types of ships and boats: lobster boats, windjammers, island ferries and even cruise ships coming in and out of Rockland Harbor, one of the busier ports on the Midcoast.

The Gulf of Maine tide edges in over the beach stones at Deep Cove on the western side of the park, offering a serene place to stroll. Seaweed brought in with the tide is always a good place to scan for small marine creatures and cast-off shells of crabs and clams.

Directions: Owls Head Lighthouse, Owls Head, State of Maine, Division of Parks and Public Lands

From the intersection of US Route 1 and ME Route 73 in Rockland, head south on Maine Route 73 for 1.9 miles. Turn left onto North Shore Drive and after 2.6 miles veer left onto Main Street in Owls Head for 0.2 miles. Turn left on Lighthouse Road to arrive at Owls Head State Park.

Dogs allowed on leash in non-beach areas only.

WebSource: www.stateparks.com/owls_head_state_park_in_maine.html
www.visitmaine.com/attractions/state_national_parks/state_parks/owls_head_state_park
http://owlshead.maine.gov/html/town_history.html
www.lighthousefriends.com/light.asp?ID=527

The high path out to the lighthouse point looks down on pocket beaches and the clear Maine seawater. Walking the edge of the coastline like this puts the visitor in intimate contact with the sea.

Red elderberry (Sambucus racemosa) *in full midsummer fruit. The spring flower is a brilliant white against the lush, dentate (toothed) leaves. Unlike the more familiar edible elderberry species (S. canadensis et al.), these berries are somewhat toxic to humans, though eaten by birds and mammals.*

Impatient Invasives

Himalayan balsam (*Impatiens glandulifera*) also called Policeman's Helmet or Impatiens, originally a native of the Himalayas, was introduced into England in the 1800s and later spread to the U.S. The genus name refers to the fact that the seeds spread very quickly and all at once. In the case of Himalayan balsam, they are propelled by an ingenious winding spring system that can launch the seeds as far as 15 feet.

In the strange case of two impatiens species, both North America and the UK have reciprocally exported their own variety to the other country with widespread impact. On this side of the Atlantic, our indigenous *Impatiens capensis* or spotted jewelweed was first introduced as an ornamental in

Himalayan balsam with fuchsia-colored flowers and thick foliage, grows in abundance at the park and is now common in the Northeast and eastern Canada, as well as the west coast from California to British Columbia. Like many invasive plants and animals, it is surely here to stay.

the early 1800s into the UK where it is now ubiquitous. *Glandulifera* first made landfall from its native home in the Himalayas to Europe in the early 1800s and was then introduced to North America later that same century, also as an ornamental planting. This plant is now categorized as an invasive here in Maine.

Himalayan balsam is not shy. It grows as high as 10 feet in a single summer, and its seed dispersal method is second to none. As if designed with young children in mind, towards the end of summer each plant creates a number of tightly wound spring-system seedpods that encompass 5–15 seeds. A single breath of wind or touch cause the springs to release with ballistic exuberance, shooting seeds in every direction. This evolved dispersal system is called *explosive dehiscence* and is particularly fascinating to young children who in my own backyard have helped to spread this invasive plant to every extreme of our seven-acre parcel. I have personally waged an annual ground offensive against this plant but seem to make little impact year-to-year in its steady advance. In one recently cut-over portion of what was formerly a spruce stand, Himalayan balsam has covered the landscape so thickly that nothing else will grow there. Pretty but sinister in its new dominance.

— D. F.

WebSource: http://www.maine.gov/doc/nrimc/mnap/features/invasives.htm

The Brown-headed Cowbird: Adaptable Parasite

Part of the sights and sounds of spring in Maine is the liquid warble of the **brown-headed cowbird** (*Molothrus ater*) signaling the arrival of the elegant brown-and-black males and drab-colored females. But hearing them elicits the mixed emotion of the joy of a new arrival with the knowledge that the cowbird will breed at the expense of other birds. This brood parasite, that derives its Latin name from the Greek word *molothrus* which means "vagabond" or "parasite," does not build its own nest but rather lays its eggs in the nests of other birds.

Males and females forage in many areas, including shorelines, fields, forests and among farm animals such as sheep. (photos: David White)

White settlers in North America called it the "buffalo bird" for its connection and co-evolution with the nomadic buffalo herds moving north and south following the seasonal grasses. It fed on the insects the huge herds turned up while grazing as well as seeds of grasses. To adapt to this feeding strategy cowbirds needed to migrate along with the buffalo and so did not spend enough time in one place in spring to build a nest, brood the eggs and feed their young. Their behavioral adaptation was to deposit their eggs in other birds' nests and forego parenting, as they moved on with the buffalo herds.

But, by the late 1800s hunters had nearly exterminated buffalo. The birds found a new host with the arrival of large cattle herds and became known as the cowbird. And as farmlands replaced aboriginal forests, edge areas became increasingly available to parasitize forest-nesting birds. The cowbird became one of the few species to benefit from the white man's arrival. Spreading east and west with the changing landscape, they have become less migratory, and it may be that in time the need to parasitize will diminish and the cowbird will begin to build its own nest again as it may have long ago.

They are known to parasitize bird nests in tree cavities, tree tops, shrubs or on the forest floor. As many as 220 other bird species, from diminutive hummingbirds to large raptors, are a target for the unwelcome foster-parenting of cowbird young. The female cowbird has evolved to be a proficient observer of other birds' nesting behavior, choosing just the right moment to lay her eggs to hatch sooner and grow faster than their adopted nest mates.

Some hosts recognize the unwanted egg and will abandon the nest or even, in the case of the yellow warbler, build another nest right on top of the offending egg. Most birds however brood it as if it were their own, until it hatches. The first-to-hatch cowbird nestling may push its smaller nest mates from the nest, or most often outcompete them for the food provided by the foster parent. Field observations have also shown "mafia behavior" whereby cowbirds destroy nests if their own eggs have been removed by the host bird, or if they are too late to have their own eggs hatch first. Adult female cowbirds can lay as many as 40 eggs in a breeding season. Such parasitism adds an additional stress on host birds, already at risk from habitat destruction, predation by domestic cats and other human-caused factors.

Cowbirds do still migrate seasonally but move south in the winter now on their own rather than at the direction of the buffalo. Ironically the cowbird, unwelcomed by other birds during the nesting season, joins large mixed species flocks in winter months. But come spring the cowbird loses its desire to socialize and once again returns north as a solitary breeding parasite.

— D. F.

♦ 18 ♦   Sears Island:
Past, Present and Future

Shorelines vary from sand beach on the east side facing the Penobscot River to the rock- and driftwood-strewn vistas on the west facing upper Penobscot Bay. It is possible to "circumnavigate" the entire five miles of coastline at low tide.

S EARS ISLAND IS 936 ACRES, two miles long, about one mile at its widest, and five miles around. (To walk the shoreline be sure to start at least two hours before low tide because a few places are impassable at high.) Along the shoreline are sandy beaches, cobbles, dunes, tidal pools and cliffs. The northern beaches are best for swimming and picnicking. Step onto one of the island's trails, or walk south along its beaches and you forget your cares. The natural environment—its sights, sounds and scents—will engulf you.

Some History

It is not common for an uninhabited island to be accessible from the mainland, but Sears Island with its 936 acres lays claim to that as well as being the largest of its kind on the East Coast. It has not always

been so: until a few decades ago the only access was by boat or by walking across a sand bar at low tide.

That didn't discourage the Native Americans who arrived by canoe to camp and fish during the summers. They named the island Wassumkeag for the "bright sand beaches."

By the 18th century, while European settlers were wheeling and dealing in land grants, they realized the island's potential for grazing, farming and logging. They began to drive the natives away from the island and named it Brigadier's, in honor of Samuel Waldo.

Farmland was cleared and leased to farm workers, beginning with grazing cattle and sheep, and expanding to include a variety of crops until it became one of the largest in the area by the late 19th century. After fire took all the buildings in 1917, they were rebuilt, but by this time farming was on the wane and ended in the 1920s. The buildings were razed in the 30's, leaving cellars, wells and miles of stone walls. Perhaps the grandest structure on the island was the Sears family summer home at the southern end, built in 1853 and burned in 1893.

After four generations of Sears family ownership, and having left their name to the town and the island, David IV sold Sears Island to the Bangor Investment Company. A failed plan to develop an island summer resort left Sears Island mostly for recreational pursuits for a while, but not completely. Smugglers were busy "rum running" during Prohibition years and arms were shipped to Europe during World War II.

The 1960s began decades of heavy industrial proposals, all of which threatened the natural resources and beauty of Sears Island. Left in their wake are the causeway, paved road and jetty, all remnants of a port proposal that ended in court in the 1990s. Squatters swarmed over the island until the State completed its purchase and drove them off.

Two planning initiatives involving many disparate interests have been conducted to decide the future of Sears Island, resulting in a 2009 conservation easement held by Maine Coast Heritage Trust on 601 acres, with the remaining land to be held for potential port development. The easement guarantees public access and preservation in perpetuity. Friends of Sears Island (FOSI) has responsibility for stewardship of the easement property.

Trails

Each of the four trails restored and maintained by FOSI creates its own aura, and each is under one-mile long and interconnect via the gravel road. The Homestead Trail, beginning at the big apple tree on the northeast beach, follows a portion of a former road to the old farm homestead, revealing cellar walls and steps gradually succumbing to nature's takeover. Several cedar bog bridges protect wetland areas, and huge oaks and white ashes recall the fields they grew up in. A vernal pool is almost hidden by summer foliage, but the chuckling of wood frogs in spring will tell you it is there.

Follow the trail to the gravel road, from which you can go on to other trails or turn back to the gate. Much of this road is lined with stone walls.

Farther along is the Loop Trail, wide and flat, with aromatic balsam firs and overarching branches. In winter snow the effect is magical. During a period of lumbering, there were four spurs leading off the arc of the main trail but now they are closed. The Blue Trail is a short distance beyond, leading downhill to the shore. There is a nice spot for lunch or to just sit and look out on the river. In the spring you may see blue flag irises just off the trail.

To access the Green Trail walk to the Homestead Trail outlet, cross over the open area and take the steps and bridge to the paved road. Turn left and walk a short distance to the Green Trail sign on your right. This trail will take you through ferns and mosses, past yellow birches, unusual stumps and multi-trunked trees, to the shore. If you are at low tide you may walk south to the jetty and go back along the paved road, or north to the gate. We recommend half tide or lower for either route.

—Marietta Ramsdell

Directions: Sears Island, 601 acres, Searsport
Maine Coast Heritage Trust and the Maine Department of Transportation

From Route 1 north & east of Downtown Searsport, turn onto Sears Island Road and continue across the causeway to the gate. Park on the causeway and note the parking restrictions near the gate.

Dogs permitted.

WebSource: www.friendsofsearsisland.org/ index.php/sears-island-maine

Two excellent reports elucidating the natural and cultural histories are available online: Report for Sears Island Joint Use Planning Committee by Lisa St. Hilaire, Maine Natural Areas Program, August 2007 (www.penbay. org/searsisland/si_mnap_review2007.pdf); and,

Natural Resource Inventory: Conservation Lands, Sears Island for Friends of Sears Island by Alison C. Dibble and Jake Maier (www.friendsofsearsisland.org)

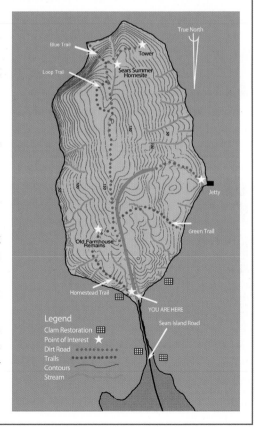

Left: The island is built up above sea level by sediments deposited by the melting glaciers. Spring melt from winter snows returns to the sea to begin the endless water cycle anew. Above: Fruiting bodies of the **scarlet waxy cap** *(Hygrocybe coccinea) emerge in the summer and fall through the soil of mixed hardwood/coniferous forests. The cap of this species starts out as the typically conic form, then flares in the later stages to flat or humped shape. (photo: Alison C. Dibble)*

Birds such as warblers and hummingbirds use lichen for nest-building material, in this case **boreal oakmoss lichen** *(Evernia mesomorpha) and* **beard lichen** *(Usnea sp.). Small mammals also use this fungus/alga symbiont for the same purpose. Numerous species of lichens are present in Maine; these long-lived, slow-growing organisms are epiphytic, existing on the surfaces of plants, especially trees. (photo: Alison C. Dibble)*

Perambulate the shoreline for the ever-changing views of tidal flats and out onto Penobscot Bay.

Skunk cabbage (Symplocarpus foetidus), *the botanical "early bird" of the vernal season, shows full leaf by early May on the west side, thriving among alders. It is salt tolerant and extremely hardy, surviving winter temperatures of well below 0°F. (photo: Des Fitzgerald)*

Rockweed (Fucus *spp.*), *with its distinctive gelatinous air bladders, rings most of the island, growing thickly in strands of up to three feet that float up vertically at high tide forming a sort of scaled down "forest."*

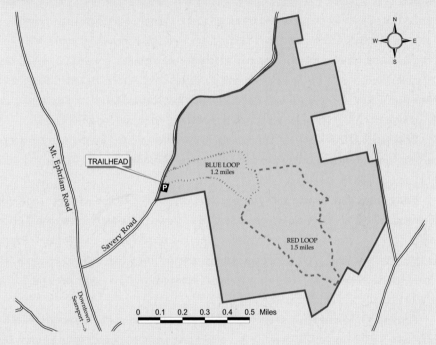

Long Cove Headwaters Preserve, 456 acres, Searsport, Coastal Mountains Land Trust

Not far from Sears Island, Long Cove Headwaters Preserve is land in recovery, an area that has served a succession of owners but now has come "home to rest." Under the protection of Coastal Mountains Land Trust, the diverse flora and fauna—including moose (*see* next page) and, no doubt, snowshoe hare—will be allowed to flourish, as nature doesn't wait long if given a chance. Abandoned logging roads are growing up in fir, spruce and pine that will become significant trees in no time. Every walk in these woods will be different. See it now. See it grow.

Directions: From downtown Searsport, drive North on Mt. Ephraim Road for approximately 2.6 miles. Turn right onto Savery Road and follow for approximately 0.6 miles. The parking area is on the right.

WebSource: www.coastalmountains.org/conserved_lands/preserves/longcoveheadwaters.htm

Maine Moose: Monarchs of the Forest

Everyone, it seems, would like to see a **moose** (*Alces alces*). Not surprisingly, during my 33-year career as a wildlife biologist in Maine, *"Where can I see a moose?"* was the most frequently asked question.

Today, as a retiree, my most popular wildlife watching trips are ones guiding people to favorite moose viewing hotspots. Moose are an iconic Maine species. The large mammals are, as one tourist guide noted correctly, "a highly charismatic, sexy species." If you're interested in seeing a moose, Maine is the place to be. With a statewide population of 76,000 moose, Maine has more "monarchs of the forest" than any state outside of Alaska. However, this does not mean that moose are easy to find. Although seen in Midcoast Maine, moose are far more abundant and more easily observed from western Maine north to Aroostook County.

Designated as Maine's official state animal in 1979, they are the world's largest member of the deer family (cervidae), inhabiting northern forests of North America, Europe and Russia. (In Europe moose are called "elk.")

Body Form. Moose have long legs, a heavy body, small tail, drooping nose and a "bell" or dewlap under the chin. Color ranges from golden brown in the summer to almost black in winter. They shed their winter coats in May to June, giving their pelage a ragged look. Standing six feet at the shoulder, adult moose are very tall animals that weigh 600-1500 pounds. They can live to be 25 years old. They are even-toed herbivores with very poor eyesight but with excellent hearing and olfactory senses.

Antlers. Only males have antlers that are shed or dropped during the winter. In healthy adult bulls, antlers may spread over five feet across and weigh 40 pounds, with as many as 30 tines (or spikes). Shape differs between individuals, depending on food quality, age and overall health. Collecting and selling shed antlers is big business. Many are made into light fixtures, rocking chairs and cribbage boards. In 1989, a Boston law firm paid a Greenville hunter several thousand dollars for a perfectly matched set of large moose antlers.

Mature bull moose shed their antlers once a year from November to January. New antlers begin growing the following spring. Antlers are formed of living tissue supplied by blood through a network of vessels covered with a soft, smooth skin called velvet. Eventually the tissue solidifies, the velvet is scraped off and the antlers become mineralized dead matter. Their main function is for display during the rutting season (mating season runs from mid-September to mid-October) and to show dominance within the herd.

True Story: One northern Maine couple tore apart a wall on their mobile home because a mounted moose head with five-foot antlers would not fit through the door. The mounted moose head was installed in the couple's living room. When the couple divorced, ownership of the head and antlers became hotly contested. The court awarded the mount to the woman because her name had appeared on the couple's moose-hunting permit. As compensation, the ex-husband was awarded the couple's two bear hounds.

Diet. They are browsers rather than grazers and obtain most of their summer food from aquatic plants such as water lilies and pondweed. Outside of summer, moose eat twigs, lichen, forest plants and bark from willows, poplars and striped maple (called moosewood). An adult bull moose consumes about 40-50 pounds of plant fiber each day; An adult cow moose with nursing twins may eat 60 pounds of plant food daily.

True Story: Varnished moose dung is sold as bracelets and necklaces in fine tourist shops in Greenville, Rangeley and other towns in the heart of moose country. A shiny dung necklace looks like a string of hamburgers.

Behavior. Moose are active throughout the day with activity peaks during dawn and dusk.

They are excellent swimmers, capable of moving through the water at six mph. They can also reach 35 mph in a burst of speed on land.

Moose are not normally aggressive, especially in water. But they can be unpredictably aggressive on land when hungry, tired or harassed by people. During mating season (mid-September to mid-October) bull moose are often antagonistic. They stop eating during the rut to breed as many cows as possible. Large bulls will lose about 200 pounds chasing, defending and breeding a harem of cows for a month. Cows with calves are very aggressive too. If you stand between a cow and a calf you'll learn firsthand why cow moose are considered the most dangerous animal in the Maine woods. (Hope that there is a nearby tree to climb. Adrenaline will make you a very fast climber.)

You can tell when a moose might attack if the long hairs on its hump are raised and its ears laid back. It may also lick its lips in a threatening gesture. That's a sign to run. Most charges are bluffs, warning you to get back. However, take each one seriously since even a young calf can cause significant injuries. A male moose may use his antlers to hold off a

(photo: Timothy C. Mayo, 2013 © all rights reserved)

predator. But when moose charge, they often kick forward with their sharp front hooves with devastating accuracy and results. And they can kick out in all directions. (You never want an ER doctor asking, "Explain again how you were bruised and cut?")

True Story: As a young teenager I was inspired by a moose radio-collaring show on "Mutual of Omaha's Wild Kingdom," a popular 1960s television program. Swimming moose in Minnesota were approached by teams of biologists in boats who jumped overboard to fit moose with a radio-collar device that gives off signals so biologists can track the animal with a receiver on land. (Attaching scientific equipment to moose in water is safer for moose and biologists.) Watching a young bull moose swimming on western Maine's Spencer Lake, a friend and I paddled our canoe alongside the animal. I hopped onto the moose's back and rode it for several minutes in the water. It was a foolish and insensitive act that I now regret, but it shows the corrupting power of television on mischievous boys.

Families. Females starting around two years of age are capable of producing young. After an eight-month gestation period, one or two young are born in early June. Calves weigh about 33 pounds at birth. Twins are somewhat common but triplets are rare. During the 1960s, moose with twins were rarely seen. Beginning in the 1970s through today, twins are more common because food resources have improved. Clear-cut harvesting of forests has benefited moose because young hardwood saplings, a favorite food, grow abundantly in the wake of extensive logging. Consequently, moose populations have doubled in the past 50 years.

Calves can follow their mother at three weeks of age and are completely weaned at five months. They stay with their mother for at least a year after birth, or if the cow is not pregnant the following year, a yearling may stay with its mother until age two. However, the cow will most likely breed again when her calf is four months old. By the following June, a few weeks before parturition, a mother moose will drive away her yearling(s), as they represent a threat to a calf. Calves occasionally become prey to black bears.

Viewing Locations. During summer, the best opportunities of seeing a moose are near freshwater wetlands, ponds and lakes in western and northern Maine. Unfortunately, moose are hard to find in the Midcoast area because they are less numerous here than in Maine's big woods. Outside of Baxter State Park, which reliably produces numerous moose sightings, the forest along the Long Falls Dam Road near Bigelow Mountain is one of my favorite moose watching areas. Bigelow and other western Maine mountains offer ideal scenery and exceptional moose habitat.

My twin brother and I were six-year-olds when we encountered our first Maine moose in 1958 on my grandparents' dairy farm near Farmington. Spooked by their border collie, a bull moose ran between the barn and farmhouse where my grandmother's clothesline stood. My grandfather's long johns were pulled off the clothesline by an antler of a frightened, bounding moose. Grandmother chased the moose across the pasture with her broom. Madder than a hornet, she returned several minutes later with my grandfather's soiled union suit.

True Story: Unlike former President George H. W. Bush, moose love broccoli. Save yourself the hassle of looking for moose in the woods by driving to the broccoli fields of Aroostook County. Smith's Farm in Presque Isle is a popular, standing-room-only moose café in mid-September when a dozen or more moose can be seen at one time eating broccoli.

Moose and Climate Change. Moose have numerous direct and indirect links to climate. They are an excellent indicator species of how climate change is affecting wildlife populations in general. They are superbly adapted to cold weather with a thick, soft winter undercoat and dark brown outer winter coat comprised of hollow hair shafts that trap air and provide wonderful insulation. Not only do they thrive in cold climates, increasing climate change data indicate that they may not be able to survive without it. As global temperatures rise, moose populations are declining throughout the northern hemisphere, from Norway to Minnesota. They are big-bodied, heavy, dark animals and as such absorb, generate and expel lots of heat. While calves begin to feel the cold at -22 degrees F, adults are able to withstand far colder temperatures. Moose are so well insulated from the cold that winter temperatures of 23 degrees F will make them pant. When winter temperatures rise above the mid-20s, moose require the shade of evergreen trees to remain cool. On winter days above 32 degrees, some moose will lie flat in the snow to dissipate body heat. Temperatures of 57 degrees F can cause moose to begin to suffer from heat stress.

Having no knowledge of where to go, Maine moose won't migrate north to Canada as global temperatures increase. They will stay in their home range and attempt to adjust by spending more time in the shade or cooling in ponds or climbing to higher elevations. The stress of high summer temperatures causes moose to stop eating. This in turn leaves them more vulnerable to winter starvation because they're unable to accumulate fat deposits needed to survive Maine's long winters. Moreover, cow moose that enter the winter in poor health are more likely to suffer poor reproductive success during the spring calving season. Pregnant cows in poor spring health have been known to absorb their fetus, deliver stillborn calves or give birth to calves that are too weak to rise and suckle.

Increasing temperature in the Northeast does not bode well for moose populations. Studies in nearby New Hampshire indicate that winter moose are suffering from blood-draining ticks (as many as 150,000 ticks per moose), brain-eating worms and disease exacerbated by climate change. Moose populations in Minnesota have dropped by nearly 70 percent since 2006. In response, Minnesota has closed its moose-hunting season for the first time in decades. Researchers there have also found that rising temperatures correlate to higher mortality rates. There is no end to the ripple effect of climate change, even for a single iconic species that has survived largely unchanged for a half-million years.

So the future of this species is unclear; perhaps the natural selective forces of nature will allow this magnificent animal to survive in Maine during the 21st century. Good luck and have fun finding Maine moose!

— Ron Joseph

Buds, flowers and bark of the red maple *(Acer rubrum)* make up part of the winter diet of moose and deer. This tree is one of the most abundant trees in the eastern U.S.

◆19◆ Sandy Point Beach Park: *Much More than a Beach*

Ospreys are nesting opportunists, such as on old pilings from a former pier, or other artificial structures like power line towers and navigational beacons. Double-crested cormorants also nest on this remnant framework. This view looks upriver toward the Penobscot Narrows Bridge.

VARIED HABITATS SUCH AS MARINE SHORELINE, upland woods, marshy spruce bog and freshwater ponds support distinct types of plants and animals adapted to the specific conditions therein. This site offers all the above in a hundred acres, just minutes from Route 1. Where industrial activity once predominated culminating in a fertilizer plant in the mid-20th century, the Town of Stockton Springs wisely conserved this land that now is returned to nature's activity.

We toured the Park in early May, just before the rise in average temperature on the Maine coast that pushes out leafy growth from trees whose buds have been swelling since late winter. The sandy beach on the northeast shoulder of the park results from the eroding bluff of the Sandy Point Esker located just to the south, a remnant of the melting glacier some 12,000 years ago. Fossil seashells eroded from marine sediments can be found on the beach (*see:* www.maine.gov/dacf/mgs/explore/surficial/sites/apr01. pdf). Excavations in the early 1900s revealed artifacts (wampum, beads, iron pots) and burial sites of native Americans dating roughly to the period of early contact with Europeans.

Above: Remains of an old dam show through the mud of the stream mouth on western side of the preserve, a sign of coastal commerce from long ago. Left: Early May on the Midcoast brings forth the ferns of many species, uncoiling from winter dormancy.

Sandy spits build up where tidal currents shape the stream sediments, this one just south of the stream. The line of dried seaweed in the foreground shows the height of the last spring tide, occurring during the full and new moon phases of the month.

Ascending into the woods brings the visitor to the beaver pond, with a wooded overlook from which to peer down to the pond through openings in the foliage. Stay here awhile in the warm months and you may see beavers swimming and hooded mergansers preening on a fallen log. Or a kingfisher (*see* sidebar) chittering from a perch, or warblers feeding in the tops of trees growing from below, their canopy visible here almost at eye level. After the pond, a loop trail leads through the swampy interior to the shoreline on the southwest side of the preserve. At lower tides, it is also possible to walk the shoreline around the point and back to the parking area.

Forward thinking by the state's Bureau of Parks and Lands led to the purchasing of this land for conservation. The Town of Stockton Springs developed the trail system and manages the park, thereby setting aside another piece of precious shorefront for the benefit of all, most importantly the animals and plants living here.

American beachgrass (Ammophila breviligulata), *highly salt tolerant, grows from Canada to the Carolinas in sandy areas and is an important plant for dune stabilization and erosion control. Each clump may grow up to 100 stems per year and spread several feet laterally by way of horizontal underground shoots called rhizomes.*

Beavers have created a freshwater habitat well worth perusing for ducks and songbirds and, of course, the beavers themselves. These opportunistic engineers of the rodent tribe were extirpated from large sections of the Northeast in the 1800s but recovered when farmland reverted to forest and trapping ceased.

A split-plank boardwalk leads through a marshy area fed by the outflow of the beaver pond. This complex plant community, dominated by spruce and sphagnum moss, is adapted to the acidic conditions (ca. pH 4) that result from the buildup of undecomposed plant material.

Sandy Point Beach, 100 acres, Stockton Springs, Maine Bureau of Parks and Lands

Directions:

From Stockton Springs, take Routes 1 and 3 East for about 2 miles. Turn right onto Hersey Retreat Road and park at the end of the road by the beach.

WebSource: www9.informe.org/lmf/projects/project_detail.php?project=1567,

Sexual Dimorphism: Vive la Différence

Sexual dimorphism is a tidy phrase that means males and females of a species can be distinguished by their size, color, shape or structure. Such phenotypic differences are familiar: male African lions have their manes; eastern whitetails, their antlers; and the peacock, his stunning plumage. The breeding plumage of many Maine birds provides other examples — the male wood duck, the hooded merganser, cardinal, pileated or other woodpeckers, or any of the spring warblers — to name a few. For the most part, we take this dissimilarity for granted, which is to say, that when one member of a pair stands out, we assume it's the male.

Typically, our male songbirds are larger and/or more brightly colored than the female. This predominant pattern is understood to be the result of sexual selection. The bigger or more brightly colored male with the robust voice selects and defends the desirable territory, as a result of which he is favored over other males by the female. By contrast, the cryptically colored female is advantaged when she sits on her nest. There, her relative invisibility makes it less likely that she will be spotted by a predator. Such typical sexual dimorphism is not universal, however. Two examples: male and female adult common loons look alike, but the male outweighs the female. On the other hand, while killdeer also look alike, in this instance the female killdeer is larger than her mate. Or consider the eastern belted kingfisher: male and female are the same size, but for some reason she is the one who is brightly colored. Such phenotypic diversity is difficult to explain in any terms other than a competition for survival, but the mechanisms — the why and how — for this are not always understood. What follows is a narrow window into the complicated world of sexual dimorphism and a couple of suggested explanations.

If the larger and/or more brightly colored male represents typical sexual dimorphism, what are the noteworthy exceptions? Raptors are the first to come to mind. Among many of these birds, the female is larger. Numerous hypotheses have been advanced to explain this phenomenon. The authors of *The Birder's Handbook* propose that reversed sexual dimorphism in raptors is closely correlated to prey agility. They support their hypothesis into three categories. The first classification includes accipiters and falcons, such as sharp-shinned hawks and peregrine falcons, i.e., birds that specialize in hunting fast-moving birds. The females of these species are much larger than their mates. The authors advance their argument with the observation that a large female is relatively safe from attack from the smaller male, while he is well equipped to provide food for her and the young. In other words, she gets what she needs without threat of violence to herself. As peregrines are superbly evolved to kill other birds, the males "represent the greatest threat to their own mates." The second category includes the buteos, such as red-tailed and rough-legged hawks, which hunt for small mammals that are relatively slower. These birds occupy a middle ground, the female being only slightly larger than the male. The last category includes the vultures, which primarily eat carrion or the relatively helpless young of

Female eastern belted kingfisher, wet from a dive. Unlike most bird species, she is more colorful than the male, an example of reverse sexual dimorphism. (photo: David White)

other species, i.e., prey that is inert or nearly so. Male and female turkey and black vultures incubate their eggs. With these birds, male and female are the same size.

Owls offer another example of reverse sexual dimorphism. In many, but not all the species, the female is larger than her mate, and again several explanations have been put forward. Arne Lundberg, a Scandinavian ornithologist writing about European owls, suggests that, given a division of labor, a small, agile male with short wings is best suited for hunting, while a larger female has a better chance of survival in cold weather without food — at least when the interval between feedings is long and food is served up by the male. In other words, unlike the peregrine, the smaller male owl is not a threat to his mate, but his smaller size provides him with a better chance of hunting success.

The **eastern belted kingfisher** (*Ceryle alcyon*) — sexes are same size, similar behavior, but different plumage — is another easy bird to recognize. (One early Maine settler, aptly observed: "Kings fishers, which breed in the spring in holes in the Sea-banks...." J. Josselyn, 1674.) The female is distinguished from her consort only by a chestnut colored band across her breast below the slate-blue band that is found on both genders. Their large, crested head, massive bill, the white spot in front of the eye, chattering call, and dramatic headfirst plunges into fresh- or saltwater — be it a stream, river, pond or tidal body — are unmistakable, especially here in Maine where it is our only kingfisher. With kill in hand, the kingfisher may retreat to an excavated burrow located near the top of a bank. This burrow may be up to 15 feet long at the end of which the female lays five to eight white eggs. (According to Audubon these eggs provide "fine eating," although extracting eggs from the protective grasp of the parents is said to be a challenge.) Unlike an open-air nest, the burrow confers protection, and there is no need for camouflage by either male or female, both of whom incubate. A kingfisher's diet includes amphibians, insects, reptiles, and small birds — sparrows, for example — as well as oysters, squid, butterflies, and moths, but small fish are its preferred prey. On occasion it will strike one that is too large to carry away and will be forced to release its victim. Just like owls, they eject the indigestible portions of their food as pellets. Parents instruct the young fledglings to retrieve morsels of food that the adult drops into the water from perches. Maine kingfishers generally

The kingfisher generally prefers to burrow into sandy banks that include a mixture of clay and fine gravel, as in this instance. Note the fresh tailings.

winter as far south as northern South America. One might describe them as reluctant migrants as they have been seen in-state during every month of the year accept January and February.

What, then, is the role of sexual dimorphism, its reverse, or its absence? There are good explanations in some instances, but not in all. Why there is a colorful breast band on the female kingfisher, for example, is hard to say—and the catch-all of sexual selection begs further study. It seems that in the end there is no "one size fits all" explanation, especially if the topic is isolated from other factors. On the contrary, there are an infinite variety of evolutionary strategies, among which the phenotype is only a single, visible parameter. Perhaps the single endpoint to keep in mind is that whatever leads to the breeding success of the individual over its lifetime will be passed on to its offspring. What holds true for raptors may not apply to other birds, and vice versa.

—T. O.

◆ 20 ◆ Three Places to Paddle: Sandy Point, Ruffingham Meadows and St. Clair Preserve

photo: Des FitzGerald

T HOUGH WALKING IS PREDOMINANTLY HOW WE VIEW NATURE, there is also the water-borne way. Paddled craft allow us to travel in a relatively quiet manner within the ecosystems of ponds, lakes, streams and rivers usually seen from afar. These three sites are all human-made water bodies with small dams creating acres of water and marshland where formerly small streams flowed; they are offered as a sampling of Midcoast paddling opportunities to nature-watch.

In whatever regard you view hunting, wildlife management areas (WMA), though created to foster game species in particular, nevertheless provide important state-owned and maintained refuges for the natural world as a whole. These shallow-water impoundments produce marshland important to wetland species, perhaps especially so for migrating ducks and geese.

Coastal fog recedes between evergreen-capped hills on an early spring morning at Sandy Point WMA.

Sandy Point Wildlife Management Area

Even if you don't have a watercraft, this is still a good quick-stop, right off Route 1, to view birds and mammals such as beavers and muskrats in and around the impounded marsh. But better yet, launch a canoe or kayak by the dam and paddle through the shallow marshland among the water lilies and wild rice and meadow sedges.

The state management plan describes the area as follows:

> This small, impounded wetland hosts an exemplary Unpatterned Fen Ecosystem and habitat for least bitterns. Sandy Point WMA (560 acres) includes 407 acres of wading bird and waterfowl habitat and 16 acres of deer wintering area. Open wetlands total 301 acres, while forested wetland total 41 acres. The parcel is within the Penobscot River drainage.

Visits in different seasons will naturally yield different displays of biota, as plants progress through their warm weather cycle, and birds migrate north then south again in various months. Mammals such as muskrat might be seen in any season. (In another locale, we once saw several in February sunning under a tent-like ice "greenhouse"

Sandy Point Wildlife Management Area, 560 acres, Stockton Springs, Maine Department of Inland Fisheries and Wildlife

Directions:

In Stockton Springs head north (east) on US 1 to the village of Sandy Point. Continue on US 1 for 0.8 mile, drive under a railroad overpass, and turn left on Muskrat Road on the immediate left (west), just past the overpass. The road to Sandy Point WMA is the first road on the right; look for a sign for Sandy Point WMA by the entrance. Drive down this road and park near the dam. Note that the road is somewhat rough, and can have deep mud puddles in spring and after summer rains.

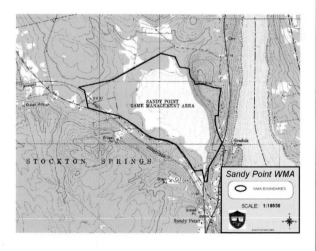

Dogs allowed on leash.

WebSource: www.maine.gov/ifw/wildlife/land/department/region_b/sandypoint.htm

---

Well-maintained beaver lodge in the central marsh is located among smaller muskrat mounds in the shallower vegetated areas. This neatly felled red maple at the parking area shows the brownish inner bark, or cambium, that nutritionally supplies the protein, carbohydrates and sugars to beavers and other dendrophagus (bark-eating) animals.

pushed up by pressure in river ice.) In fact, a muskrat farm existed here starting in the 1920s when the area was first impounded.

For birders seeking to check off a hard-to-find species, the **least bittern** *(Ixobrychus exilis),* observed here by state biologists, provides one of many incentives. The state's inventory of wildlife cites over 75 bird species, 16 fish, 17 reptiles and amphibians and 31 mammals, all living within the complex wetland and upland plant communities.

Above: Territories are established early in the season: this pair of Canada geese will nest in the marsh, raise a brood and return south in the fall.
*Right: Much of Sandy Pont WMA comprises what is termed an Unpatterned Fen Ecosystem, prime habitat for the **least bittern** (Ixobrychus exilis), a Maine species of special concern. (photo: David White)*

Ruffingham Meadows Wildlife Management Area

There's nothing more satisfying then setting off by canoe on a glassy calm morning in search of quiet adventure, be it for plant, beast or something more personal. This is what Ruffingham Meadows can offer—and deliver. Ruffingham is wide open, but it's also intimate: a place for binoculars, an old-fashioned magnifying glass or a glass-bottomed tube with which to watch underwater life in the shallow waters. It is also a place to sit still, perhaps covered over by camo-netting, and let the curious muskrat come to you, the wary duck emerge from the wild rice, the turtle take a breath. Bring a seat for your canoe and make yourself comfortable. Go at dawn or go at sunset, but go. Don't let the stillness deceive you. In a quiet way, there's a lot going on here.

— T. O.

Wild rice has been planted by the state and grows in abundance at Ruffingham Meadows, as seen from the put-in on a calm fall day, perfect for paddling.

Above: Male **hooded merganser** *(Lophodytes cucullatus.* photo: *Karl Gerstenberger).*
Left: Decaying pond lilies and fall colors signal the coming of nature's winter dormancy.

196

Nesting boxes are used by hooded mergansers, wood ducks and goldeneyes—sometimes by more than one species at once, called "egg-dumping," an attempt by each female to reproduce letting the other do the incubating. State biologists check boxes during the winter (see next page) when ice affords easy access. (photo: Ashley Malinowski.

Ruffingham Meadows Wildlife Management Area, 704 acres, Searsmont
Maine Department of Inland Fisheries and Wildlife

Directions: From Belfast, travel west on Route 3 for approximately 12 miles to North Searsmont. Parking is on the right side of the road in a gravel parking lot marked by a sign.

WebSource: www.maine.gov/ifw/wildlife/management/wma/region_b/ruffinghammeadow.htm

Duck Box Maintenance

Maine Department of Inland Fisheries and Wildlife (MDIFW) biologists take advantage of the thick ice and cooler temperatures of winter to investigate activity that may have occurred during the past spring in duck boxes across the state. Duck boxes are placed 5–10 feet off the ground or water surface in wetlands areas where natural snags and dead trees necessary for cavity-nesting waterfowl are absent. These boxes are ideal for wood ducks, hooded mergansers and goldeneyes. Metal sheeting is wrapped around the tree or pole below the box to prevent predators like raccoons, squirrels and snakes from climbing up to the box. The bottom is filled with about four inches of pine shavings to supply an insulating layer in which the female duck can lay her eggs.

The eight on the left are hooded merganser eggs. The nine on the right are wood duck eggs. Both of these species are capable of "dump nesting." (photo: Ashley Malinowski)

Each winter, biologists head out to bogs and streams to check and refresh the nest boxes. The box number is recorded along with the contents of the box and how many species used the box. Some cavity-nesting species are parasitic nesters: they will "dump" their eggs in a box being used by another hen of the same or different species in an attempt to have that hen raise the intruded eggs. When this happens, the box is often abandoned. The failed eggs are identified by species, counted and removed from the box. The number of eggs hatched—indicated by the presence of eggshells and the soft membrane found on the inside surface of the hard shell—is also recorded. Old shavings and any other refuse such as rodent droppings, leaves and moss that may have been dragged into the box are removed and fresh shavings are installed. This box cleaning helps reduce diseases that may be spread to the duck or her eggs.

In the spring, when the ducks are incubating eggs, biologists return to boxes to catch and band them and check for overall health before returning them to the nests. After hatching, when the ducklings have left the box to follow their mothers, biologists return again to conduct brood surveys, conducted multiple times in a season to determine how many survive to a certain age. Boxes can increase reproductive success, and banding and brood surveys are an important step in determining population growth and the dynamics of Maine's duck species. Most of the duck boxes that the MDIFW monitors and maintains are located in our Wildlife Management Areas. The duck box program is but one example of how Maine's wildlife biologists improve wildlife habitat on these public lands.

— Ashley Malinowski

Sedge Wren

One of the more elusive members of the Ruffingham Meadows bird community is the diminutive 0.32-ounce **sedge wren** (*Cistothorus platensis*)—probably more often heard than seen, but nonetheless present. These are highly secretive birds, so much so that not much is known about their natural history. *C. platensis* was once referred to as the short-billed marsh wren, but the name was too easily confused with its larger Troglodytidae cousin, the **marsh wren** (*Cistothorus palustris*), also present in Ruffingham. Both are difficult to spot and are frequently identified only by song. Dependent as they are on wetlands, one might assume that they are an at-risk species. Who, after all, has not read about a local marsh being replaced by a mall, or an inconveniently located wetland being filled in to make room for a "vital" parking lot? Multiply these reports throughout the year-round range of the sedge wren, and how could they not be at-risk? It therefore came as a surprise to learn that the International Union for the Conservation of Nature (IUCN) Red List identifies *C. platensis* as a species of Least Concern, with an upward trending population. What does that signify?

One way to appreciate the sedge wren's survival strategy is to consider its complicated, highly nomadic, short distance, and difficult-to-simplify migration and breeding pattern (a fuller understanding of which can be gained from an article by Herkert et al. in *Birds of North America*). An essential aspect of this is the wren's extensive and fragmented seasonal distribution. The range map in the *Sibley Guide to Birds* has green dots that indicate "rare occurrence." Taken as a whole, these dots reveal how the species finesses the ephemeral nature of its preferred breeding habitat—the result of fluctuating water levels, grazing, mowing, planting, etc. It turns out that sedge wrens respond with a combination of high mobility, low nest fidelity, and a really long, double-barreled breeding season that begins as early as May and continues into September. The earlier nesting period is concentrated in the upper-midwest and Canada, while the second occurs mid- to late summer. Certain birds fly north and breed; then, in late summer, they go south and breed a second time. The result is that breeding on the eastern fringe of the sedge wren's range may not take place until July or August, later than one might expect. According to Herkert, "Late nesting may represent re-nesting attempts by individuals arriving from elsewhere within their range or could be an adaptive response of local birds to delayed availability of moist but unflooded grassland habitat." In either event, breeding cannot be further delayed, as insects are the wren's primary source of nourishment, and their abundance tapers with the onset of frosty temperatures.

There is another curious and tantalizing dimension to sedge wren behavior. "The sedge wren's communication system also appears to be adapted to high population mobility, suggesting that opportunistic breeding has occurred for a long time rather than being of recent origin, such as in response to recent agricultural changes or habitat loss." (Herkert, et al.) In other words, the disjunct populations and nomadic behavior have been around for millennia and are not the result of human activity. There is, incidentally, no plumage change during this five-month breeding window.

Sedge wren on **reed canary grass,** *Phalaris arundinacea.*
(photo: Chris Buelow)

The upshot is that *C. platensis* seasonally goes where it may not have gone before, de-camps in response to local circumstance, then retreats to a second, more southern location to raise another family well into the time when many other species are heading to their winter range. This behavior is not dramatic; it's barely visible. And, though incompletely understood, it's no less astonishing.

Another question: What are sedges, and how do I distinguish them from grasses? It seemed an appropriate question to ask while paddling around in a sedge meadow filled with wild rice, especially as *C. platensis* selects upright sedges for its nest sites. According to biologist Glen Mittelhauser, one of the authors of *Sedges of Maine: A Field Guide to Cyperaceae* (University of Maine Press, 2013), an easy way to keep the three plant families apart is to remember the ditty: "Sedges have edges. Rushes are round. Grasses have joints down to the ground." Next spring when we return to watch the courtship of bitterns and look for sora rails, I'll be checking the plants as well. It will be easy to tell one from another.

What Does Least Concern Mean? The goal of the IUCN Red List is "To provide information and analyses on the status, trends and threats to species in order to inform and catalyze action for biodiversity conservation." An easy way to get a handle on this immense undertaking is to look at the established categories of risk.

Least Concern (LC) means that a species or taxon has been identified and evaluated but does not qualify as Threatened, or even Near Threatened. There are two rankings below LC. The bottom category is Not Evaluated (NE); above that is Data Deficient (DD). Organisms in these groups have not been assessed and therefore are not eligible for risk categorization. Put another way, it is good to be of Least Concern, at least if you believe that there is safety in numbers. Least Concern means the IUCN has its eyes on you. They'll know if your world starts to come apart. But here's the rub: As a member of the Least Concern Club, you are one of many and may possibly be overlooked during the next IUCN review. But, sooner or later, should your circumstance deteriorate, you will be "promoted" from LC to Near Threatened (NT). From there, if the world is still against you, you may progress to Vulnerable (VU). Thereafter, if your luck has truly run out, you may progress — one might better say "fall" — past a series of way-points laid out as if the IUCN powers-that-be were reluctant to admit defeat: Endangered (EN), Critically Endangered (CE or CR), Extinct in the Wild (EW). And, finally, Extinction (EX), the irreversible end of the road. Or is it?

In 2012, 2000 species were added to the Red List, four of which were designated Extinct. But then, according to Wikipedia, two species were rediscovered and withdrawn from Extinction. This is not as bizarre as one might imagine. The ivory-billed woodpecker, now presumed to be irrevocably extinct, walked back and forth across this boundary for years, becoming a poster child for a generation of wishful birders. Cryptic or other hard-to-see species can understandably be overlooked, only to be subsequently found. (When queried, an IUCN respondent informed me that, as far as he was aware, three amphibian species had been down-listed in 2012 from EX to CR. He referred me to the IUCN Summary Statistics website: http://www.iucnredlist.org/about/summary-statistics#Table_7, where I might find the names of all species whose status had changed since 2006.)

The work performed by the IUCN is both a window beyond our Midcoast landscape and a reminder of how interconnected all the inhabitants are, ourselves included. In fact, the IUCN can unexpectedly warp one's own perspective. As it happens, just like the sedge wren, we too are a data point: in 2008 the IUCN designated *Homo sapiens* a species of Least Concern.

Still nagged by a sense of uncertainty about the status of the sedge wren, I checked the Endangered Species list for the Maine Department of Inland Fisheries & Wildlife. There it was: *C. platensis.* It was also on New Hampshire's list. And that of Massachusetts, as well as Vermont's. In fact, according to the aforementioned Herkert et al. (http://bna.birds.cornell.edu/bna), the reference of choice for what's what in the birding world, at least nine states have expressed concern for the sedge wren, as has the National Audubon Society (from 1982 to 1986). Even the United States Fish and Wildlife Service (USFWS) was worried. The Service has categorized the species as a "Migratory Nongame Bird of Management Concern" owing to its dependence on vulnerable or restricted habitats.

— T. O.

St. Clair Preserve

This preserve is made up of mostly hardwood and spruce-fir forest with cedar swamps and bog surrounding the 95-acre Knight Pond. The preserve is bounded to the south by a conservation easement held by Coastal Mountains Land Trust and the 680-acre Ducktrap Wildlife Preserve to the west. The original 240 acres was donated by the Bok family in 1962 and named after the caretaker of that property, Eugene St. Clair. In 1988 a second 53-acre tract along the southwestern shore of the pond was donated by Hans and Brigitta Gautschi.

For access to Knight Pond and the thoroughfare through to Pitcher Pond canoeists and kayakers can launch at the town beach. The only walking trail on the preserve is a 500-foot woods road out to Stubby Point on Knight Pond.

The preserve is a rarity in being a freshwater pond so close to the coast that is uninhabited and open to the public. The 50-acre bog within the preserve that forms the north and south boundary of the thoroughfare gradually conducts water west from Knight Pond into Pitcher Pond. This half-mile stretch of shallow stream-like water can only be paddled by canoe or kayak and may be too shallow to traverse in the drier late summer months.

The northern portion of the bog is populated with the rare **Atlantic white cedar** *(Chamaecyparis thyoides)*, one of the first trees in this country to have been used for organ pipes because of its natural resonance. This is one of only a dozen stands of this species in Maine and it may well be the most northern stand of these trees on the East Coast. The trees are scattered and are small to medium in size. In addition the **New England bluet** *(Enallagma laterale)* has been seen in both Knight Pond and Pitcher Pond. This striking damselfly is more common to the south and is becoming increasingly rare throughout its limited, mostly coastal range from Maine to the mid-Atlantic states. Knight Pond is populated by a number of fish species including small mouth bass, chain pickerel, yellow perch and in the spring of the year anadromous spawning alewives which reach the pond via the Ducktrap River and its tributary Kendall Brook.

*Above: Blooming in late May, the showy **rhodora azalea** (Rhododendron canadense) is easy to spot among the emerging foliage of the wetland plants. Its alternate name, swamp azalea, identifies its wetland habitat. Right: Widely distributed throughout the U. S. and Canada, the **American white water lily** (Nymphaea odorata) blooms principally during the morning hours; its rhizomes (spreading roots) are a favored food of muskrats.*

St. Clair Preserve, 293 acres, Northport, The Nature Conservancy

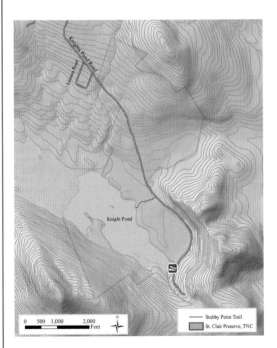

Directions: Take US Route 1 to Northport and turn west onto Beech Hill Road. Go approximately 2 miles and make a left onto Knight Pond Rd. The preserve begins just south of the stone wall beyond the red farmhouse. The road ends at the town beach and the preserve is located to the north of beach and to the southwest of the pond. The southwest portion of the preserve can be accessed via canoe from the boat launch at the town beach.

No pets are allowed.

WebSource: www.nature.org/ourinitiatives/regions/northamerica/unitedstates/maine/

Macrobdella decora. (photo: Tripp Davenport)

Hirudotherapy: The Diverse Roles of Leeches

"Dr. Rinker, what are these things attached to my legs?" asked one of my students years ago during our springtime field work in a freshwater marsh in New York State.

I replied with more fascination than with sensitivity to my student's concern: "Wow, Andrea, those things are leeches! A bunch of them, too." But then, in an attempt to turn her mounting panic into a teachable moment, I added, "And each student gets an extra-credit point for every attached leech!"

Andrea and her lab partner literally hopped back into the muck, splashing and yelping like crazed marsh-muckers, refusing to emerge from the cool dark water without counting at least a dozen of these bloodsucking worms attached to their ankles and calves. Other students, less courageous, quietly edged their way to the shore to shake off the hungry horror awaiting them at water's edge. (I knew some of the boys were thinking anxiously about that much-fêted scene from Rob Reiner's 1986 movie, "Stand by Me," when four young male friends take a short cut through a local swamp only to discover leeches in their underpants.) Andrea received high marks for her lab work that day!

Altogether we added up about 20 individual specimens of the **North American medicinal leech,** *Macrobdella decora.* None had begun to feed so were easily removed with a fingernail slipped slightly under their oral and anal suckers. However much leeches are reviled by the world at-large, Andrea and her classmates quickly focused on the unknown with a childlike sense of wonder. "Dr. Rinker, these animals are really beautiful."

Indeed, the segmented, two-inch-long relatives of the common earthworm have an olive-green color with dark, sometimes reddish spots along their upper surface and a reddish-orange undercoating. Further, with five pairs of eyes, both male and female sex organs, and a mouth full of tiny teeth arranged in a tripartite jaw (much like the Mercedes Benz emblem), the North American medicinal leech presents a full biology lesson with each writhe and wriggle in its unique natural history. And, like other sanguivorous leeches—some kinds don't suck blood at all, but consume their prey whole like those giant worms in the ravine portrayed in "King Kong"—the saliva of the North American medicinal leech contains a gumbo of enzymes that act as an anesthetic, vasodilator and anticoagulant. For a much-maligned animal found throughout eastern North America from southern Canada to the Carolinas and along the Mississippi River drainages, it provides a trove of pharmaceutical treats for molecular biologists and health professionals.

Scientists have identified over 65 kinds of leeches in North America — about a tenth of the 650–700 species or more recognized worldwide. They are probably present in most Maine lakes but, being chiefly nocturnal, are observed infrequently. Found in a variety of habitats including lakes, ponds, marshes, springs and slow streams protected from wave action, they show their greatest abundance in areas with stones, sticks, plants and other debris to which they can adhere and find concealment from predators and sunlight. Disturbances in the water, such as splashing and marsh-mucking, alert the worms via tactile stimulation that a blood meal awaits. They are important in forest and stream food chains, serving as both predator and prey. Some invertebrates, fish, turtles, frogs and birds feed upon leeches that, in turn, feed upon some invertebrates, turtles, frogs and birds, and mammals such as deer, beaver, skunks and humans. Adding to their oddity, a few species of leeches even nurture their young by providing food, transportation and protection—unusual behavior among the vermiform. Altogether leeches in North America and around the planet carry out an undervalued but irreplaceable ecological link in nature too often overlooked in our repugnance toward their blood-sucking behavior.

Leeches are members of the Phylum Annelida that includes polychaetes (also referred to as bristleworms, the class includes lugworms and sandworms) and oligochaetes (a second class that includes aquatic blackworms and terrestrial earthworms). Structurally, leeches resemble the oligochaetes. Like them, leeches are composed of a series of body segments. Unlike oligochaetes, however, they lack the bristles (or chaetae) used for locomotion by other annelids, replacing them instead with oral and anal suckers. Employing DNA sequencing, tax-onomists believe that the ancestors of leeches were probably freshwater worms feeding off the surface debris of fish and crustaceans. Then, as the earliest land vertebrates emerged from their watery environment, the ancestors of modern-day leeches surfaced with them, using a pene-trating proboscis to drink the vital body fluids of their prey.

Later, some types evolved a set of three jaws to rasp the skin, complemented with salivary chemicals to drink their host's blood clot-free and to prevent inflammation. And, since blood does not make for a balanced diet (though it's a good energy source), leeches also evolved special chambers in their throats to house endosymbiotic bacteria, some of which are found nowhere else on the planet except in these little chambers of gore, to help synthesize nutrients otherwise unavailable. The North American medicinal leech seems descended from an aquatic ancestor that evolved first in freshwater, then became terrestrial and finally returned to freshwater. Nonetheless, *M. decora* still emerges from water to lay its egg cases on land; the young leeches must crawl back into the water. The meandering evolutionary path of leeches is just as engaging and odd as their present-day ecology.

Apart from their ecological roles, another benefit of leeches is their therapeutic potential. In 2004, the U.S. Food and Drug Administration approved them as "medical devices." Their saliva contains protease inhibitors that are antiviral compounds. Their blood-sucking habits prevent venous congestion in plastic and reconstructive surgery. And, as mentioned previously, leeches have a soup of chemicals in their bodies now under study for their pharmaceutical properties as anesthetics, anticoagulants and vasodilators. In fact, some of their wide-ranging medicinal applications stretch back into ancient Rome.

Hirudotherapy (from the Latin word *hirudo*, meaning "leech") is a widespread treatment that uses medicinal leeches in healing various kinds of illnesses and diseases. Approved by many countries, it is an efficacious remedy based upon centuries of experimentation. Metaphorically, hirudotherapy is also a treatment that extends beyond human health into the ecological and even ethical realms. Leeches can be said to have a significant healing influence in their respective ecosystems to bring balance in waterways and wetlands damaged by human activity. They also challenge what we value in the world around us. We've unhinged the natural world thus far with our proliferation; our biases reveal a disordered view of Earth's essential biodiverse richness. Maybe, if we confront our inordinate fear of creatures such as parasitic leeches, and understand their roles fundamentally in the economy of nature, we may exercise that eternal maxim of "Physician, heal thyself."

— H. Bruce Rinker, Ph.D.

Epilogue: Coastal Maine's Past and Uncertain Future

Somewhere about 10,000 years ago the Redpaint People arrived on the coast of Maine where they found a wealth of resources, notably Atlantic cod, which were big, easy to catch and wonderful to preserve by drying. For millennia they subsisted on this and other species because the Gulf of Maine was an extremely productive ecosystem.

What is so unique about coastal Maine, the Gulf of Maine and the western North Atlantic is that despite the abundance of fish along this coastal ecosystem there are relatively few species. Shockingly few, in fact. Maine's coast has no native intertidal crabs, no tide pool sculpins and no abalone, whereas similar coasts worldwide have those critters. In addition, Maine's coast has only a few species of kelp, only one sea urchin and one limpet snail. Compare this to central California where there are a bunch of kelp and kelp-eating species, including three species of sea urchins, five species of abalone and 17 species of limpet snails. Maine has only about 100 species of fish in its coastal water compared to twice that number at our latitude along the European coast.

The low number of species is likely because the North Atlantic is a relatively young ocean (it wasn't around during most of the time dinosaurs roamed the world). It was warm until the poles cooled around 14 million years ago. The northern cold water biota at that time was primarily in the North Pacific so that became the source for "inoculating" the North Atlantic. Our cod, sea urchins, kelp, limpets and lots of other critters came from the North Pacific. However, the inoculation was incomplete, so we only have a subset of the species found in the vast North Pacific. For example, harbor and gray seals came from the Pacific, but sea lions and fur seals did not. Other species such as sea otters made it into the North Atlantic, but failed to persist and went extinct.

So we have a beautiful rocky shore with the fewest species of any rocky shore in the world. So what? One consequence of having a productive ecosystem (lots of plankton and nutrients in our waters), but low diversity is that all that productivity must channel through relatively few species. This has a tendency to create booms and busts. Perhaps the abundance of cod was one such boom (although that is a species best known for its "bust" these days). Cod declined precipitously as fishing capacity increased. The species that had been prey to cod and other predators — now rare due to overfishing — increased explosively. As a result, we've seen remarkable increases in sea urchins, crabs and, of course, lobsters.

Lobsters are a special case. First of all, they are a homegrown North Atlantic species (there is no Pacific equivalent to our clawed lobster). However, they are also vulnerable to attack from big predators. They have claws, but a large cod or wolfish can dispatch a slow moving Maine lobster easily (often by attacking the tail). So lobsters had to be near shelters and forage at night in a sea of hungry and abundant predatory fishes. Centuries of heavy fishing on cod, hake, haddock and other large predatory fish provided a risk-free coastal zone for lobsters. One could argue that we have *"domesticated"* the Gulf of Maine by removing predators and adding food (bait) for this highly valued marine resource.

Beginning in the early 1940s lobster abundance increased and held steady for nearly 40 years. Then beginning around the early 1980s lobster abundance began steadily increasing along the coast of Maine and the Canadian Maritimes. Landings went from under 10,000 metric tons in the early 1980s to over 50,000 metric tons in recent years. The egg-bearing lobster abundance increased and expanded offshore. The catch per unit effort has been steadily increasing over that time, which means that the lobster population is outpacing our ability to catch them.

Add to the predator-prey feedback I just described the socio-economic feedback we face today. While the loss of predators results in lower risk of predation, the hyper-abundance of lobsters today (exceeding two per meter square in large areas) creates a higher risk of collapse from disease and certainly a higher consequence of such as decline.

In recent years, over 80% of Maine's marine resource value has come from the lobster. However, this benefit comes with greater costs and risks than ever before. The cost of bait, for example, has increased in terms of price per pound because as lobsters increased in abundance so did traps and the need for trap bait. Until recently, the greatest tonnage of landings in Maine was herring (the predominant bait for traps). Now, the tonnage of lobsters landed exceeds that of herring. Herring must be imported along with other bait species. Some of this bait is being shipped to Maine from as far away as New Zealand.

Add to that increased cost the increased risk of fishing a lucrative monoculture. Boats, traps and licenses are specific only for Maine's lobster. If anything happens to this one species, the maritime fabric that defines the Maine coast would be in jeopardy. Today, because so many more fishermen have borrowed money to purchase their fishing boats, they need considerable annual income to persist. Even a downturn for 5 to 10 years could be catastrophic for Maine lobstermen. Their valuable coastal property may have to be sold, resulting in a rapid gentrification of the Maine coast.

The risks are exacerbated by climate change. Today, Maine is in an oceanographic "sweet spot" with temperatures ideal for baby lobsters and adults. As sea temperatures warm, the environment becomes more hostile to the lobster. In southern New England a shell disease broke out in 1998 (warmest year on the planet at the time) that resulted in an 80% decline in lobsters. Lobster stocks in coastal Rhode Island never recovered. This could happen in Maine. However, with so few species in our ecosystem, what might replace the lobster?

One possible plus to climate change in the Gulf of Maine is that more fish species, and even blue crabs, are becoming established. This well-documented northern shift in many species along the East Coast of North America is evident in Maine: more black sea bass and red hake are seen here than ever before. Exactly where this will end up is anyone's guess.

What we need to do is learn how to manage a complex ecosystem so that our management can react to the rapid changes we are already seeing. Only by increasing our agility to manage this ecosystem will we likely be able to secure Maine's maritime heritage.

— Bob Steneck

(*See* additional technical reading in support of all statements in this essay in Bibliography)

General Bibliography

Bent, A. C., *Life Histories of North American Birds*, Dover Publications, New York, 1961

Bigelow Henry R. and Schroeder, Wm. C., *Fishes of the Gulf of Maine*, U. S. Govt. Printing Office, Wash. D. C., 1964

Birkhead, Tim, *Bird Sense: What It's Like to Be a Bird*, Walker & Co., 2012

Borror, D. J. and White, R. E., *Peterson Field Guide to Insects*, Houghton Mifflin, Boston, 1970

Caldwell, D. W., *Roadside Geology of Maine*, Mountain Press Publishing Co., Missoula, Montana, 1998

Dwelley, Marilyn, *Spring Wildflowers of New England*, Down East, 1973

Erlich, Paul R. et al., *The Birder's Handbook: A Field Guide to the Natural History of North American Birds*, Simon & Schuster, 1988

Foster, Steven and Duke, James A., *Peterson Field Guides: Eastern/Central Medicinal Plants*, Houghton Mifflin, Boston, 1990

Godin, Alfred J., *Wild Mammals of New England*, Johns Hopkins Univ. Press, Baltimore, 1977

Katona, Steven K. et al., *A Field Guide to the Whales, Porpoises, and Seals of the Gulf of Maine and Eastern Canada*, Charles Scribner's Sons, 1983

Kenney, Leo P., and Burne, Mathew R., *A Field Guide to the Animals of Vernal Pools*, Massachusetts Division of Fisheries and Wildlife, 2000

Linsenmaier, Walter, *Insects of the World*, McGraw-Hill, 1972.

Marley, Greg A., *Mushrooms for Health*, Down East, Camden, Maine, 2009

Odling-Smee, F. John et al, *Niche Construction: The Neglected Process in Evolution*, Monograph in *Population Biology*, 2003

Martin, Scott M., Terrestrial Snails and Slugs of Maine, *Northeastern Naturalist*, 2000

Palmer, Ralph S., *Maine Birds, Bulletin of the Museum of Comparative Zoology*, 1949

Romer, Alfred S., *Vertebrate Paleontology*, Univ. of Chicago Press, Chicago, 1958

Sibley, A. S., *Sibley Guide to Birds*, Alfred A. Knopf, New York, 2000

Sibley, David Allen, *The Sibley Guide to Trees*, Alfred A. Knopf, 2009

Terres, John K., *The Audubon Encyclopedia of North American Birds*, Alfred A. Knopf, 1991

Epilogue

1997 Acheson, J. M., and Steneck, R. S. Examining the bust then boom in the Maine lobster industry: the perspectives of fishermen and biologists. *North American Journal of Fisheries Management* 17: 826–847.

1997 Steneck, R. S. Fisheries-induced biological changes to the structure and function of the Gulf of Maine Ecosystem. Plenary Paper. Pages 151–165 in Wallace, G. T., and Braasch, E. F. (eds). *Proceedings of the Gulf of Maine Ecosystem Dynamics Scientific Symposium and Workshop*. RARGOM Report, 97–1. *Regional Association for Research on the Gulf of Maine*. Hanover, NH.

Spring peeper *(Pseudacris crucifer).*

2001 Steneck, R. S. and Wilson, C. J. Long-term and large scale spatial and temporal patterns in demography and landings of the American lobster, *Homarus americanus, in Maine. Journal of Marine and Freshwater Research.* 52: 1302–1319.

2001 Steneck, R. S. and Carlton, J. T. Human alterations of marine communities: Students Beware! pages 445–468 in Bertness, M, Gaines, S., and Hay, M. (eds). *Marine Community Ecology.* Sinauer Press, Sunderland, MA.

2004 Steneck, R. S., Vavrinec, J. and Leland, A. V. Accelerating trophic level dysfunction in kelp forest ecosystems of the western North Atlantic. *Ecosystems.* 7(4): 323–331

2006 Butler, M., Steneck, R. S and Herrnkind, W. The ecology of juvenile and adult lobsters. Pages 263–309 In. Phillips, R. (ed). Lobsters: the biology, management aquaculture and fisheries. Blackwell Publishing Ltd. Oxford UK.

2006 Steneck, R. S. Is the American lobster, *Homarus americanus* overfished? A review of overfishing with an ecologically-based perspective. *Bulletin of Marine Sciences.* 78: 607–632.

2008 Bourque, B. J., Johnson, B., and Steneck R. S. Possible prehistoric hunter-gatherer impacts on food web structure in the Gulf of Maine. Pages: 165–187 In.

Erlandson, J. and Torben, R. (eds) *Human Impacts on Ancient Marine Environments.* Univ. of California Press.

2011 Steneck, R. S., Hughes, T. P., Adger, N., Arnold, S., Boudreau, S., Brown, K. Berkes, F., Cinner, J., Folke, C., Gunderson, L., Olsson, P., Scheffer, M., Stephenson, E. Walker B., Wilson, J. and Worm, B. Creation of a gilded trap by the high economic value of the Maine lobster fishery. *Conservation Biology* DOI: 10.1111/j.1523–1739.2011.01717.

2013 Estes, J. A., Steneck, R. S., Lindberg, D. R. Exploring the Consequences of Species Interactions through the Assembly and Disassembly of Food Webs: A Pacific/Atlantic Comparison. *Bulletin of Marine Sciences. 89*(1), 11–29.

2013 Steneck, R. S., and Wahle, R. A. American lobster dynamics in a brave new ocean. *Canadian Journal of Fisheries and Aquatic Sciences.* 2013, 70(11): 1612–1624

2013 Steneck, R. S., Leland, A., McNaught, D.,Vavrinec, J. Ecosystem flips, locks and feedbacks: The lasting effects of fisheries on Maine's kelp forest ecosystem. *Bulletin of Marine Sciences.* 89: 31 – 55

2014 Travis, J., Coleman, F. C., Auster, P. J., Cury, P.M., Estes, J. A., Orensanz, J., Peterson, C. H., Power, M. E., Steneck, R. S., Wootton, J. T. The invisible fabric of nature: species interactions and fisheries management. *Proceedings of the National Academy of Sciences.* (doi/10.1073/pnas.1305853111).

Luna Moth

Boettner, G. H., J. S. Elkinton and C. J. Boettner. 2000. Effects of a biological control introduction on three non target native species of saturniid moths. *Conservation Biology* 14:1798–1806

Brown, S. G., G. H. Boettner and J. E. Yack. 2007. Clicking caterpillars: acoustic aposematism in *Antheraea polyphemus* and other Bombycoidea. *The Journal of Experimental Biology* 210: 993–1005.

Kellog, S. K., L. S. Fink and L. P. Brower. 2003. Parasitism of native luna moths, *Actias luna* (L.) (Lepidoptera: Saturniidae) by the introduced *Compsilura concinnata* (Meigen) (Diptera: Tachinidae) in central Virginia, and their hyperparasitism by trigonalid wasps (Hymenoptera: Trigonalidae). *Environmental Entomology* 32: 1019–1027.

Lindroth, R. L., G. E. Arteel and K. K. Kinney. 1995. Responses of three saturniid species to paper birch grown under enriched CO_2 atmospheres. *Functional Ecology* 9: 306–311.

Tallamy, D. W., M. Ballard and V. D'Amico. 2010. Can alien plants support generalist insect herbivores? *Biological Invasions,* 12, 2285–2292.

Tuskes, P. M., J. P. Tuttle and M. M. Collins. 1996. *The Wild Silk Moths of North America: A Natural History of the Saturniidae of the United States and Canada.* Cornell University Press. Ithaca, NY.